W9-BJQ-407

MY HEART FOR THY CAUSE: ALBERT N. MARTIN'S THEOLOGY OF PREACHING

Brian Borgman

Mentor

Dedication

I affectionately dedicate this work to my wonderful wife and companion, Ariel (Prov. 18:22), and to my children, whom I love more than life, Ashley, Zachary and Alex (Psalm 127:3).

Christian Focus Publications publishes biblically-accurate books for adults and children. The books in the adult range are published in three imprints.

Christian Heritage contains classic writings from the past.

Christian Focus contains popular works including biographies, commentaries, doctrine, and Christian living.

Mentor focuses on books written at a level suitable for Bible College and seminary students, pastors, and others; the imprint includes commentaries, doctrinal studies, examination of current issues, and church history.

Copyright © Brian Borgman 2002

ISBN 185792 716 8

Published in 2002 by
Christian Focus Publications, Geanies House, Fearn,
Ross-shire, IV20 1TW, Great Britain.

www.christianfocus.com

Cover design by Alister MacInnes

Printed and bound by WS Bookwell, Finland

Contents

PART FOUR: THE MAN OF GOD IN THE PULPIT: THE ACT OF PREACHING

Foreword

It is difficult to write a foreword to a book based on one's own views of preaching without giving a strong impression of self-serving. However, my personal affection for the author of these pages coupled with my deep appreciation for his labors, have constrained me to yield to his gracious insistence regarding this matter.

Little did I know when I began preaching at age seventeen that a time would come when I would be placed in the position of having to subject the activity of preaching to the kind of thorough and critical analysis essential to the composition of a series of lectures on this subject - lectures which would mold the thinking and practice of fledgling pastor-preachers. However, in 1977 I was placed in that very position with the opening of the Trinity Ministerial Academy and my responsibility to teach the courses in Pastoral Theology.

As I approached this daunting task I did so with two deeply rooted convictions as to the sources that should determine my formulations. The first of these convictions was that of the absolute authority and sufficiency of the scriptures as the primary source for any sound theology of preaching and pastoral work. The second conviction was that of the necessity for the constant "quality control" of historical theology over all the tentative conclusions with respect to my emerging understanding of the teaching of scripture on these issues.

Since I taught the entire course in a three and four year cycle, I was constrained to subject the lectures to various degrees of serious revision and editing every three to four years. As I did this I became increasingly convinced that there was a third body of data to which careful attention must be paid in constructing an adequate and comprehensive theology of preaching. That body of data is the voice of general revelation as it is revealed in the science or art of rhetoric. I am using the term "rhetoric" to signify the observed principles of effective oral communication. As a younger preacher I was uncomfortable with the original title given to R.L. Dabney's lectures on preaching which was SACRED RHETORIC. To me it bordered on being an oxymoron! However, with the passing of the years and a more careful reading of the list of books which Dabney says most influenced his thinking in the composition of his lectures, I have come to see the wisdom of the original title.

In reading Dr. Borgman's analysis of my lectures it will soon be evident to the reader that I indulged a profuse use of quotations of the older writers. A word of explanation and justification for this fact is in order. By the time I began to compose the lectures I had come to a deep appreciation of the creeds and confessions of the historic Christian church. I had also come to the persuasion that along with the creeds and confessions the church has bequeathed to us a body of wisdom and insight, which though never above Scripture in its authority is meant to function, along with the creeds and confessions, as a quality control upon our independent insights from the Scriptures.

The more I sought to analyze the activity of preaching, I found myself coming to tentative conclusions that seemed either novel or radical in terms of current consensus. It was at this time that I intensified my examination of that gold mine of wise, scripturally sound, and rhetorically astute wisdom deposited in many of the writers of the past.

As I fed my mind upon these writers a general pattern of the authorship of their books on preaching began to emerge. It became evident that most of the older books on preaching and pastoral work were written by men who had attained substantial long-term competence in these endeavors. It was their recognized competence which led their brethren in their particular ecclesiastical circles to constrain these men to write on the subject. In many cases such men were pressured to leave their proven sphere of ministerial usefulness and to pass on their experiential knowledge of these things to a rising generation of pastor-preachers in a seminary context. Then, in many cases after many years of teaching the subject in the classroom setting, these same men committed to writing the substance of their classroom lectures as their most ripe reflections on the subject of preaching and pastoral work.

In other cases there were eminent preachers who did not leave the pastoral ministry to teach in seminaries, but at the height of their powers they were asked to give lectures on the subject of preaching at various seminaries. These lectures then became the basis of their literary productions.

The common denominator in these various patterns is that the recognized excellence of the practitioner of preaching undergirded and gave validity to the wisdom and counsel of the lecturer and author on the subject of preaching. This pattern is in marked contrast with the plethora of books written by men with no proven long-term competence as practitioners who have taken upon themselves to be the instructors of potential practitioners.

Because of my desire that relatively young and inexperienced men should feel the weight of the perspectives of these seasoned practitioners that my lectures were deliberately top-heavy with extensive quotations. Dr. Borgman has added to that weight additional judiciously chosen ;quotes from men of the past and the present who themselves are competent practitioners.

I have received continuing pressure from many to put my pastoral theology lectures into print. Until such time as this is done (if ever) I commend Dr. Borgman for capturing and stating in his way the heart of what I attempted to say in these lectures and what I would say if I were to commit them to writing. May God be pleased to use this book to challenge many to become better men and more competent spirit-filled preachers of the Word. As I have entered my fortieth year of laboring in one congregation, the work of preaching, both in the disciplines of preparation and in the act of preaching continue to be the most arduous but the most rewarding sphere of labor I have experienced in my lifetime.

These pages contain an accurate synopsis of my efforts to set forth a sound theology of preaching - a theology rooted in the data of special revelation, sensitive tot he voice of general revelation, and disciplined by the boundaries of historical theology. My labors and those of Dr. Borgman will be more than amply rewarded should God use this book to cause His servants to "stir into flame" the gift of sacred utterance.

Albert N Martin

Acknowledgements

This work started out as a Doctor of Ministry Project for Westminster Theological Seminary in California. Therefore, the place to begin giving thanks is with my fellow-elders, Andrew Winans, Dan Holler and Dave Gamble. They were gracious in giving me the time to complete the degree and the project. They were always supportive. Special thanks goes to Dave Gamble for his proof-reading and helpful suggestions and intense interest in preaching and this project. God has richly blessed me with excellent co-laborers.

My wife, Ariel, a true lioness of God, held the fort down while I was gone for extended periods of time taking classes and writing. Even through two knee surgeries, she never complained but only supported and served. If every pastor could have a wife like her, the church of God would be all the richer.

The congregation of Grace Community Church of Gardnerville, Nevada, loves the preaching of the Word of God and loves the God of the Word. It is a pleasure to serve them as their pastor. I have no greater joy than opening the Word for them Lord's Day after Lord's Day.

Pastor Albert Martin deserves special thanks. He has not only served the church of Christ faithfully for four decades, and uniquely contributed to the area of pastoral theology and homiletics with his incredible lectures, but he has also become my friend and mentor. I have a very large heart for Pastor Martin. His help through the entirety of this project, in spite of cancer surgery and his own dear wife being diagnosed with cancer, was of inestimable value. Pastor Martin is living out 'My Heart For Thy Cause'. This next generation will thank him for restoring to us through God's Spirit the old paths of pastoring and preaching.

Both Mrs. Ann Rimbach, of Trinity Baptist Church, and Harry Heist, of Trinity Pulpit, were of inestimable help. They both were always prompt and efficient in assisting me. Thank you.

Finally, God, my Heavenly Father, who in His sweet providence has brought these people into my life, is worthy of all praise. May He see fit to revive preaching in our day for the glory of Christ and His Church!

Soli Deo Gloria!

Brian Borgman

INTRODUCTION: WHY ALBERT MARTIN?

The great theologian John Murray was a favorite at the Leicester Conference for Ministers. He had helped in founding the conference, and his influence was widespread. The established tradition was that that outstanding spokesman for the Reformed faith would take the final session of the conference. In 1967 Professor John Murray wrote the following note to Iain Murray:

> If Al Martin is to be there I really think he should be asked to take the three evening services you propose for me. He is one of the ablest and moving preachers I have ever heard. In recent years I have not heard his equal. My memory of preachers goes back sixty years. So, when I say he is one of the ablest, this is an assessment that includes very memorable preachers.[1]

John MacArthur, popular radio Bible teacher and Pastor of Grace Community Church in Sun Valley, California, stated, 'I find Al Martin's preaching to be sound, compelling.... He cuts it straight.'[2] Renowned theologian, Dr. J I Packer, notes that Albert Martin's preaching is 'very clear, forthright, articulate.... He has a fine mind and a masterful grasp of Reformed theology in its Puritan-pietistic mode.'[3] Writer Iain Murray has commented, 'I esteem Al Martin very highly and have seen something of the worldwide influence of his ministry. Consistency and simplicity in his personal life are among his characteristics – he is in daily life what he is in the pulpit.'[4] Dr. Joel Beeke said, 'Al Martin's preaching excels in bringing home God's truth to the consciences of people for every sphere of life. He aims to bring the whole Word of God to the whole man for the totality of life.'[5] Pastor Edward Donnelly of Newtownabbey, Ireland, wrote,

> His preaching is powerful, impassioned, exegetically solid, balanced, clear in structure, penetrating in application. He is able to combine profundity with simplicity, so that all are fed. I have seen him touch audiences of several nationalities, of all ages and social backgrounds,

> ranging from well-instructed believers to pagans. His ministry is often attended by a peculiar degree of unction from the Spirit.[6]

Donnelly goes on to describe a most amazing scene which occurred at the South-Eastern Reformed Baptist Family Conference, in the summer of 1990 at William Jennings Bryan College, in Dayton, Tennessee.

> The main auditorium was filled with six or seven hundred people and he was preaching on Jesus in Gethsemane. Towards the close of his sermon, all the lights went out and Pastor Martin finished preaching in the dark. As he led in prayer at the end, the lights came on again. It was discovered that the building was equipped with a system for switching off the lighting when there was no-one in the auditorium. The large audience had been so gripped by the preaching that there was, literally, not a single movement among them. The engineers had not calculated that it would be possible for people to sit so motionless and the instruments were calibrated accordingly. When Pastor Martin had announced the closing prayer, we must have leaned forward in our seats and triggered the lighting. It was a startling example of the power of the Word. I regret to say that the lights did not go out while I was preaching![7]

The preaching ministry of Albert N. Martin has been blessed by God. Pastor Martin has not only been used by God through the preaching of the Word, but he has hammered out on the anvil of education and experience a thorough theology of preaching. It is obvious that Albert Martin is unique in his God-given gifts and abilities. In fact, it would be wrong to attempt to mimic him in the pulpit. Spurgeon warned his students: 'Indeed, all mimicry is in the pulpit near akin to an unpardonable sin.'[8] Nevertheless, the theology of preaching which he propounds and practises is in great need today. Preachers today can learn much from one who preaches with such passion, clarity and power.

The contemporary church is glutted with preaching which can barely be called by that noble name. The 'seeker' model of preaching, which is common among churches which have imbibed the church growth philosophy, is topical, laden with stories and anecdotes, and non-confrontational.

The 'benign Bible' talkers escape the curse of topical and anecdotal preaching, and although committed to the text of Scripture, rarely provide the deep application of the truth. Their hearers receive Bible information, but leave week after week without going under the knife.

Others, revolting against the man-centeredness of contemporary preaching, espouse a Christo-centric preaching, which faithfully preaches Christ from all of Scripture, but fails to drive the truth home to the heart with penetrating application. To be sure, there are happy exceptions. This is not a blanket condemnation of all contemporary preaching but it must be admitted that much of what takes place in the modern pulpit is weak and insipid.

Albert Martin's theology of preaching is a strong remedy to many of the ills of preaching today. Many of the notes he strikes with forceful clarity have been neglected for decades. He is thorough, God-centered, radically biblical, believing that the Scriptures are sufficient to lead the church into a sound theology of preaching which glorifies God and does good to the souls of men.

This writer, with multitudes of others, has been deeply affected by Pastor Martin as a person, a preacher and a teacher of homiletics. But who is this esteemed preacher? What providential events influenced and shaped him and his thinking? Before his theology of preaching is presented, a brief biographical sketch will be provided. It is not the purpose of this section to give a comprehensive biography. That will be left to an abler writer. However, it is important that an outline of fundamental facts about the man is given. For some, this will be an initial introduction to the pastor from Montville, New Jersey. For others, it might fill in a few biographical details of one they have admired and profited from for years.

Early Years

Albert N. Martin was born on April 11, 1934 in Alexandria, Virginia. He was the second of ten children. His father, George Martin, was at that time an officer in the Salvation Army. Shortly after the birth of Albert, George was offered work at the new

Schick Electric Shaver plant in Stamford, Connecticut. The family moved to Connecticut, and the Martin household began to grow.

His childhood was one marked by security and love. The home was filled with the air of strong leadership by a kind and dependable father, and wonderful support from a loving and firm mother. Strong, principled discipline administered in love kept the children in loving obedience. In the home, the word 'no' to a parental directive was as bad as any four-letter word. At supper time the children had a preview of the Judgment to come, as mother would give a report on each child's behavior for the day. If a spanking was in order, the child was marched upstairs to the bathroom, where he or she would close the blinds while father locked the door. If the attitude was not changed, mother would say, 'Spank him again, George, he's not sweet yet.'[9]

According to Albert's mother, his temperament was compliant, non-aggressive and very sensitive. On one occasion, at around nine years old, he received a set of pressed cardboard shoulder-pads and a little football helmet. He went off to the park to play football with the boys. When the boys told him he was too little, he ran home crying, broken-hearted. His mother comforted him and then told him to go back and try again until they let him play! This sensitivity also manifested itself when young Albert went to set up his own shoeshine business. When an older boy told him to scram because the corner was his, he once again ran home with tears in his eyes.

During his school days a report card was sent home which had a letter grade for the academics and a number grade for attitude and behavior. In the Martin home, character and integrity were more important than academics. His mother would often tell him that the letter grade on his report card reflected what God had given him by nature. However, the number grade reflected the development of his character. Diligence and detail were ethical imperatives in the home. 'Any job worth doing is worth doing well' was the dictum. His sister, Joyce, recalls:

> I can remember Dad, when we had to take turns doing dishes, coming in and making us wash the whole group of dishes over again if just one dish was dirty. We didn't have dishwashers. The dishwashers

> were the children. I can remember Mother saying that if young men can lift weights, then they can scrub a floor. So they often scrubbed the floors. Then she would take a toothbrush and have them use it in the corners. You did not allow a piece of dirt, not even a little speck of dirt, to get in the way or the job was not done completely. I can remember her making us do the same with the windows. I've heard my brother Al say that was one of the things that formed his approach towards the Scriptures. He can't just skim over a scripture. He must dig to get as much as he can out of it.[10]

The household was a disciplined, meticulous home. It was a home where the all-seeing eye of God was a reality. Mother often reminded, 'God sees the dirt in the corners, son.' In this flabby age, such structure and discipline may be seen as stifling. Although the discipline was firm, the structure non-negotiable, and the work ethic fueled by the 'God who cares for details'; it was a happy home, where love abounded. Everyone knew his role and there was love and respect for parents and siblings alike. Most importantly, the fear of God was a reality.

Conversion and Call to the Ministry

The Martins at first attended the Salvation Army, where George was an officer and a band leader. In the context of those early Salvation Army days, Albert remembers the sense of being a great sinner, being lost and in fear of hell. When the Salvation Army would have their Decision Sunday, he would often go forward to the 'penitent form'[11] while singing,

> 'Into my heart, into my heart, Come into my heart Lord Jesus;
> Come in today, come in to stay, Come into my heart, Lord Jesus.'

Both George and Mildred felt a deep responsibility to rear their children in the Scriptures. Mildred began to listen to M R DeHaan and the Radio Bible Class. After a while, some of the doctrines and practices of the Salvation Army caused the Martins to rethink their involvement, and they left. The family ended up at a Baptist church, where there was in some degree a commitment to expository preaching. Although in retrospect, it was not the kind of preaching which dealt with the soul, there was an attempt to explain the Scriptures.

During these years, Albert can only remember being an awakened sinner. He was often afraid to go to sleep because of a terror of eternal hell. As he grew and developed, he was popular and a good athlete, especially in football. However, at the close of 1951 and beginning of 1952 God began to do a real work of grace in his heart. Natively timid, he found a great boldness in confessing Christ as a teenager. Shortly after his conversion, in his zeal for his Savior, he passed out tracts at the football awards banquet. At about the same time, some old saints at a Gospel Mission Hall had been praying for the young people in the community. The prayers of these old saints were answered, and a stir was caused by many young converts, who were zealous for Christ and for the conversion of others. The older men from the Gospel Hall welcomed the young people, and encouraged them to preach and witness.

In February of 1952 Albert left his home on a snowy night, with snow crunching under his feet. He marched resolutely to the Ligget's drugstore to preach on the street corner. He felt like a man going to his execution, knowing that his peers would be there and would witness this event. As they gathered, a few of the young people sang 'What can wash away my sin?' Then he stood with a pocket New Testament and opened his mouth. He recalls:

> Whatever I preached that night, I don't know. But two things happened to me; it was as though God took a pair of invisible scissors and cut the last ribbon that tied me to the frowns and smiles of men and took a rod of steel and drove it down my backbone, and I was free. That was the most memorable thing that night.[12]

Those early days were marked by great zeal in prayer, Bible reading, preaching and witnessing. Many times he missed supper so he could pray for an hour before he would preach on a street corner or at the Mission Hall. During this time he also worked. Even on the job he was zealous for Christ. He recalls:

> I was working for Western Union, borrowing my sister's old blue balloon tire bike to deliver telegrams. I would give out a tract whenever I would deliver a telegram. On a Saturday morning, the man who was the manager for the station called to the secretary, and she said, 'The manager wants to see you.' I thought, 'Uh, oh. Somebody called in about me passing out tracts and I am going to get fired.'
>
> The manager said, 'Are you Albert Martin?'
>
> I said, 'Yes.'
>
> He said, 'We sent in over our wires an article to the *New York Times* last night, maybe you would like to see it.' He showed me the article about a former Stamford High football player who was at the center of a religious revival. [Author's note: Joyce believes the article was called 'Bible Study Replaces Friday Night Dances'].
>
> The manager went on to commend me, 'With young people getting a reputation for doing this, that and the other, I am glad to know that someone out there is doing something good and religious.' I walked out of there, wiping my brow![13]

With that job he saved money for a Thompson Chain Reference Bible, and he devoured the Word. An uncle also gave him a *Strong's Concordance*, and he studied the Word. Even in these early years, where zeal can sometimes override truth, God framed into his soul the principle that the Bible alone would govern him in all of life. With diligence he gave himself to searching the Scriptures, digging deep in order to bring out the treasure of truth for his soul.

When God laid hold of him through the new birth, he came out of the womb preaching. There has always been a visceral sense of the call. Although not all the elements of the call which will be outlined in the following pages were immediately present and understood, there was some quality guidance through some of the older saints. Pastor Scofield, from the Mission Hall, was a great support to him and his young companions. While the mainline churches were offended by their fervor, and the evangelical churches were taken aback, not knowing exactly what to do with them, Pastor Scofield gave them solid counsel and wise leadership.

Albert entered Bob Jones University after graduating from high school in 1952. His sister Joyce remembers walking into the kitchen one day, and finding her mother crying. Joyce asked, 'Mama, what's the matter?' She said, 'Now that Al is off to college, I not only miss my son, I miss my friend.'

After two years at Bob Jones he transferred to Columbia Bible College and enjoyed very happy times there. There was a spiritual vitality on campus, and the school had a strong emphasis on missions. In fact, he had a desire to go to the mission field. Perhaps the only aspect of his time at Columbia which was not positive was his struggles with the higher life teaching. When a prominent higher life teacher came to the college, Albert wrestled in his soul between the description of the higher life and what he would later know as Puritan pietism (i.e., the biblical Christian life). Nevertheless, in his senior year he became the student body president. And in 1956 he graduated Magna Cum Laude.

Marriage and Early Ministry

Shortly after his conversion he was asked to speak to a church's young people's group in Concord, New Hampshire. He met the president of the group. She was an attractive brunette and he said, 'When I saw her I freaked out!'[14] The relationship grew over the next few years and this attractive young woman named Marilyn went on to become Mrs. Albert Martin in June, 1956. Shortly after the wedding he served on the staff of Columbia Bible College; all the while both he and Marilyn had a strong desire to go to the mission field. During this time, however, the potential for the mission field was crumbling. He had asthma, which excluded him from candidacy. Although the mission field was fading from the picture, there was no doubt that they would serve God somewhere.

In 1957 a friend recommended him as a Camp Evangelist. God's hand had been on his preaching, even in front of Ligget's drugstore in Stamford. God continued to use him, and thus began his itinerant ministry, where he traveled in a Volkswagen and preached in many different evangelical churches. In this itinerant ministry he saw first-hand many of the serious deficiencies caused by the gospel of easy-believism, the carnal Christian theory and the separation of repentance from faith. He himself never preached that kind of gospel. From the earliest days of his new life in Christ, he saw the necessity of repentance, the necessity of a changed life and the necessity of Christ as Lord as well as Savior.

On one particular occasion, a friend lined up a speaking engagement at Wheaton Graduate School chapel. Albert stood and challenged these young 'cream of the crop' academicians. With no intimidation from his prestigious surroundings, with passion and directness, he appealed to them to be people of courage, like John the Baptist. The devil didn't care about their Wheaton degree, or the education, but what he would tremble at would be their godliness and zeal for Christ. After the chapel service, an elderly man with a shock of white hair came up, took his hand and simply said, 'Thank you, young man. As you preached the text came to mind, "He was a burning and shining light." When you preached there was light and heat.'[15] That man was Merrill Tenney, and the heat and light has continued to burn from that day to the present.

Although in retrospect, Pastor Martin looks at those days of itinerant ministry as 'lacking in many biblical perspectives', he also views them as 'ordered by God'. Much was built into him as a teenage street preacher. He was greatly shaped by his college experience. He was also deeply influenced by his time on the road, in church after church. God uses these kinds of experiences to mold His men. Yet another formative influence would come into his life, which would indeed change his very direction of ministry.

Four and a half years after their wedding, Albert and Marilyn had a son, Joel. It was the birth of Joel in 1961 that impressed Albert of the necessity of being more frequently at home. He was now a father; he had a family. With such a rich legacy and high standard from his own father, he decided he ought to seek a ministry consistent with this conviction. He was between ministries in 1962, looking and waiting for an open door. During this time he was willing to engage in any form of legitimate employment that would provide for his family.

A pastor friend was involved in a church planting effort in northern New Jersey. The fledgling church had purchased a Roman Catholic retreat center. One of the buildings they were renovating was a barn which had dried dung plastered to the concrete floor.

His pastor friend offered him a job scraping the dung off the floors for $15.00 a day. While engaged in this less than glamorous job, that open door of opportunity finally came.

One day he accepted a call for the pulpit supply for the Christian and Missionary Alliance Church of North Caldwell. He preached in the morning on 'What is a real Christian?' from Luke 14:25-33 and in the evening, 'Why Should Christ Give You a Pastor?' The elders asked him to come for a week of meetings. They also requested him to fill the pulpit for the summer. That interim pastorate turned into a full-time call to a settled ministry. Later, he and Marilyn had two daughters, Heidi and Beth.

The Doctrines of Grace

Albert had always embraced conversion as the work of God alone. He always preached that the new birth was a pervasive and life-changing event. He had heard of Edwards and McCheyne, and knew they were Calvinists. He even picked up Thomas Boston's *Human Nature in its Fourfold State*, in 1958. Yet it was not until he was in the pastoral ministry, where he had to labor consecutively passage by passage, that he was confronted with the doctrines of grace. One of his early heroes, Charles Grandison Finney, had thoroughly disappointed him with his treatment of Romans 5:12 and original sin. Seeing that Finney's *Systematic Theology* was not a sure guide, he picked up W G T Shedd's *History of Doctrine*. He argued with Shedd, marking up the margins with points of contention.

Through the friendship of Ernest Reisinger, he read A W Pink's *The Sovereignty of God*, but it was the necessity of teaching a basic doctrines class to his new congregation that brought him to a more thorough understanding of the sovereignty of grace. One day as he was preparing to teach an adult Bible class on regeneration, he said to his wife that he wondered whether or not he ought to leave the ministry until this basic issue was settled. This issue over what comes first, regeneration or faith, was too much, and Sunday was coming. But as from his earliest days, he let the Bible guide his thinking, and he taught it straight, leaving the chips to fall where they might.

The supposed Achilles' heel of Calvinism, limited atonement, was settled for him when he was given John Owen's classic treatment, *The Death of Death in the Death of Christ*, by Ernest Reisinger. The pilgrimage took a decade, yet after that time of reading, praying, studying and wrestling, he came into the settled conviction that classic, reformed Christianity is nothing less than biblical Christianity.

One interesting side note is the subject of baptism. When he was reaching the end of his journey, and was embracing Reformed theology, he assumed he would end up a Presbyterian. However, it was upon reading Professor John Murray's book, *Christian Baptism*, that he became a convinced Baptist! The writer asked if he ever told John Murray this bit of information, and Pastor Martin's response was to be expected. 'No, no. I esteemed our friendship too much to ever make this an issue.'[16]

In 1966, he came out with his 'manifesto', sixteen sermons on the sovereignty of God.[17] He laid out powerfully this doctrine which had gripped his soul. The series is expositional, with careful biblical exegesis of passage after passage. It is clear, forceful and compelling. In fact, even to this day, over thirty years later, Pastor Martin runs into people who have heard this series and profited from it. In a real sense, it was his public, ministerial declaration of where he stood. He had come home theologically, and from then on he would be one of the outstanding advocates of Reformed theology and piety.

It should be kept in mind, however, that he had been introduced to Reformed doctrine earlier in his ministry. In fact, he had been exposed to some men who held to the five points of Calvinism, but did not manifest in practical ways a commitment to genuine godliness. However, it was not from that womb that a love for Reformed doctrine was born. Albert had read the biographies of McCheyne and Edwards and others, and these were the things they believed, but their lives were a totally different calibre. If he had to judge the doctrines of grace by his first exposure to men who said they held them in his generation, he would have rejected them on the basis of the lack of godliness and humility in many of these men's lives.

It was in the context of the warmth and piety of solid Reformed and Puritan literature and the warmth and piety of living men, like Ernie Reisinger, Walt Chantry, Iain Murray and John Murray that his love for Reformed theology was born. He grew, not only in his understanding of the doctrines of grace, but also in the genuine piety which grows out of the doctrine. One of the themes that has been a constant landmark in his ministry has been 1 Timothy 4:16, 'Give heed to yourself and to your teaching; persevere in these things, for as you do this you will ensure salvation for both yourself and for those who hear you.'

Trinity Baptist Church

From 1962 until the end of 1966, he pastored the Alliance Church in North Caldwell. The church was doing well, and lives were being changed, but part of his pilgrimage was dealing with the pastoral ministry and the New Testament pattern for the local church. Once he had come to the realization that he could in good conscience no longer pastor an Alliance church, he went to the local leaders of the denomination and told them his dilemma. These men did not seem to understand that the man they were dealing with was led by a firm commitment to maintaining a good conscience before God. Finally, he offered his resignation to the congregation.

At this very time another opportunity for ministry came up with a large church near Philadelphia. This church held out high hopes for an enlarged sphere of ministry and usefulness. The sanctuary sat 750, it was close to Westminster Seminary, and a daily radio broadcast was included.

There was a small detail that had not been factored into this process: the North Caldwell congregation refused his resignation. They told their pastor that he was their leader. As a result, they would be willing to disband as a CMA church, focus on the issues which had caused him so much consternation, and make up their minds. In January 1967 they began to meet in a local school, having voted to continue the pastoral relationship. This involved leaving behind church buildings and eventually the parsonage, when efforts to reach a righteous settlement to secure the church properties failed. After approximately seven months of digging through the Scriptures corporately, that little flock decided that the convictions which he had developed were indeed what the Bible taught and what they now believed. In September 1967 the church reconstituted, embracing the 1689 Baptist Confession of Faith and becoming Trinity Baptist Church.

This was a fruitful time for Albert and the church. Many of the issues which would be the hallmark of later ministry were hammered out in these days. The issue of the call to the ministry, which is given in this project, was developed. The nature of pastoral oversight began to evolve, according to the biblical pattern. There were other issues too which settled into deep convictions. The bottom line of this formative period of his ministry was that a man with his Bible and reliable guides of the past will be led into the truth. He could genuinely say that for him the proverb, 'Buy truth and sell it not' (Prov. 23:23), was an obsession. Wherever this obsession led him, he would follow. Whatever the results, he would live with them. His conscience was too alive to God's Spirit to do otherwise.

Expanding Ministry

Ernie Reisinger not only put books into Albert Martin's hands, he also introduced him to a new world of friends. Iain Murray and Professor John Murray were two men who would make an indelible imprint on him. His friendship with these two men would prove to be ordained by God for the good of His church beyond the borders of North Caldwell, Essex Fells and Montville. At the age of thirty-four, he was invited to the Leicester Conference for Ministers. At Leicester many were blessed as they heard this young man from New Jersey. He was also instrumental in keeping unity between the Baptists and paedo-Baptists in the U.K.

The testimony of long-time friend, Pastor Achille Blaize, is indicative of the kind of impact that was being made and the kind of friendships which were being forged.

> A young minister friend of mine came from a conference in which Pastor Martin was preaching and said to me enthusiastically, 'You

must come and hear this young American preacher. He is all over the place in his preaching!'

The previous summer I had a bad experience with an American preacher and had said to myself that only chewing gum and bad preachers come from America! My friend insisted that next spring I should hear him. I sat in the Conference Hall in the front row about one meter from where the preacher would stand to preach. Suddenly, someone sat on my right. I noticed the size of his feet, they were like West Indian banana boats! To my surprise the stranger whispered in my ear, 'I am Al Martin, what is your name?'

He preached for about 80 minutes. I was so overwhelmed and moved that I could not leave my seat. I discovered the secret behind his sermon: the burning piety of his own heart and life. I learned one thing among many: the preacher who does not cultivate daily communion with God and personal piety will be stultified.[18]

Then came the family conferences and pastors' conferences which were springing up. Albert Martin became a frequently invited speaker to these, where multitudes sat under the anointed preaching of the Word of God. One of the reasons that so many were coming to hear this man with a burning message in his heart was because of sermons they had heard on tape. From the beginning of his ministry, tapes have been a way to get the word out. If the present writer were to start listing the testimony of those who have been enriched through the tape ministry of Trinity Pulpit, it would be lengthy. There can be no doubt, however, that God has spread His Word through the tape ministry of Trinity Baptist Church.

From the beginning, the church, even before 1967, believed that tapes for shut-ins and others would be beneficial. One man volunteered his time to make reel-to-reel copies. Soon, the request for recorded sermons snowballed. The elders found out that this poor man was sleeping for one hour intervals through the night, so he could wake up and change the tapes! The church made him an offer of employment so that he could devote more of his time to the growing tape ministry, without killing himself in the process. Since 1971, Trinity Pulpit has sent out more than 750,000 tapes throughout many parts of the world. They have never put copyrights on the tapes, and so the actual number of taped sermons is incalculable.

Books have also been important to Trinity Baptist Church. A book table with solid Reformed and Puritan literature has promoted sound doctrine and piety through the printed page. Trinity Baptist Church found a man who was operating a book service out of his church, and offered him the opportunity to run the book service under the auspices of Trinity Baptist Church. The man accepted the invitation and Trinity Book Service was born. With a mailing list of over 10,000 and an annual gross over $500,000,[19] it is clear that the promotion of God-centered literature has also been at the heart of the church.

Conferences, tapes and books all formed a part of the expanding ministry and influence of Trinity Baptist Church and their Pastor. Reformed Baptist Churches were popping up here and there. With the increased interest in new churches, many were voicing their opinion that Trinity Baptist Church had a stewardship and duty to train pastors for these churches. Out of that sense of stewardship, Trinity Ministerial Academy was born.

> What events and influences led to the establishment of Trinity Ministerial Academy? For an answer to this question, we must look back to the 1950s, when a resurgence of interest in the historic confessions of the Protestant Reformation began to be felt on both sides of the Atlantic. Gradually the writings of men whose names had all but been forgotten were once more being read and studied.... In Great Britain, God raised up the Banner of Truth Trust, which in 1955 began publishing Calvinistic writings and did a brisk business in books which a generation earlier almost no one would buy....
>
> Large numbers of young men and women, converted from Catholicism, liberalism, and agnosticism, were interested not only in reading and talking about biblical doctrines, but in putting these truths into practice in daily life and witness.
>
> God also began to lay His hand on Baptist men of Calvinistic persuasion and put into their hearts a desire to prepare themselves for the gospel ministry. As these men, however, looked for schools where they might receive solidly biblical ministerial training, they found that their only option was in seminaries which, although Reformed in theological perspective, did not share their deep

appreciation for experimental theology (in large measure derived from the great Puritan heritage) or their commitment to Baptist distinctives.

Some investigations were made into the possibility of placing a qualified man of Baptist persuasion on the faculty of the non-Baptist Reformed seminaries. For various reasons this possibility was never realized. Also, it became increasingly evident that these faculties would continue to be divided and inconsistent in regard to those facets of Puritan theology and experimental Calvinism which we believe to be of fundamental importance in the training of men for the ministry. Thus our thoughts were turned more and more toward the establishment of a school where men who gave evidence of having necessary gifts and grace could be prepared for the work of the ministry. At a meeting of the Reformed Baptist Association in the spring of 1970, Pastor Albert N Martin gave a lecture on 'A Theology of Ministerial Training'. This lecture subsequently was given again to several Reformed Baptist churches in the Northeast. During the following years, from 1971 to 1975, the elders of Trinity Baptist Church made three specific efforts to engage a man spiritually and scholastically to join with them in establishing a school for preparing men for the ministry. In each instance, it was clear to all concerned that the time was not yet right to move ahead in this endeavor.

Meanwhile, theological students continued to request instruction in certain aspects of practical theology which would supplement what they were receiving in their regular training. In response to this desire for an articulation of the principles of experimental Calvinism (particularly as these principles related to the work of the ministry), regular monthly classes were held from 1973 to 1975 under the leadership of Pastor Martin. The response to this meager effort was so encouraging that it intensified our desire to do something more extensive. Early in 1976 it was felt that the time had come to initiate a program of more specific theological training for young men in our congregation. Saturday morning classes were opened at the beginning of February and continued until the end of May. Pastors Albert Martin and Robert Fischer taught courses in systematic and biblical theology. The evident blessing of God on this endeavor encouraged us to think and pray in terms of expanding these efforts into a full-time training program. At a congregational meeting in January 1977, Trinity Ministerial Academy gave enthusiastic endorsement to the proposal of its elders that Trinity Ministerial Academy be opened in the fall of 1977.[20]

The Academy served many in the Reformed Baptist community of churches well for twenty years. It was in the Academy that Pastor Martin's Pastoral Theology lectures were given. But like only a few institutions, Trinity Ministerial Academy decided to close its doors in May 1998 due to some issues of stewardship. The Academy never built its own buildings, which meant it would never perpetuate itself in order to make mortgage payments on brick and mortar. The Academy was a stewardship of the Church, and that stewardship was examined and found wanting.

In a congregational meeting on January 11, 1998, Albert outlined five reasons why the Academy would close its doors.

(1) The stewardship of funds was an issue. The Church supported the Academy and it was decided that the amount of funds needed to keep the school running, in light of the other four reasons, was unwarranted.

(2) The stewardship of the time and labor of the Pastors involved in the school was also an issue. The Pastors who were involved both at Trinity and outside of Trinity found it difficult to maintain their pastoral duties, which are explicit in Scripture, while maintaining their duties at the Academy, which were only inferred duties.

(3) The stewardship of academic standards also became a concern. As times have changed over twenty years, the point of whether the men were receiving the highest standards of academic training came into focus.

(4) The counsel from other established churches which had longstanding relationships with the Academy was also significant. These other churches were finding it difficult, economically, to send men and support them.

Finally, (5) other options had arisen over the years which had not existed in the 1970s. Various seminaries and other institutions, holding to the Reformed faith, had arisen. There were more churches than there had been twenty years ago to help oversee the education of promising men.

Although the closing of the Academy was sad, it really was just another reflection of his commitment, and the commitment of Trinity Church, to bring everything under the scrutiny of the

Word. It is a good conscience which ultimately matters at the end of the day.

Conclusion

Pastor Albert N. Martin has much to offer this flabby generation of preachers. His life is a challenge to greater heights in godliness and lower depths in humility. One of his close friends, Pastor Randy Pizzino, has observed:

> Pastor Martin is simply the finest Christian I have ever known. His passion is to know Christ, to be like Him, to please Christ. He has lived with an obsession so to know the Word as to obey it and not just preach it. I would not be able to count the number of times that I have observed Pastor Martin go out of his way (in a way many would think absurd) so that he could maintain a good conscience before God and men. For 25 years there has hardly been a week that his godliness of life has not served as a prod to seek to keep this foul heart of mine in a right and blood-washed condition before God.[21]

His sister Lois has paid an enormous tribute to her brother's character when she penned these words,

> I would liken my brother's life from the moment of his conversion until the present to the symbolism found on Calvin's coat-of-arms: a hand holding a flaming heart with these simple yet profound words, 'My heart for Thy cause, I offer Thee, Lord, promptly and sincerely.' The flaming heart of service to God has never diminished in my brother's soul – rather it has only burned brighter and with intensity as God's 'cause' has been progressively revealed through the pages of Scripture in the years which have followed my brother's conversion.[22]

The preaching of God's Word deserves nothing less than men with flaming hearts, with a desire to give their hearts for His cause. In order for God-owned preaching to be revived in this day and the coming generation, the church needs to recover an understanding of the call to ministry, the life of the man of God, and what preaching is, in its essence and act. For a clearer understanding, which stirs the soul, look to Christ's gift to the church, Albert N Martin, and learn.

PREFACE

A word must be said concerning the research and writing of this book. The author has listened to hundreds of Albert Martin's sermons, as well as his pastoral theology lectures. He has read the relevant literature, the expanse of which is seen in the footnotes. The author initially wrote the material contained in this book as a project when he was a Doctor of Ministry candidate, eager to learn and grow in his own ministry. He can testify that not only has his own preaching improved, but his walk with God has been strengthened. The reason is actually simple: 'My heart for Thy cause' is not only the pervasive theme of Albert Martin's theology of preaching, but also his life. Preaching involves the whole man in and out of the pulpit, yielded up to God, in order to reach the whole man sitting in the pew. This view of the ministry impacts preaching and living.

After the research began, it became obvious that some choices had to be made regarding the actual writing of the material. The author has not simply given, verbatim, Pastor Martin's lectures. The writing of this project follows Pastor Martin's lectures, includes most of the quotations Pastor Martin used, but the style is somewhat hybrid. To many this will be disappointing. However, there are two fundamental reasons why this road was taken. The first is owing to Pastor Martin himself. Pastor Martin has read widely in the area of preaching. He has culled from the great works, not a few of which are relatively unknown today. It was this gleaning in the fields of the greats that caused the author also to root around in the same fields. The first 'hybrid' aspect of this project relates to the variety of sources which are used. The author has added quotations which were not in the original lectures, but which he believed would strengthen or add color to the point at hand. The reader will notice that there are many lengthy quotations, which may seem to hamper the readability of the project. The author does not apologize for the length of these, nor does he regret that they give the book the appearance at some points of being an anthology. Pastor Martin's lectures are somewhat anthological themselves. The reason is simple: nothing new is being said here; in fact it is gloriously old. The masters of the past knew much more than the communication theorists of today. Therefore, anything in Pastor Martin's lectures or in this book which can point a man back to those sources, stimulating his interest to take up and read, is well worth the effort.

Furthermore, sprinkled throughout the section on preaching are many illustrations which the author has taken straight from Pastor Martin's own preaching. The examples, which were not part of the lectures, were thought to be fine illustrations of the point under consideration. Pastor Martin is too humble always to be pointing students to his own preaching for examples, but this author has thought it fitting to use the exemplary preaching of the man to illustrate his own theology.

The second 'hybrid' aspect of the project is the style. First, there will be a multitude of *Martinisms* which will not be in quotation marks. Only if a given quotation is longer than two sentences is it actually in quotation marks, usually with an appropriate footnote. If the author had footnoted every sentence which actually belonged to Pastor Martin, the project would be very cumbersome. Unfortunately, there will also be some *Borgmanisms*. The author has a style of writing which cannot be extracted from the project (that is not to say he did not wish it to be so). One cannot approach a subject like this, having one's heart greatly stirred, and keep one's own affections from dripping onto the page.

One final word about the research and writing of this book. The author comes to this project as one who has a deep love and admiration for Pastor Martin. His own soul has been enriched, not only by the preaching and pastoral theology he has been immersed in, but also by the kind and encouraging friendship of Pastor Martin. In many ways, this project is a labor of my love for Albert Martin, who has helped this pastor to love Christ more fervently, see God more clearly, and understand preaching more biblically. His humility, gentleness and godliness have made a deep impression on this pastor's heart. It is also a labor of love to all who have profited from Pastor Martin's ministry and want something in print. Finally, it is a labor of love for the body of Christ, which is in dire need of God-owned, passionate preaching. May the great Head of the church be pleased to use this book to stir pastors, to preach and to live out 'my heart for Thy cause'.

PART ONE:

THE CALLING OF THE MAN OF GOD IN THE PASTORAL OFFICE[23]

1

THE CALL: FOUNDATIONAL PRINCIPLES, FUNDAMENTAL ERRORS AND FALSE REASONS

Introduction

The place to start exploring powerful preaching is the calling of the preacher. Although the subject of calling has been blurred today, one cannot separate a true call of God to the pastoral office from preaching. Men who enter seminary and subsequently the ministry with no theology and conviction of personal calling are a blight upon the church. Spurgeon's words ring as true today as they did over a hundred years ago, 'That hundreds have missed their way, and stumbled against a pulpit is sorrowfully evident from the fruitless and decaying churches which surround us.'[24]

Just as it is irresponsible and dangerous to separate the call of God from the act of preaching, so it is equally dangerous to separate preaching from the life of the preacher. 'Unless we would degrade preaching to a mere elocutionary art, we must never forget that the soil out of which powerful preaching grows is the preacher's own life.'[25] It is a shame today that among the multitudes of books which deal with preaching, so few touch on this vital subject. With so many being disqualified from ministry today, it appears that there is a desperate need to return to an examination of the soil of good preaching, which is the life of the preacher. The words of McCheyne are compelling:

> I am persuaded that I shall obtain the highest amount of present happiness, I shall do most for God's glory and the good of man, and I shall have the fullest reward in eternity, by maintaining a conscience always washed in Christ's blood, by being filled with the Holy Spirit at all times, and by attaining the most entire likeness to Christ in mind, will, and heart, that is possible for a redeemed sinner to attain in this world.[26]

In the following section, the term 'man of God' will be used for a man who has been called to the pastoral office. The pastoral office will be viewed from the perspective of the elder (*presbyteros*) who governs and labors in preaching and teaching within a local assembly (1 Tim. 5:17) and makes his living from the gospel (1 Cor. 9:16).

It must first be stated that there is clear biblical warrant for addressing the subject of a call to the ministry. Romans 12:3-8 reveals the responsibility believers have in making a sober, self-assessment regarding their gifts. Some gifts are given for the pastoral office, and if one believes he might be in possession of them, the natural question is whether God has called him to the office. Edmund Clowney states, 'This principle of stewardship in Christ's kingdom leads us to an unavoidable conclusion: *The call of the Word of God to the gospel ministry comes to ALL those who have the gifts for such a ministry.*'[27] The clear responsibility of each individual to evaluate his gifts to see if he is in possession of ministerial gifts, is warrant to address the subject of the call to the ministry.

Other passages, such as James 3:1 and Hebrews 13:17, set forth the sober reality of stricter judgment for one's teaching and giving an account for those under one's charge on the Great Day. This thought, of course, should steer all clear of the pastoral office unless they know they are called. Since there should never be a light-hearted entrance into the ministry due to such weighty realities, it is concluded that the subject of the call demands attention.

Finally, the God-given standard for the pastoral office (1 Tim. 3:1-7; Titus 1:5-9; 1 Pet. 5:1-3) makes it clear that not only must there be a desire, but there must also be commensurate qualifications. If a man reads his Bible personally, he is driven to ask himself, 'Do I meet the biblical standard? Has God given me a desire with commensurate qualifications?' The fact that some are qualified while others are not, gives rise to the consideration of the call to the ministry.

In summary, the clear responsibility believers have in assessing their gifts, the sober warnings to those contemplating the pastoral office, and the setting forth of a God-given standard for the office make it evident that the consideration of the subject of a call to the ministry is not only legitimate, but also warranted.

In light of the biblical warrant for addressing the subject of the call to the ministry, there is a looming fear in doing so. The fear is summed up in Ezekiel 13:22, where God condemns the false prophets: 'Because you disheartened the righteous with falsehood when I did not cause him grief,' and also 'have encouraged the wicked'. There is an element of fear in discouraging the truly called with imbalance or error in this subject. Equally fearful is the thought of encouraging one who has not been called. It is with this sense of caution that the subject is handled.

The foundational principles which must regulate one's thinking and judgment regarding a call to the pastoral office

There must be a consciousness that this subject is in the realm of 'experimental divinity' or 'the theology of Christian experience'. When anyone moves into the arena of 'experiential' theology, he runs into a number of variables which have a bearing on the final equation. Each man is conditioned by temperament, experience, ecclesiastical environment and so on. Because these variables are so significant, many good men who agree in other areas of objective theological truth, come to this subject with a tremendous diversity of opinion.

For instance, C H Spurgeon and R L Dabney would cross a multitude of theological 't's' and dot doctrinal 'i's' with the same pen. On the subject of the call, however, they are apples and oranges. Pastor Martin's assessment is that Spurgeon's theology of the call probably exempted some who were called, while Dabney's approach probably encouraged some who were not. The advice at this point then is not to put all of the eggs in one basket. In other words, don't imbibe only one source, and don't imbibe any source without 1 Thessalonians 5:21 discernment. These opinions must be held up to the light of Scripture, that which is true and helpful should be embraced, and that which doesn't square with the plumb line of the Word should be jettisoned.

Another foundational principle is that this subject must be

approached with the full awareness that the consideration is for the call to an ordinary and not an extraordinary office in the church. The Bible is full of extraordinary calls to extraordinary offices, such as those to Elijah, Isaiah, Jeremiah and Paul. When hammering out a biblical theology of the call, it is a mistake to think that one's call needs to be similar to that of an Old Testament Prophet or a New Testament Apostle. There have always been those willing to get on a horse and see what happens, but those Damascus road calls are extraordinary because they are for an extraordinary office. A pastor's call is an ordinary call to the ordinary office.

Finally, if one is to tread safely in this matter he must think of the call to the ministry primarily in terms of the biblical teaching concerning an elder who 'labors in the Word and teaching'. Since this is the case, he is driven to the biblical texts which define this ministry (1 Tim. 3:1f; Titus 1:5f; Acts 20:17f; 1 Pet. 5:1f). All elements of the call that may be experiential must not be allowed to override the clear precepts of the written Word. Dabney is helpful at this point, 'While the call of prophets and apostles was by special revelation, that of the gospel minister may be termed a scriptural call.'[28] Clowney echoes this truth: 'God has not left his will shrouded in mystery. He has spoken, plainly and fully. The man who wishes to know God's will must turn to the "oracles of God", the written revelation of the Bible.'[29]

This leads us to add another important class of texts by which the Holy Spirit will inform the judgment, both of the candidate and his brethren, as to his call. It is that class in which God defines the qualifications of a minister of the gospel. Let every reader consult, as the fullest specimens, 1 Timothy 3:1-7; Titus 1:6-9. The inquirer is to study these passages, seeking the light of God's Spirit to purge his mind from all clouds of vanity, self-love, prejudice, in order to see whether he has or can possibly acquire the qualifications here set down. And his brethren, under the influence of the same Spirit, must candidly decide by the same standard whether they shall call him to preach or not.[30]

The fundamental errors with respect to what constitutes a call to the pastoral office

Throughout church history, the subject of the call to the pastoral office has been shot through with erroneous thought. Some have entered the ministry under the influence of ignorance or a misguided zeal. Untold numbers of young people have probably answered a call never given because of an imprudent missions speaker. Although zeal and earnestness are good, if it is ignorant zeal or zeal not restrained by a biblical rationality, then it can breed uncalled men entering the ministry.

Others have set their hopes on a call to the ministry based on fanaticism or a mystical piety. Often related to this erroneous thinking are false signs and wonders, which seem to give an extraordinary claim to an extraordinary office. Although today examples could be multiplied, one thinks of the French Prophets of Whitefield and the Wesleys' day. Charles Wesley's words remind us of such presumptuous claims,

> I lodged at Mr. Hollis's, who entertained me with his French Prophets – equal, in his account, if not superior, to the Old Testament ones. While we were undressing he fell into violent agitations and gobbled like a turkey-cock. I was frightened and began exorcizing him with, 'Thou deaf and dumb devil,' etc. He soon recovered out of his fit of inspiration. I prayed and went to bed, not half liking my bed-fellow. I did not sleep very sound with Satan so near me.[31]

Apart from the fanaticism and mysticism, there is the rank individualism in this age, out of which many self-proclaimed calls come into being. Although the importance of the church's recognizing the call as an essential element will be covered shortly, it is sufficient at this point to say that any claim of a call to the ministry which is crassly individualistic is erroneous. A call takes place within a corporate body, involving not just the individual, but the body.

Finally, there is one other erroneous view on the call which is abominable, that is the pragmatic or rationalistic approach to the call. 'If the need exists we must put someone in the office, qualified or not!' This writer knows of a rural church which had been searching for a pastor for a long time. One day a man attended who had 'given a few sermons' in various gospel mission halls, and the church asked him on the spot to be their pastor. The need was there, and here was a man who had the gift of speaking, and yet his wife was a professing atheist! Christ will gift His church (Eph. 4:11-12), and yet where He has not seen fit to provide a qualified and called man, the church should never take it upon itself to put unqualified men into her offices.

Some common false reasons for assuming or desiring a call to the pastoral office

Just as there are men misguided in their thinking, so there are also men who are misguided in their reasons for entering the ministry. False reasons for entering ministry abound. The term 'false' is used to refer to 'that which is based upon wrong or mistaken ideas – such as "false pride" ' (Webster's Dictionary of American English, Third College Edition). The following is a catalog of seven common false reasons.

1. The pressure of a falsely (wrongly) instructed conscience. This false reason is connected to the earlier expressed concept of misguided zeal. The over-zealous conference speaker cries out, 'If you really love Christ, if you are really grateful for His dying on your behalf, then what prevents you from entering full-time Christian service? Is it selfishness? Fear?' As this earnest, yet unrestrained speaker lays on the guilt of a blood-stained cross, young people are manipulated into ministry through a falsely instructed conscience.

2. The pressure of unwise and sometimes unsanctified ambitions of other people. A serious Christian couple may 'dedicate' their child to the Lord's service, and raise that child with unceasing reminders of their dedication of him to the ministry. As he grows, if he does not outright rebel, he may be pressed into entering Bible college and seminary and then the ministry, not because of a Divine call, but because of unsanctified parental ambition. Or take the case of a pastor who keeps track of the number of his young people who have entered full-time Christian service, like notches on a gun. It is one of his marks of ministerial success to say, 'We've had 24 young people enter the ministry from our church.' As this pastor moves among the young people he is always pushing and pulling to get more notches.

3. *An unbalanced and unbiblical concept of spirituality.* Here the false reason is based on the false assumption that those in ministry are the real Christian warriors, the truly spiritual among God's elect. There is a deadly confusion here between graces and gifts. The fruit of the Spirit, genuine godliness, and character are set aside, while gifts are exalted and seen as what makes one truly spiritual.[32]

4. *An inaccurate assessment of oneself and one's gifts.* This false reason is likened to the man who at the carnival walks into the room of crazy mirrors, which thoroughly distort reality. In the arena of their Christian life, they have a distorted view of what they are and what gifts they possess. This false reason could be rooted in pride, or ignorance, and is usually accompanied by an unwise unwillingness to seek counsel.

5. *An unmet psychological need for personal identity.* The sadness of a man who seeks self-identity in a ministerial office due to its position, influence and popularity, cannot be overstated. The man is looking for self-identity in the wrong place. He is like the teenage girl who longs for identity and affection and so does what will bring her satisfaction of those longings, or so she thinks. The love and recognition she desired is met with unkind and selfish young men. The result is heartache, disappointment, bitterness and a bloodied conscience. The parallel to a man seeking personal identity through ministry is sobering. Anyone who has been in the ministry for any amount of time knows that the unkind treatment of God's people can be devastating. He must realize that his personal identity comes from understanding the biblical doctrines of anthropology and soteriology, not in ecclesiastical office.

6. *An inaccurate and inadequate view of the breadth of the biblical qualifications for and the responsibilities of the pastoral office.* The danger here is that an outgoing, loquacious extrovert is either told by those around him that he would make a good

preacher, or the pulpit holds an attraction for him as an outlet for his fertile mind and mouth. He may be a people person and quite a talker, but totally void of any understanding of the qualifications and responsibilities attached to that pulpit. There is a grave mistake of confusing a proficiency in language with the necessary graces which correspond to the qualifications for the pastoral office.

7. An unmortified lust for authority, attention, influence and monetary gain[33] *connected with the pastoral office*. The Bible is full of warnings against this kind of man (Matt. 23:6-7; 1 Tim. 3:6, 6:3-5; 1 Pet. 5:3). This is obviously the most blatant and sinful false reason for desiring the pastoral office and there aren't enough words to condemn such lusts, other than 'their judgment from long ago is not idle, and their destruction is not asleep' (2 Pet. 2:3).

One of the concerns in dealing with the subject of the call to the pastoral office is that men may enter into studies and subsequently ministry without any serious evaluation of their own motivations. Covering the fundamental errors of what constitutes a call to the pastoral office and false reasons for desiring a call is an integral preliminary consideration. It would greatly benefit the body of Christ if churches were more conversant with these errors and false reasons.

2

THE FOUR ELEMENTS WHICH COMPRISE A BIBLICAL CALL

The four elements which comprise a biblical call to the pastoral office are (1) an enlightened and sanctified desire for the work of the pastoral office, (2) a proven fitness for the work of the pastoral office, (3) an adequate external confirmation for the work of the pastoral office, and (4) a providential opportunity and proper ecclesiastical recognition for the office and work of a specific pastoral charge.

Element One: an enlightened and sanctified desire for the work of the pastoral office

This desire is both necessary and legitimate, as Paul reminded Timothy: 'If any man aspires to the office of overseer, it is a fine work he desires [to do]' (1 Tim. 3:1).[34] It must be a willing desire (1 Pet. 5:2), not coerced in any way. It must be an enlistment, not a draft.[35] It must be a strong and prevailing desire.[36] Spurgeon notes:

> We must feel that woe unto us if we preach not the gospel; the Word of God must be unto us fire in our bones, otherwise, if we undertake the ministry, we shall be unhappy in it, shall be unable to bear the self-denial incident to it, and shall be of little service to those among whom we minister.[37]

This desire must also be based on a proper recognition of the work, not the romanticized notions of youth overtaken by the glory-lust of the pulpit.

The focus of the desire is threefold in nature. First, there must be a longing to be used in self-denying service to edify the people of God. In other words, a man must be absorbed with the end for which the ministry was instituted (Eph. 4:11; Acts 20:28ff; 1 Pet.

5:2ff; Heb. 13:17). If a man is not captured with the vision of building up the people of God, he should abandon the notion of being called. God does not call men who love to preach but can't stand the people.

The second focus of the desire must be a longing to be used in a Spirit-filled ministry of calling out God's elect. The concept that God would use the preacher's voice to be as it were the voice of Christ (John 10:27), and that He would use the preacher's voice to be His voice in creating faith (Rom. 10:14-17), ought to be a great desire. If the candidate for ministry is not consumed with a longing to preach to a valley of dry bones, knowing the Word of the Lord can make them live (Ezek. 37), then he should resign his candidacy for the ministry. Spurgeon pulls no punches in his comments on this subject: 'It is a marvel to me how men continue at ease in preaching year after year without conversions.... Brethren, if the Lord gives you no zeal for souls, keep to the lapstone or the trowel, but avoid the pulpit as you value your heart's peace and your future salvation.'[38]

The third focus of the desire is a longing to discharge a growing sense of God-given stewardship. God is the one who bestows the gifts and gives the stewardship (1 Cor. 4:1-2). There are times when the discharge of the stewardship is pure delight. There are other times when the compulsion to discharge comes simply from the weight of the stewardship (1 Cor. 9:16-17).[39] Bridges notes: 'This constraint rises above all difficulties, takes pleasure in sacrifices for the work's sake, and quickens to a readiness of mind, that (were it not restrained by conscious unfitness and unworthiness) would savor of presumption.'[40]

This desire for the pastoral office must not only have proper focus, but it must also be immersed in the context of a local church. Ideally, the local church should be a biblically structured, biblically healthy, biblically functioning church. This is an important factor for two fundamental reasons. First, it is within the context of a healthy, biblically functioning church that a man's fitness for the ministry can be most accurately recognized. Secondly, the potential ministerial candidate gains a realistic and accurate view of the work of the ministry in such a context.

Finally, the desire for the pastoral office has proper channels of expression. The man who begins to sense God's call must express this desire first and foremost to God in the secret place of prayer. As the man grows in his own desires, having had those desires sifted and sanctified by prayer, he may approach his overseers. The man must be in subjection to his elders (Heb. 13:17), and it is to them he must look first and foremost for wisdom, guidance and confirmation. He may also seek counsel from other trusted, mature friends and counselors, thereby following the wisdom of the Proverbs (12:15, 13:10, 19:20).

Element Two: a proven fitness for the work of the pastoral office

A proven fitness for the work is seen in three major areas, namely Christian character, Christian experience and gifts.

1. There must be manifested grace indicative of genuine, matured, balanced and proven Christian character (derived from an overview of the requirements of 1 Timothy 3:1-7 and Titus 1:5-9).

It is evident, however, that this ministerial standard presupposes a deep tone of experimental and devotional character – habitually exercised in self-denial, prominently marked by love to the Savior and to the souls of sinners, and practically exhibited in a blameless consistency of conduct.[41]

Because God's purposes work in harmony, those men whom He calls not only will have an enlightened and sanctified desire for the work, but will also demonstrate a proven fitness for it, manifesting Christian graces and character. This is not optional, rather it is absolutely critical, as is made clear by the particle of necessity in 1 Timothy 3:2, 'The overseer must (*dei*) be'. As one looks at the qualifications for the office, one is struck by the fact that the primary focus is on character, not gifts. The man who possesses the desire for the work must also manifest graces indicative of genuine, matured, balanced and proven character.

On the next page is a comparison of the two critical passages delineating the qualifications for those who would serve in the pastoral office. It is given for quick reference.

1 Timothy 3:1-7

1 It is a trustworthy statement:
if any man aspires to the office
of overseer, it is a fine work he
desires [to do.]
2 An overseer, then, must be
above reproach,
the husband of one wife,
temperate,
prudent,
respectable,
hospitable,
able to teach,
3 not addicted to wine
or pugnacious,
but gentle,
uncontentious,
free from the love of money.
4 [He must be] one who
manages his own household
well, keeping his children under
control with all dignity
5 (but if a
man does not know how to
manage his own household, how
will he take care of the church of
God?),
6 [and] not a new convert, lest
he become conceited and fall into
the condemnation incurred by
the devil.
7 And he must have a good
reputation with those outside [the
church], so that he may not fall
into reproach and the snare of the
devil.

Titus 1:5-9

5 For this reason I left you
in Crete, that you would set
in order what remains and
appoint elders in every city as
I directed you,
6 [namely,] if any man is
above reproach,
the husband of one wife,
having children who
believe, not accused of
dissipation or rebellion.
7 For the overseer must be
above reproach as God's
steward,
not self-willed,
not quick-tempered,
not addicted to wine,
not pugnacious,
not fond of sordid gain,
8 but hospitable,
loving what is good,
sensible,
just,
devout,
self-controlled,
9 holding fast the faithful
word which is in accordance
with the teaching, so that he
will be able both to exhort in
sound doctrine and to refute
those who contradict.

A number of observations emerge from these two passages as non-negotiable standards. First, it is required that there be no just grounds to charge an overseer with a pattern of inconsistency with respect to godly character (1 Tim. 3:1; Titus 1:7). Secondly, there must be unquestioned sexual integrity (1 Tim. 3:2; Titus 1:7). Thirdly, there must be exemplary domestic piety (1 Tim. 3:4-5; Titus 1:6b). Fourthly, there must be the graces indicative of sound judgment (1 Tim. 3:2; Titus 1:8). Fifthly, there must be graces essential to good relationships, that is, he must be a people person (1 Tim. 3:3; Titus 1:7b). Sixthly, he must manifest the essential graces of patterned self-control (1 Tim. 3:2; Titus 1:8b). Seventhly, there must be pure motives, or a non-mercenary mentality (1 Tim. 3:3b; Titus 1:7). Eighthly, he must demonstrate the graces of having an aggressive love for people (1 Tim. 3:2; Titus 1:8). Ninthly, he must have the graces essential for effective and wise leadership (1 Tim. 4:5). Tenthly, he must have a good testimony before the unconverted (1 Tim. 3:7). Finally, he must show the graces which accompany experience, and must have in some measure neutralized pride (1 Tim. 3:6).

2. There must be clear indications of an enlarged, balanced and tested Christian experience (identifying the major aspects of such Christian experience).

The character qualification of Christian experience (1 Tim. 3:6), should lead to the question, what are the major aspects of Christian experience? They would be, at least, a proven love for and devoted attachment to the person of Christ; a personal and perceptive acquaintance with the fundamental workings of sin and grace in the soul; a chastened disposition of humility and self-distrust; a presence of a deep and growing love for people. These aspects of Christian experience all deal with the inner life.

The inner life of the preacher, as was noted, is unparalleled in importance. Has the inner life of the man equipped him to do what he is called to do in the lives of his people? Many who excelled in the academics of the seminary classroom fail in the hospital room, board room, living room, counseling session and pulpit. This proven fitness which comes only from Christian experience is a non-negotiable for the ministry.

For instance, how can one preach Christ if in his life there is doubt as to his own devoted attachment to Christ? Is this one who says he is called, willing to follow Christ (Mark 1:16-20; Luke 14:26-33)? Can this ministerial candidate say, 'For me, to live is Christ and to die is gain?' James Stewart states, 'You may preach Paul's Christ or Calvin's Christ, and not break a single shackle of sin or bind up one broken heart. There is not authority enough in second-hand religion to rouse the listless and set the captives free.'[42] Whitefield, in his heart-felt passion, cried, 'You will never preach with power feelingly, while you deal in a false commerce with truths unfelt. It will be but poor, dry, sapless stuff – your people will go out of the church as cold as they came in. For my part, I would not preach an unknown Christ for ten thousand worlds.'[43] The man of God must know Christ! He must be gripped with a love for and devoted attachment to his King! Without this major aspect of Christian experience, he is unfit for the pulpit and ought to spend his time seeking Christ, not the office.

Furthermore, the man of God is called to be a physician of souls. He trafficks in the arenas of sin and grace. He therefore, must be well acquainted experientially with these great realities. He must be able to say, 'What we have seen and heard we proclaim also to you that you too may have fellowship with us; and indeed our fellowship is with the Father and with His Son Jesus Christ' (1 John 1:3). John Owen's words are immortal:

> If the word does not dwell with power *in* us, it will not pass with power *from* us.... The want of this experience of the power of gospel truth on their own souls is that which gives us so many lifeless, sapless orations in words and dead as to power, instead of preaching the gospel in the demonstration of the Spirit.[44]

3. There must be the presence of the gifts essential for fulfilling the purposes and ends of the pastoral office (necessity, source, identity and basic elements).

Although much more could be said (and will be in the next section) about Christian experience and the inner life of the man of God, the point is sufficiently clear. There is more to a proven fitness than proven character and tested Christian experience; there must also be the presence of gifts essential for fulfilling the ends and purposes of the pastoral office.

These gifts, which obviously grow and develop, must be present at the time when a man is called actually to do the work of the ministry. That certain gifts are absolute prerequisites is the plain testimony of Scripture. The most relevant texts make it clear that he must be 'able to teach' (1 Tim. 3:2), which means he must be able to take revealed truth and impart it to the saints for their edification and to sinners for their conversion. It is interesting to note that Spurgeon would not admit men into the Pastors' College unless they were able to show some fruit in their preaching labors, thus illustrating this qualification. John Newton's comments provide a balance: 'These [gifts] are to appear in due season; they are not to be expected instantaneously, but gradually, in the use of proper means. They are necessary for the discharge of the ministry; but not necessary as pre-requisites to warrant our desires after it.'[45]

The other clearly required gifts are of leadership (1 Tim. 3:4-5) and the ability to exhort in sound doctrine and refute those in error (Titus 1:9). The man of God will find himself in a place of spiritual and organizational leadership, as well as training other men (2 Tim. 2:2). Therefore, he cannot be inept as a leader. He will find himself in positions where he must defend the truth and engage in conflict for the sake of truth. Paul, knowing the difficulties, tests, trials and battles, makes certain that these graces are clearly required for the man who would take the office. Not only are there clearly required gifts, there are also gifts which are inferred from the demands of the revealed tasks of the pastoral office (Acts 20:28; Eph. 4:11; 1 Tim. 5:17; Heb. 13:17; 1 Pet. 5:1-5).

There is a clear and inescapable logical connection which exists between the pastoral office and the intention of Christ who gives men to fill it. Those whom Christ calls, He equips with the requisite gifts (Eph. 4:8; Jer. 3:15). At this point, it would prove beneficial to examine the source of the gifts and identify the specific gifts which Christ bestows upon the men He calls to pastoral ministry.

It is obvious that the ultimate or immediate source of all gifts is God Himself. Paul says that it is the Spirit Himself who sovereignly bestows His gifts (1 Cor. 12:4-11). It is noteworthy to remember that some gifts are imparted primarily in conception (Ps. 139:13-16), as God wires men together in their mother's womb. Other gifts are imparted germinally in regeneration, as God gives new life in Christ. Still others are imparted gradually through a process of growth and maturation, such as Solomon's gift of wisdom (1 Kgs. 3:9). There are also times when some gifts come directly by the Holy Spirit, especially gifts dealing with public utterance (Eph. 6:19; Matt. 10:19-20). Whether a gift comes through creation and common grace or redemption and special grace, they all must be consciously cultivated (2 Tim. 1:6; 1 Tim. 4:14).

The identity of specific gifts requisite for the pastoral office can be categorized under five headings:

(1) those gifts which come to expression in the disposition, capabilities and acquisitions of the mind;

(2) those gifts which come to expression through the various faculties connected with the facility of sanctified utterance;

(3) those gifts which come to expression in a proven ability to oversee, guide and govern the people of God with sanctified leadership;

(4) a more than ordinary degree of spiritual disposition consistent with the unique nature of rule in Christ's church;

(5) a more than ordinary degree of spiritual force of character.

Those gifts which come to expression in the disposition, capabilities and acquisitions of the mind. The mental gifts of the pastoral office cannot be over-emphasized. Pastoral work is not simply people work, mouth work, or leadership work; rather an essential aspect is rigorous mental work. The nature of this work demands a number of mental qualifications for the man of God. He must have a mind which is reverently and lovingly submissive to the absolute authority of the Scriptures. In biblical terminology, this is the mind 'holding fast the faithful word' (Titus 1:9), which 'trembles at My word' (Isa. 66:2). See also 1 Corinthians 2:13; John 17:8; Jeremiah 15:16; 2 Timothy 2:2.

The man of God must also have a mind furnished with a grasp of the basic contents of Scripture, that is, a general familiarity with the contents of the Bible (2 Tim. 2:15, 3:15). He must have a basic understanding of and a love for the meaning, inter-relatedness and self-consistency of Scripture. The man of God must be growing in his grasp of the theological disciplines. He must also be furnished with the necessary tools and spiritual dexterity to discover and make plain the meaning and application of Scripture to others (2 Tim. 2:7, 3:16-17; 1 Tim. 3:2; Titus 1:9).

Finally, his mind must be disposed to and furnished with sound practical judgment. The pastor must be able to take what he knows of Scripture, not only to teach others in a public setting, but also to apply it with skill to individual cases. John Owen addresses this subject with his usual precision:

> The proper ways whereby pastors and teachers must obtain this skill and understanding are, by diligent study of the Scriptures, meditation thereon, fervent prayer, experience of spiritual things, and temptations in their own souls, with a prudent observation of the manner of God's dealing with others, and the ways of the opposition made to the work of His grace in them. Without these things, all pretenses unto this ability and duty of pastoral office are vain; whence it is that the whole work of it is much neglected.[46]

Those gifts which come to expression through the various faculties connected with the facility of sanctified utterance. It is obviously necessary that for one to be duly qualified for the pastoral office he needs more than gray matter. He must possess gifts in the area of speech, or public utterance. Too many have been the victims of a brilliant man with extraordinary mental gifts, yet who could not preach his way out of a paper bag. It is torturous to saints who love God's Word and want to learn. It is with scriptural warrant, therefore, that the absolute non-negotiable requirement of the gift of sanctified utterance is asserted.

The pastoral epistles are clear in their testimony (1 Tim. 3:2; Titus 1:9; 2 Tim. 2:2). The apostolic models of pastoral labor reveal this truth (Acts 20:20, 35; Col. 1:28-9; 1 Thess. 2:11). The apostolic injunctions concerning pastoral labor confirm it (1 Tim.

4:11, 13, 16; 2 Tim. 2:2, 15; 4:2; Titus 1:13; 2:8, 15). The New Testament requirements and examples make sanctified utterance a non-negotiable requirement. Furthermore, the apostolic description of one who is sent by Christ is of an ambassador[47] (2 Cor. 5:19f.), and a herald[48] (2 Tim. 1:11). Both of these word pictures demand gifts of public utterance. John Stott, in his classic study, notes:

> Heralding is not the same as lecturing. A lecture is dispassionate, objective, academic. It is addressed to the mind. It seeks no result but to impart certain information and, perhaps, to provoke the student to further inquiry. But the herald of God comes with an urgent proclamation of peace through the blood of the cross, and with a summons to men to repent, to lay down their arms and humbly accept the offered pardon.[49]

Is not this whole subject of the gift of utterance a missing note in today's churches? Is not the curse of the modern church that pulpits have been opened to nice guys who can't preach? One does not doubt the sincerity and even godliness of many men, but let the church affirm with a holy boldness that if a man cannot preach then he is not one of Christ's pastoral gifts to the church.

Now the vital question: What is a sanctified gift of utterance? Is it mere oratorical skill? Is it the ability to weave a good tale? Is it Ciceronian eloquence? Four basic elements which comprise the gift of sanctified utterance are set forth. These will be unpacked one at a time.

(1) *A natural, acquired and cultivated ability to speak so as to secure the listening ear of the average listener.* This is not necessarily the kind of beautiful utterance described in Ezekiel 33:32: 'Behold, you are to them like a sensual song by one who has a beautiful voice and plays well on an instrument; for they hear your words, but they do not practice them.' But the utterance, although perhaps not filled with such melodious sonnets, is not one of the stammering tongue. It should be noted that those who have physical impediments which are so distracting that only the highly motivated and devoted can listen are not called to labor in the Word.[50] Spurgeon noted:

> A man with a big tongue which filled up his mouth and caused indistinctness, another without teeth, another who stammered, another who could not pronounce all the alphabet, I have had the pain of declining on the ground that God had not given them those physical appliances, which are as the prayer-book would put it, 'generally necessary'.[51]

The element here is natural in that it is an ability endowed by God in nature. It is an acquired ability in that it takes learning and experience. It is a cultivated ability in that it demands constant efforts at improvement.

(2) *A natural, acquired and cultivated ability to express one's thoughts clearly and convincingly to the average person.* This is a logical deduction from the 'able to teach' qualification in 1 Timothy 3:2. How can a pastor comfort, incite to action, motivate to godliness, or bring the heretic and his heresy to the bar of man's judgment with conviction unless he has this ability? The plain answer is that he cannot. How can he feed with knowledge and understanding (Jer. 3:15)? It must be granted by all that the gift of sanctified utterance includes the ability to get thoughts out of the preacher's head into the heads and hearts of the listeners.

(3) *A natural and conferred ability to be received as a messenger of God without torturing the discernment of the true people of God.* On numerous occasions, in homiletics classes and church services, many have been tested by the well meaning, even zealous man (usually young), who 'preaches' his heart out. Everything from the organization, to the flow, to the grammar, to the actual speech patterns have tested the patience of the listeners. One of the indispensable elements of sanctified utterance is the ability to speak in such a way that the people of God are not tempted to lie when one asks them how he did. In other words, they know that God has spoken (1 Thess. 2:13). They will sense the spiritual authority (Matt. 7:28-9). They will be edified in their souls, nourished on the Word. Even though there may be many rough edges, there will be a settled conviction by true saints that the man is a messenger of God.

(4) *A supernatural endowment of the Holy Spirit enabling one to speak with divine unction.* Unction is something which is difficult to define, but there is no doubt left in the preacher's mind when it has occurred. Martyn Lloyd-Jones defines unction in these terms:

> It is the Holy Spirit falling upon the preacher in a special manner. It is an access to power. It is God giving power and enablement, through the Spirit, to the preacher in order to that he may do this work in a manner that lifts it up beyond the efforts and endeavors of man to a position in which the preacher is being used by the Spirit and becomes the channel through whom the Spirit works.[52]

Marcel defines unction in terms of 'the freedom of the Spirit'.[53] It is the extraordinary development of the faculties; the soul, the tongue, the mind, the affections. This unction 'belongs only to the spoken style'.[54]

Some have described the experience of unction as if they were being carried along, preaching without effort. There is the felt power of the truth. There were fresh thoughts coming to mind, an extraordinary fluidity of speech in communicating those thoughts, and an unusual intensity in delivering them. Many times such unction comes in declaring the glories of Christ or in application of the truth, especially to the unconverted. There are never any regrets or second guesses about the content of the extemporaneous flow (which is not always true about other extemporaneous, unplanned comments). There is transaction between preacher and congregation, an empathetic involvement with their hearts and minds. Unction is the preacher and the congregation experiencing the truths of 1 Corinthians 2:4, 1 Thessalonians 1:5, 2:13 and 1 Peter 4:11.

There are a couple of precautions, however. Unction has nothing necessarily to do with a particular level of physical animation, eloquence, volume or fluency. On the other hand it may be reflected in all these factors. One may with great unction preach quietly, almost in a whisper, whereas another may expand his lungs to full capacity. Another caution is that the preacher will not experience the same degree of unction in every sermon. At times he may feel as if alone in the pulpit, only to find that God had mightily used the message. Other times he may have sensed tremendous unction, only to have his wife ask if he was feeling well that day.

Those gifts which come to expression in a proven ability to oversee, guide and govern the people of God with sanctified leadership.

The specific gifts which are requisite for the pastoral office are being identified. Those gifts which come to expression in the disposition, capabilities and acquisitions of the mind have been covered. Also covered are those gifts which come to expression through the various faculties connected with the faculty of sanctified utterance. Finally, the gifts of oversight and leadership will be explored.

The New Testament is unambiguous in its testimony regarding the absolute necessity of such gifts of leadership. First, the term used for 'overseer'[55] implies governing abilities. Such texts as 1 Timothy 3:4-5, Romans 12:3, 6-8 and 1 Corinthians 12:4-7 and 12:28 make the gift of leadership an absolute necessity. Further testimony comes from other passages where 'shepherd' is employed as the image (e.g. Acts 20:28).

There was a man who graduated from seminary who is representative of many. He had an incredible gift of teaching. He had great exegetical skill, a craftsman's ability to outline a passage, and the skill to communicate with clarity. Yet he failed miserably in the area of leadership. His wife was the head of the house. Away from the pulpit and lectern he was shy and introverted. He ended up going to a church and although he taught the people well, he was never able to lead them. This is indeed a tragedy. The pastoral office demands men of strong enough character that not only do they have mental gifts and speaking gifts, but they can oversee, guide and govern the people of God with sanctified leadership.

Part of this sanctified leadership are gifts of more than ordinary spiritual discernment, wisdom and courage. These elements are combined with a more than ordinary degree of spiritual disposition consistent with the unique nature of rule in Christ's church. In other words, there is a servant's heart operating in the midst of leadership. Jesus reminded His disciples of this quality:

> But Jesus called them to Himself, and said, 'You know that the rulers of the Gentiles lord it over them, and their great men exercise authority over them. It is not this way among you, but whoever wishes to become great among you shall be your servant, and whoever wishes to be first among you shall be your slave; just as the Son of Man did not come to be served, but to serve, and to give His life a ransom for many' (Matt. 20:25-28, see also 1 Pet. 5:3).

Finally, there must be a more than ordinary degree of spiritual force of character.

> The man whose Christian character does not command confidence and respect would, as a minister, only dishonor God and His cause.... The minister must have some force of character. The feeble, undecided, shuffling man, who cannot rule his own family, nor impress and govern his inferiors by his moral force, had better not preach.[56]

Element Three: an adequate external confirmation of fitness for the work of the pastoral office

> While sober self-assessment of our desire, graces, and gifts, is a personal responsibility which no man can righteously evade, an external confirmation of that assessment by a cross-section of spiritually-minded people is essential to a valid call to the pastoral office.[57]

The necessity of sober self-assessment has already been emphasized. If a call to the ministry is based on self-assessment alone, it is neither safe nor biblical. There must be an earned and recognized credibility by those in the assembly who are spiritually-minded. The testimony of Scripture on this point is abundant. Paul's command to Timothy in 2 Timothy 2:2 gives the principle in propositional form. Timothy was assessed by Paul and others, and then he, in turn, must entrust these things to others who are likewise approved. Acts 15:38 and 16:2 give a description of this principle in the negative and positive. Paul believed that John Mark had lost his credibility and Paul could no longer give him his confirmation in the ministry. On the other hand, it was the brethren's positive and confirming assessment which launched Timothy into the apostolic band of ministry.[58]

This element to the call to the ministry cannot be ignored. The *Zeitgeist* is crassly individualistic and subjective. Nevertheless, the inviolable principle of external confirmation by the mature and spiritually-minded is a quality control on the ministry. A man who is a part of a healthy body with solid leadership has a tremendous advantage at this point. Edmund Clowney cogently expresses the role of the church in external confirmation:

> The same gifts of the Spirit that give assurance to the man of God regarding his own calling also mark him out to the people of God. The church does not call in its own name, but in Christ's. The function of the church is to recognize and acknowledge the calling of God.[59]

Element Four: a providential opportunity and proper ecclesiastical recognition for the office and work of a specific pastoral charge

This element has some providential variables in it. For instance, in God's providence there may be some time between the external confirmation and the actual opening of a door for ministry. A biblical example would be David's anointing to be king and his actual reign over Israel. There was obviously a providential interval which included Saul, desert experiences and the like. Paul's call and ministry also saw a providential hiatus (Gal. 1:13-24).

This element of the pastoral call stresses that after sober self-assessment, after an external confirmation of character, experience and gifts, there is a crowning validation to this call when a man is ordained and installed into a specific pastoral charge. It is here where the ministry of the Holy Spirit and the human decisions of the church meet in providential concurrence (Acts 20:20, cf. 14:23; Titus 1:5). The notion that a man can be called and ordained to the pastoral office and then not fill any office is ridiculous. Although a man may have to wait for a full-time charge, if he is called, gifted and recognized by the church, then he will have a providential opportunity in a specific charge.

John Newton's words of advice to a young man provide a fitting conclusion:

> That which finally evidences a proper call is a correspondent opening in Providence, by a gradual train of circumstances pointing out the means, the time, the place of actually entering upon the work.... If it be the Lord's will to bring you into His ministry, He has already appointed your place and service; and though you know it not at present, you shall at a proper time.[60]

Conclusion

If the church is going to be serious about renewing God-owned, passionate, applicatory preaching, then she must be gravely serious about her understanding of the call to the pastoral ministry. One is reminded of the Great Awakening and the uncomfortable emphasis which Whitefield and the Tennents placed on an unconverted ministry. Today the church must warn against not only an unconverted ministry, but also an uncalled ministry. There must be foundational principles which regulate her judgment and thinking in this area. She must be aware of fundamental errors regarding the call. Pastors should examine themselves and ministerial candidates for false reasons for assuming a call. And there must be rigorous efforts to maintain the true biblical elements which constitute a true call to the pastoral office. The call, however, constitutes only the starting point of powerful preaching. There is a corollary, and that is the life of the man of God.

PART TWO:

THE LIFE OF THE MAN OF GOD IN THE PASTORAL OFFICE[61]

3

THE MAN OF GOD IN RELATIONSHIP TO GOD

General Introduction

The call of God comes to a man who is 'living before God', with all that that life entails. God does not call automatons, He calls living, flesh and blood men. As a result, the healthy life of the man of God is critical for efficient, God-owned ministry. The central axiom to this section is: As a general rule, sustained effectiveness in pastoral ministry will be realized in direct proportion to the health and vigor of the whole redeemed humanity of the man of God.

There are a number of elements in this axiom which deserve the utmost attention. First, the phrase 'sustained effectiveness in pastoral ministry' means week in, week out, year in, year out, labor in the pastorate, which has as its major component the preaching and teaching of the Word in the context of a local church. The preaching of the Word and the pastoral care of the flock are in view here. The effectiveness spoken of here is simply that which accomplishes the biblical goals, namely, to glorify God, to save sinners and to build up the saints.[62]

The second phrase, 'general rule', acknowledges that God has used unregenerate men to convey his Word (e.g., Matt. 7:21-3). This, however, is the exception, not the rule. The axiom also emphasizes that there should be no disparity between the man of God as a solid, growing, mature Christian and the man of God as a pastor. He must be an example in the basics of the faith (1 Tim. 4:12; Titus 2:7); he must be above reproach (1 Tim. 3:2; Titus 1:6); he must not be like the Pharisees, who do not practice what they preach (Matt. 23:3). This cannot be overstated, because the Scriptures set forth a cause and effect relationship between what a servant of God is as a man and what he accomplishes as a minister of the Word (1 Thess. 1:4-5, 2:10-12; 1 Tim. 4:16, 5:22-3).

Is this not why there is so little power among ministers of the Word today? The church is plagued today with weak pulpits. Men who know little, feel little and live little of the Christian faith fill pulpits and bring reproach on the biblical enterprise of pastoral preaching. Others have all the communication gimmicks, and can hold a crowd, but there is no power, no genuine spiritual effectiveness. In recent years it has been tragic to see some popular preachers who have been found out to have been carrying on like pagans for years! If there is to be serious sustained effectiveness in pastoral ministry, the man of God must have health and vigor in his redeemed humanity. In this present day, when pastors are given advice only on how to run a bigger and better dog and pony show, Spurgeon's words ring true:

> We are, in a certain sense, our own tools, and therefore must keep ourselves in order. If I want to preach the gospel, I can only use my own voice; therefore I must train my vocal powers. I can only think with my own brains, and feel with my own heart, and therefore I must educate my intellectual and emotional faculties. I can only weep and agonize for souls in my own renewed nature, therefore must I watchfully maintain the tenderness which was in Christ Jesus. It will be vain for me to stock my library, or organize my societies, or project schemes, if I neglect the culture of myself; for books, and agencies, and systems, are only remotely the instruments of my holy calling; my own spirit, soul, body, are my nearest machinery for sacred service; my spiritual faculties and my inner life, are my battle axe and weapons of war.[63]

The man of God must see it as his primary duty to nurture his own soul, growing in the graces of true Christlikeness and godliness. Thomas Murphy does not exaggerate, when he states,

> It should be laid down as our first principle that eminent piety is the indispensable qualification for those in the ministry of the gospel. By this is not meant simply a piety the genuineness of which is unquestionable, but a piety the degree of which is above that of ordinary believers. It is meant that there should be a more thorough baptism of the Holy Ghost, a more absolute consecration of all powers

and faculties to the service of God, a more complete conformity to the likeness of the Lord Jesus, a greater familiarity with the mind of the Spirit, a nearer approach to the perfect man in Christ Jesus, in those who take upon themselves the privileges and the responsibilities of the pastor, than are commonly expected even in true Christians. The pastor should not be satisfied with reaching the general standard of spirituality. He has devoted himself to a high and holy office to which he believes himself called, and hence he has need of a very high tone of piety. As a minister appointed to serve in the sanctuary and wait upon souls, how deep should be his humility! His great aim is to save men, and it will not therefore suffice for him to have merely the ordinary sympathy with the suffering and the lost. He is to be a leader in the spiritual host of God; must he not go before others in spiritual attainments? To draw men up to a more and more elevated standard and devotedness is the appointment he holds from the great Head of the Church; surely he must rise still higher?

The first thing for the young minister to consider is how he may attain to this high degree of holiness in heart and life.

We dwell long and minutely upon this branch of our subject because of its superlative importance. There is no other point in the whole subject that needs to be so thoroughly impressed as this.[64]

The contemporary climate, perhaps in reaction to an undue exaltation of the clergy or perhaps only because of the anti-authoritarian air, revolts against this type of statement. It is common for men in pastoral office to so 'level the playing field' that their growth in holiness becomes sub-standard in order to 'relate' to the rest of the congregation. It is not a false piety that pastors are after. Neither is it the arrogance of a triumphalistic spirit. Neither is it being advocated that pastors should avoid being transparent in their faults and open about their own shortcomings (although this seems to be a bit overdone today too). What is being asserted is the simple fact that the man of God must make personal holiness and spiritual growth his primary duty before God. If he is to be effective, he must have a health and vigor in the totality of his redeemed humanity.

The Life of the Man of God in Relationship to God

The Scriptures are clear, the man of God lives life before the eye of God (2 Tim. 2:15; 2 Cor. 2:17) as a steward who is examined by God Himself (1 Cor. 4:1-5). Everything the man of God is, he is before God. Therefore, he must be assiduous to cultivate his life, spiritually, intellectually, physically and emotionally. To echo the axiom once again, 'As a general rule, sustained effectiveness in pastoral ministry will be realized in direct proportion to *the health and vigor of the whole redeemed humanity of the man of God.*' The whole of his redeemed humanity includes the man spiritually, intellectually, physically and emotionally.

Spiritually: The man of God must strive to maintain a real, expanding, varied, and original acquaintance with God and His ways.

Striving is part and parcel of the minister's life. Indeed, it is part and parcel of the Christian's life (Luke 13:24)! If the man of God is to have sustained effectiveness in his ministry, he must strive to maintain an acquaintance with God and His ways. This acquaintance must be *real,* as opposed to feigned, formal or professional. He must be apostolic in the sense that he can say, 'What we have seen and heard we proclaim to you also, so that you too may have fellowship with us; and indeed our fellowship is with the Father, and with His Son Jesus Christ' (1 John 1:3). He must be a man who knows God other than by hearsay.

Furthermore, his acquaintance with God and His ways must be *expanding*. He is called to be transformed 'from one level of glory to another' (2 Cor. 3:18), he is called to 'grow in the grace and knowledge of our Lord and Savior Jesus Christ' (2 Pet. 3:18). This progressive transformation and growth is locked into the fact that God and His holy Word are both inexhaustible. If the man of God is not expanding in his acquaintance of God and His ways, he is failing as a Christian and his effectiveness as a pastor will be neutralized.

This acquaintance must not only be real and expanding, it must be *varied*. The ups and downs, the joys and sorrows, must be experienced. The Psalms, which cover the entirety of human emotion and experience, serve as a good guide. If the man of God is to know God, he must know Him in the darkness of night and the brightness of day, in the fullness of His presence (Ps. 16:11) and in the absence of His presence (Ps. 77:7-10).

This varied experience of God and His ways is obviously a first-hand experience. The acquaintance must be a *personal and individual* acquaintance. In this day of crass individualism, there is the danger of overemphasizing the personal and individual at the expense of solidarity and the corporate. Nevertheless, the Bible in its broad context of solidarity (in Adam, in Christ, in the faith, etc.) also presents a noble individualism where the hairs of a man's head are numbered (Matt. 10:30) and each one is called by name (John 10:3). So the man of God not only walks with his God corporately, but also individually.

The question arises as to how the man of God attains and maintains this acquaintance of God and His ways. God has not only ordained the ends, but He has also ordained the means. Likewise in the realm of attaining and maintaining this relationship with Himself, God has established means which are integrated and interdependent. In other words, although the means will be considered separately, they cannot be separated in the life of the man of God. Also, these means are basic and foundational, they are not the 'secrets' of the mystics, rather they are plain, ordinary, biblical means.

Among the means which God uses, in the lives of all His children, and in particular, in the life of His called servants, are suffering, tribulation, affliction, temptation and opposition. Although these means are not among our favorites, they are deeply rooted in the biblical testimony. Paul and Barnabas, in Acts 14:22, were said to be 'strengthening the souls of the disciples, encouraging them to continue in the faith, and saying, "Through many tribulations we must enter the kingdom of God."' Jesus Himself taught His disciples on numerous occasions that trials and tribulations would be inescapable realities in the lives of His followers (John 16:33; Matt. 5:10-12). If our Master suffered, then certainly His followers must endure suffering (Heb. 5:7-8; John 15:18-21).

Both Psalmist and Apostle recognize suffering as a means of growing in grace (Ps. 119:67, 71; 2 Cor. 1:3-7; Heb. 12:5-11). Octavius Winslow eloquently states,

> But affliction is one of the Lord's moulds for shaping you into an experimental Christian. And to be an experimental Christian His Word must be inwrought into our soul. What can we know of the promises, the succourings, the sympathy of God's Word, – its perfect adaptation to our crushed and sorrowful condition of our humanity, – but for trial?[65]

Paul even understood suffering as a way to propagate the suffering of Christ (1 Cor. 4:8-13; 2 Cor. 1:3-11, 4:7-12; Col. 1:24). Although Paul never taught that his sufferings were atoning, he did see them as an extension of Christ's own suffering, for the sake of making Christ's atonement known.

> Paul's suffering completes Christ's afflictions *not* by adding anything to their worth, but by extending them to the people they were meant to save. What is lacking in the afflictions of Christ is not that they are deficient in worth, as though they could not sufficiently cover the sins of all those who believe. What is lacking is that the infinite value of Christ's afflictions is not known and trusted in the world.... And those ministers of the Word 'complete' what is lacking in the afflictions of Christ by extending them to others (through their suffering).[66]

Suffering as a means of growing in acquaintance with God and His ways is really outside the man of God's control. They are ordered by God alone. There are, however, numerous other means that are within his control and by which he can cultivate his walk with God. The primary means is the devotional assimilation of the Word of God (Ps. 119:9-11; Josh. 1:8; Ps. 1:1-3; John 17:17 1 Pet. 2:2; 1 John 2:14b). This devotional assimilation of God's Word ought to have a few essential elements to it, namely: it ought to be structured and consistent; it ought to be systematic and comprehensive; it ought to be prayerful and meditative. Murphy instructs his readers once again,

> Ministers are liable to get into the habit of studying the Word of God simply so that they may be the better prepared to teach others. It is all important, however, that they should do more than this. They should not read the Bible merely for others, nor simply as a book of science, or history, or geography, or profound wisdom only, but that they may also bring it home and apply it to themselves. The faintest impression that it is not intended for their own personal benefit should never be admitted. Their hearts should be so applied to it that they themselves be brought nearer to God. They should listen to it that they may hear God's voice addressed to their own souls, and that for themselves they may see His glory beaming upon every page. For their own personal benefit, as if there were no others in the world who needed it, for their own spiritual strength and instruction and comfort, they should meditate upon it profoundly everyday.[67]

Another means of cultivating that acquaintance with God and His ways is the habit and spirit of secret prayer (Luke 18:1; Ps. 5:1-3; 55:16-17; Mark 1:35; Matt. 6:5-6; Eph. 6:18; Jd. 20). The habit and spirit of secret prayer, as a discipline, has multifaceted benefits. Vital, personal communion with Christ is renewed and increased (Eph. 3:14-19). One's perspective on reality is kept in focus (2 Cor. 4:18; Ps. 73, esp. vv.16-17). One's own sins are seen in their true light (Ps. 90:8; Isa. 6:1ff.). One's pardon and acceptance before God are sealed afresh to the heart (Ps. 130:3; 1 John 1:9). Finally, although not exhaustively, one receives grace for the work at hand (Heb. 4:16; Jas. 4:4; Isa. 40:29-31).

Thomas Brooks states,

> Our Saviour in the text takes it for granted that every child of God will be frequent in praying to his heavenly Father; and therefore He encourages them so much the more in the work of secret prayer. 'When you pray;' as if He had said, 'I know you can as well hear without ears, and live without food, and fight without hands, and walk without feet, as you are able to live without prayer.'[68]

> Luther long ago has said – 'Prayer, meditation and temptation, make a Minister.' No one will hesitate to admit the importance of the first of these qualifications, who has ever realized the weight of Ministerial responsibility, who has been led to know that his 'sufficiency is of God', and that prayer is the appointed channel of heavenly communications.[69]

Pastors must pray! They must pray because they are children of God. They must pray because of the enormous ministerial responsibility placed upon them. Pastors must pray, lest they be found out to be hypocrites. Jonathan Edwards puts it in plain language,

> The spirit of a true convert is a spirit of faith and reliance on the power, wisdom, and mercy of God, and such a spirit is naturally expressed in prayer. True prayer is nothing else but faith expressed. True Christian prayer is the faith and reliance of the soul breathed forth in words. But the hypocrite is without the spirit of faith. He has no true reliance or dependence on God, but is really self-dependent.[70]

As the man of God disciplines himself in the Word and secret prayer, he should find that the fruit of these disciplines is increasing ethical conformity to the will of God. As this becomes a central concern, he can say with Paul, 'I also do my best to maintain always a blameless conscience before God and before men' (Acts 24:16). Maintaining a good conscience, therefore, is another interdependent means of growing in acquaintance with God and His ways. Maintaining a good conscience means that there is no controversy with God in terms of unconfessed sin, duties neglected and unperformed, and truth not being believed. Maintaining a good conscience also means that one has sought to resolve any area in which abnormalities have occurred, with one's wife, children, fellow workers, the flock of God and the world. In the present time, when conscience is a neglected area of humanity, the pastor must have the realization that this is vitally important. A defiled conscience dampens zeal for the Word and causes estrangement in prayer.[71]

Pastor Martin tells of an incident which reveals the seriousness with which men of God must work at maintaining a good conscience. At an evening worship service he called out the wrong number to a hymn, and in the next second made a false excuse as to why he did it. After the hymn he had to admit to the congregation that he had just lied. Some may say, 'A mere peccadillo! No big deal!' But what constrained him to be so meticulous? He was about to pray and he knew he had lied. Before he could lead the congregation in prayer, he had to keep his conscience void of offense, thus he confessed his sin.

The man of God must keep a blameless conscience! The Scriptures are clear, it is casting aside of a good conscience which leads to the shipwreck of the faith (1 Tim. 1:18-19). Whether it is a harsh word to his wife, impatience with his kids or a domineering spirit with a fellow elder, the man of God must be relentless in keeping a blameless conscience. A defiled conscience will cloud a man's judgment in ministry and make him ripe for a fall. It must be remembered, it was the same David whose conscience smote him for cutting the hem of Saul's garment, who also defiled another man's wife. Somewhere in the course of life, David failed to maintain a good conscience. One of the ministerial falls in the last decade involved a man who was preaching a series on Christian marriage, while carrying on an affair for eight years! Oh, how a defiled conscience can become a dull conscience, and a dull conscience can lead a man down the road of apostasy.

Some ministerial candidates and even some seasoned pastors may say, 'Bible reading and prayer. How basic. Give me something more substantial.' The battle will be won or lost in the arena of the basics! The conscience will be kept clear as the man of God exercises himself in the basics of Bible reading, meditation and prayer. The most telling fact of a pastor's ministry is his private life before God, with his heart opened before an open Bible, and his heart lifted up in secret prayer. Men who are mighty in God are mighty in the secret place, not just in the pulpit.

Engaging in periodic seasons of intense self-examination and protracted seasons of prayer is another means of growing in acquaintance of God and His ways. The biblical examples are numerous. Moses spent forty days with God. Daniel set himself to fasting and prayer. Our Lord Jesus spent time alone with God for extended periods of time. Great saints have also engaged in these seasons of self-examination and prayer, underscoring the benefit of such times.[72] These times are absolutely necessary for spiritual health and vitality because remaining, indwelling sin is so powerful. One would think that trafficking in holy things, day in and day out, would be gloriously refreshing. But because of indwelling sin, the man of God many times gets dulled rather than sharpened through his excessive contact with holy things. There is also the draining influence of the tasks and burdens of the ministry. Paul knew this (2 Cor. 11:28), and in fact placed it above the physical suffering he endured. Therefore, if a man of God is going to maintain a growing acquaintance with his heavenly Father, he must get away for self-examination and protracted seasons of prayer.

Finally, a regular exposure to the masters of the inner life will yield rich reward for the man of God. Anyone who has come into close contact with the Puritans has felt the stimulating, challenging effect of their writings. Owen, Flavel, Brooks, Baxter, Edwards, Winslow and others are masters of the inner life. The man of God must make friends with these types of writers if he is to grow in his acquaintance with God and His ways.

The life of the man of God in the pastoral office, if it is to be marked by sustained effectiveness, must strive to maintain a thriving relationship with God. If he is to be an effective pastor, he must first be a holy child of God. Erroll Hulse captures this connection,

> Preaching is not lecturing. It is not merely the presentation of scientifically accurate materials. Of course, the preacher is concerned with the world of exegesis, with structure and flow, with simplicity and rhetoric; but without piety he will never be and cannot be a preacher. Moreover, his effectiveness and power as a preacher will be directly connected to his piety. Expressed negatively, if a glaring blemish of manner obstructs the message, how much more a moral inconsistency in the life of the preacher, as the Scripture says, 'As dead flies give perfume a bad smell, so a little folly outweighs wisdom and honor' (Eccles. 10:1).[73]

Intellectually: The man of God must seek a maturing spiritual perception of the truth of God, both in its objective essence and in its practical application to the world of men and things.

The life of the man of God must not only be marked by pre-eminent piety, that is, he must be experientially acquainted with God and His ways, but he must also be a man who rigorously engages his mind before God. In dealing with the spiritual and intellectual separately, one might think that a sharp distinction is being made between head and heart, the spiritual and the intellectual. That is not the case. Many have rightly criticized that distinction, but it is possible for a man to have a genuinely humble walk with God and be inept intellectually. It is also possible for a man to have great intellectual capacity, and yet be sterile in his walk with God. Murphy brings this issue into balance,

> The pastor must study, study, study, or he will not grow, or even live, as a true workman for Christ. The want of this is the cause of innumerable failures which are seen in the ministry. Here is a young man who enters the office with fine talents, a fair amount of preparation, an encouraging field of labor and every prospect of success. But the promise is not fulfilled. He does not come up to the expectations which were excited, and which he himself entertained. On the contrary, his preaching decreases in interest, his congregation falls away and his whole work declines. The reason is that he has not kept his mind polished up by constant study, or continued to replenish it with the rich stores of thought which he might have gathered from other sources. This process is well described by Vinet in his admirable work: 'We must study to excite and enrich our own mind by means of other men's. Those who do not study find their talents enfeebled and their minds become decrepit before the time. In respect to preaching, experience demonstrates this most abundantly. Whence comes it that preachers much admired in the beginning decline so rapidly or remain so much below the hopes to which they had given birth? Most frequently it is because they did not continue their studies.'[74]

Evangelical pastors have three to four year pastorates on the average. Could it be that because of this very issue they cannot sustain a long pastoral ministry? Could it be that all the freshness is gone because there is no maturing perception of God's truth that keeps preaching fresh? It is worth considering this area of the intellectual life before God, Who has commanded men to love Him with all of the mind (Matt. 22:37).

The principal focus of the life of the man of God in his intellectual relationship to God is the truth of God. This includes all the verities which God has revealed in general and special revelation. It is God's truth which must occupy the mind of the man of God. It is the truth of God which determines the field of intellectual growth and maturing perception. Alexander makes the point well when he says,

> If we might have our choice, it is better to converse with truth than with error; with the rudest, homeliest truth, than with the most ingenious, decorated error; with the humblest truth, than with the most soaring, original and striking error.... Again, while error leads to error, truth leads to truth. Each truth is germinal and pregnant, containing other truths. Only upon this principle can we vindicate the productiveness of solitary meditation. Link follows link in the chain, which we draw from unknown mysterious recesses. A few elementary truths are the bases of the universal system.[75]

The man of God must grow and expand in his grasp of God's truth. His understanding must be maturing, his appreciation of the organic unity of God's truth must be deepening. His whole life is given to learning more and more of God's revelation. Spurgeon identifies this quality in the Apostle Paul from 2 Timothy 4:13:

> How rebuked are they [preachers who won't study] by the apostle! He is inspired, and yet he wants BOOKS! He has preached at least for thirty years, and yet he wants BOOKS! He had seen the Lord, and yet he wants BOOKS! He had a wider experience than most men, and yet he wants BOOKS! He had been caught up into the third heaven, and had heard things which it was unlawful for a man to utter, yet he wants BOOKS! He had written the major part of the New Testament, and yet he wants BOOKS! The apostle says to Timothy and so he says to every preacher, 'Give Thyself unto reading.'[76]

The man's perception, however, must be spiritual, that is, given by the Holy Spirit. When the Spirit is revealing truth to the mind, there is light and heat. There is understanding with the mind and the engagement of the affections. The mind lays hold of the objective essence of a truth and the heart is delighted as it feels the truth. The mind then sees the truth, by the power of the Spirit, with its ramifications and connections with other truths. The man of God then begins to work out these things in their application to the world of men and things.[77]

The importance of this one principle must again be stated. How many pastors degenerate into dullness, needless repetition and sterility? How many because of lack of freshness in the study, bore the people of God? They ought to be edifying their people, equipping them to persevere, not be an occasion for them to prove their perseverance! Let him bring light and with it heat! 'As surely as we abominate all interesting and attractive preaching of falsehood, may we equally abominate all dull and unimpassioned proclamation of the truth!'[78]

How is this principle to be implemented? If indeed effective preaching and pastoral ministry are inextricably linked to the pastor's spiritual and intellectual development, then how is this axiom applied? Four lines of advice are drawn here. (1) He must make time for general reading beyond specific sermon preparation. (2) He must seek to establish a balanced reading program. (3) The man of God must seek to preserve the fruits of his reading. (4) He must take heed to some serious warnings, 'Therefore let him who thinks he stands take heed that he does not fall' (1 Cor. 10:12).

(1) *The man of God must take time for general reading beyond specific sermon preparation.*

There is a tremendous temptation for a pastor who is reading constantly to think that he has done his intellectual duty. Alexander is sagacious when he says:

> What theologians say of preparation for death, may be said of preparation for preaching; there is *habitual*, and there is *actual* preparation; the current of daily study, and the gathering of material for a given task. It may be compared with what is familiar, in another faculty, that of Law: the lawyer has his course of perpetual research, in the great principles of general jurisprudence, or the history of statutory enactment, or the systematic arrangement of practical methods, and he has laborious and sometimes sudden reading-up for an emergent case. Should he confine himself entirely to the latter, he must become narrow, though perhaps an acute, practitioner. So likewise the clerical scholar, however diligent, punctual, and

> persistent, who throws his whole strength into the preparation of sermons, and who never rises to higher views, or takes a larger career, through the wide expanse of scientific and methodic truth, must infallibly grow up stiff, cramped, lopsided, and defective. His scheme of preaching may never take him through the entire curve of theology and Scripture; or the providential leadings of his ministry may bring him again and again over the same portions. These are evils which can be prevented only by the resolute pursuit of general studies, irrespective of special pulpit performance. Such habits will tend to keep a man always prepared; and instead of getting to the bottom of his barrel as he grows older, he will be more and more prepared, as long as his faculties last.[79]

(2) *The man of God must seek to establish and maintain a balanced reading program.*

The balance comes in covering a wide range of literature through the course of a given year. Obviously the man of God must have consistent contact with *devotional literature*, the kind that stirs the soul. Here is where many have met their best friends – the Puritans. Such authors as Sibbes, Brooks, Flavel, Bunyan, Owen, and others have a special affinity for reaching the heart. If the heart is to be on fire, in life and in the pulpit, then there must be an acquaintance with the experimental divines.[80]

Theological literature must also make its way on to the plates. Although one will get much theology in the devotional literature of the Puritans, he must also set aside time for works dealing with theological issues. Beware of the novel, and stick with the old standards: Calvin's *Institutes*, *The Works of Jonathan Edwards*, Owen's theological treatises, Charles Hodge, R.L. Dabney, J.H. Thornwell, J.P. Boyce and J.L. Dagg. The mistake may be made in thinking that more recent works lack depth, but there should be a solid acquaintance with many theologians of the twentieth century, such as B.B. Warfield, Geerhardus Vos, John Murray and the superb recent work of Robert Reymond, *A New Systematic Theology of the Christian Faith* (Nashville, TN: Thomas Nelson Publishers, 1998).

In addition to the devotional and theological, there should be *biographical and historical literature.* Experience and Scripture (Heb. 12:1; 13:7) teach that the lives of great saints stir the soul.

With the 'great cloud of witnesses' surrounding God's people at any given generation, there ought to be an awareness of their lives. How many can remember a time of great growth in one's walk with Christ, which sprung from the reading of a stirring biography. Indeed, 'time would fail me if I tell of' Whitefield, Edwards, McCheyne, Luther, Calvin, Newton, Bunyan, Judson, Carey, Paton, Cameron and others.

However, the pastor must not only know the lives of the great saints, he must also be aware of the times in which they lived. He no doubt will get great historical information in a biography like Dallimore's on Whitefield, but he needs to be acquainted with church history. The standard historical works are fine, but focusing on a specific era is especially helpful. For instance, Iain Murray's book, *Revival and Revivalism: The Making and Marring of American Evangelicalism 1750-1858* (Banner of Truth, 1994) is a historical treasure house. Both biographical and historical reading will keep the man of God fresh in a multitude of ways.

The menu must also include *pastoral and homiletical literature*. Books dealing with issues such as pastoral oversight, counseling, church discipline and preaching keep these vital issues before the pastor in such a way that he keeps his balance and freshness in ministry. In other words, a contempt-breeding familiarity can develop in the pastor since he is always trafficking in these things. However, reading them brings new insights and perspectives. The pastor can always counsel better, lead better and preach better, regardless of what many pastors think.[81]

Polemical literature is also a necessity in the ministry. With the warning from Alexander on exposing the mind to error still fresh, the man of God must also keep in mind his duty to refute false doctrine and contend for the faith (Titus 1:9; Jude 3). He must keep abreast of such issues as theonomy, the health and wealth gospel, 'evangelical feminism', the self-cult of Robert Schuller, 'revival' movements, new expressions of antinomianism, post-modernism and the resurgence of paganism. In the context of the local church, many people have questions about a variety of issues, and the pastor must be prepared to give intelligent, thoughtful responses.[82]

Technical literature, such as that which deals with textual criticism, archeology, hermeneutics and the lexicon and syntax of original languages: the occasional reading of such materials keeps the pastor fresh in those more technical, yet vital aspects of the ministry. As one called to be an expert in the Word of God, he cannot afford to neglect such things totally. Yet, he must not only be familiar and comfortable with the culture and literature of the ancient biblical world, he must also be in touch with his world, so that he is constantly bringing biblical truth into contact with where people live. Therefore, *contemporary literature* is also important. Newspapers, news magazines and other materials which are current with the world are a great resource.

(3) *The man of God must also seek to preserve the fruits of his reading by note-taking, underlining, indexing and filing.*

If Jonathan Edwards studied with a pen in his hand, and incessantly wrote out his thoughts on scraps of paper, how much more ought the mental pygmies[83] of today attempt to preserve their thoughts which come from their reading?

(4) *The man of God, as one who is a reader, must also give heed to some warnings.*

The first warning is that he must not make reading a substitute for thinking. All thinkers are readers, but not all readers are thinkers. His reading should compel him to trace out a thought, apply truths to various situations, think through the ramifications and implications, and compare, contrast and synthesize thoughts. Too many pastors simply gather thoughts from books, instead of using books to stimulate thought.[84]

The next warning is critical because when a man comes to see the beauty of the Reformed faith, it transforms him into a new kind of reader. This is a glorious thing, but it can lead to dangerous pride, therefore he must not make a status symbol out of the amount of reading he does. Carnal pride can creep in here without notice – even if he is reading Owen, Volume VI, on sin and temptation! Boasting about the amount of reading he does will inevitably reveal that the amount of reading is not doing him much good. The man of God should allow the amount of his reading to seep out of his pores through his life and preaching.

> Not to read or study at all is to tempt God: to do nothing but study, is to forget the ministry: to study, only to glory in one's knowledge, is a shameful vanity: to study in search of the means to flatter sinners, a deplorable prevarication: but to store one's mind with the knowledge proper to the saints by study and prayer, and to diffuse that knowledge in solid instructions and practical exhortations – this is to be a prudent, zealous, and laborious minister.[85]

Sustained, effective preaching and pastoral ministry will be realized as the man of God grows spiritually in his walk with God and as he grows intellectually, grasping God's truth with maturing spiritual perception. Pastors must be men of heat and light, of head and heart. In addition to the head and heart, the man of God must also be concerned about his physical and emotional health, as vehicles through which he serves God with all that he is.

Physically and Emotionally: The man of God must seek to attain and maintain an accurate understanding of his present physical and emotional constitution and engage in a regular but flexible discipline aimed at keeping these two aspects of his redeemed humanity in optimum health and vigor.

A concern for the pastor's physical and emotional health and vigor is necessary because he is a body-soul entity (Gen. 2:7). Although there is a distinction between the body and the soul (Matt. 10:28), the Bible also teaches that there is a recognizable interplay and interdependence between man's body and soul, as numerous Proverbs demonstrate (Prov. 3:7-8; 4:20; 17:22; 18:14). Furthermore, Psalms 6, 32 and 51 reveal the physiological effects of unconfessed sin. Elijah needed rest and food to help cure his depression (1 Kgs. 19:2ff.). Again and again the Bible shows that delicate interplay between soul and body.

The man of God is not a disembodied spirit ministering to God's people. He is a human being, who is designed to bear only so much, as is seen in the metaphor of the body being an 'earthen vessel' (2 Cor. 4:7). He must, therefore, take care of his body as a stewardship from God. The Westminster Larger Catechism, on the sixth commandment, 'You shall not murder' (Exod. 20:13), is relevant to this subject, both positively and negatively.

Q. 135. *What are the duties required in the sixth commandment?*
A. The duties required in the sixth commandment are, all careful studies, and lawful endeavors, to preserve the life of ourselves and others by resisting all thoughts and purposes, subduing all passions, and avoiding all occasions, temptations, and practices, which tend to the unjust taking away the life of any; by just defense thereof against violence, patient bearing of the hand of God, quietness of mind, cheerfulness of spirit; *a sober use of meat, drink, physic [medication], sleep, labour, and recreations*; by charitable thoughts, love, compassion, meekness, gentleness, kindness; peaceable; mild and courteous speeches and behaviour; forbearance, readiness to be reconciled, patient bearing and forgiving of injuries, and requiting good for evil; comforting and succouring the distressed, and protecting and defending the innocent.

Q. 136. *What are the sins forbidden in the sixth commandment?*
A. The sins forbidden in the sixth commandment are, all taking away the life of ourselves, or of others, except in the case of publick justice, lawful war, or necessary defence; *the neglecting or withdrawing the lawful and necessary means of preservation of life*; sinful anger, hatred, envy, desire for revenge; all excessive passions, distracting cares; *immoderate use of meat, drink, labour and recreations*; provoking words, oppression, quarreling, striking, wounding, and whatsoever else tends to the destruction of the life of any.[86]

The biblical doctrine of salvation also demands this concern for the health of the body. Redemption is designed for the totality of the sinner's humanity, body and soul (Rom. 8:23; Phil. 3:20-1; 1 Thess. 4:14). God shows His concern for His people as body-soul entities by His promise to redeem their bodies as well as their souls. This attitude is seen in Paul's practical concern for Timothy's health (1 Tim. 5:23), in light of the heavy ministerial demands (1 Tim. 5:19-22). Our Father knows the frames of His people (Ps. 103: 14), and although there are providential exceptions, He calls them away from time to time to rest (Mark 6:31).

A holy life is vitally connected to the stewardship of the body. Those who have experienced the mercies of God are to present their bodies as living sacrifices (Rom. 12:1). The body is the temple of the Holy Spirit (1 Cor. 6:13, 20). Paul's desire was for Christ to be magnified in his body (Phil. 1:19-20). If this is the calling for all Christians, how much more ought men of God to be committed to the care of their bodies? If they are to excel in grace and piety, as models for their people, shall they undermine their credibility because of a neglect of their bodies? This concern has multiple ramifications as it relates to effectiveness in pastoral ministry and preaching.

Furthermore, the biblical doctrine of preaching requires a concern for the physical and emotional health of the preacher. Preaching requires the engagement of the whole man,[87] not only the spiritual, but also the physical faculties. Preaching which engages the whole man makes tremendous demands on the preacher: physically, spiritually and emotionally. Just as preparation for preaching demands mental rigor, so the act of preaching demands physical rigor. R C Sproul notes, 'Though preachers differ in the expenditure of energy given in a sermon, it has been estimated that a half-hour address can use as much physical energy as eight hours of manual labor.'[88]

Special revelation is unambiguous regarding the necessity of this concern, but so is natural revelation through the past and present experiences of men of God. The testimony of John Owen's biographer is significant,

> Still, the hours which are taken from needful rest are not redeemed, but borrowed, and must be paid back with double interest in future life. Owen, when he began to feel his iron frame required to pay the penalty of his youthful enthusiasm, was accustomed to declare that he would willingly part with all the learning he had accumulated by such means, if he might but recover the health which he had lost in the gaining of it.[89]

Robert Murray McCheyne's memorable words are even more stinging when one realizes that he died at the tender age of 29, 'God gave me a message to deliver and a horse to ride. Alas, I have killed the horse and now I cannot deliver the message.'[90]

The necessary starting point is attaining and maintaining an accurate assessment of one's own condition, physically and emotionally. He must realistically face the truth that the outward man is decaying (2 Cor. 4:16). A realistic evaluation of oneself (Rom. 12:3) must extend to his own physical and emotional constitution, which God has sovereignly and providentially designed (Ps. 139:13-16). In light of this evaluation, one must establish a regular but flexible discipline of activities related to these issues. Everyone needs physical exercise and mental and emotional relaxation. If these things are neglected, the man of God is not being a good steward of the purchased property of Jesus Christ. He must keep in the forefront of his mind that he not only glorifies God with his rigorous mental work for the pulpit and the holy sweat of a sanctified walk, but he must also glorify God in his body (1 Cor. 6:19-20).

Concerning physical health there are a number of cautions. First, one must beware of fundamental ignorance of or indifference to the basics of health and nutrition. If the man of God is to glorify God in his body, how can he be indifferent to or ignorant of what is good for him? How can he glorify God by eating (1 Cor. 10:31), without knowing the basics of health and nutrition. There is an element of hypocrisy if he carelessly loads his system with excessive amounts of salt, saturated fats and other medically proven toxins, and then asks the congregation for prayer when he is diagnosed with high blood pressure or other self-induced health problems.

Secondly, beware of the 'no planned physical exercise syndrome'. Some have misconstrued 1 Timothy 4:8 as a negative statement on physical exercise. Paul, however, is affirming that there is profit in bodily exercise, although compared to godliness it is 'little'. Jonathan Edwards chopped wood and rode his horse for exercise. However, most pastors don't need firewood, or have a horse. Those things belong primarily to a bygone day, and so the man of God must be more innovative. Running, swimming, racketball, basketball, or a treadmill are a few ideas out of dozens if not hundreds of available forms of exercise.

Thirdly, he must beware of the pattern of cheating on the

necessary measure of sleep. Although there are warnings in Scripture about a carnal love of sleep and laziness (Prov. 6:6-11), and the man of God may be called upon from time to time to forego the necessary amount of needed sleep (Matt. 26:40), it is clear that in order to maintain optimum health, sleep is vitally important and ordained by God (Ps. 127:2). The Lord's sound sleep puts a sanction on taking necessary rest, even a daytime nap (Mark 4:35ff.; Luke 8:22ff.). It is a matter of creaturehood, not sinnerhood.

Fourthly, the man of God must beware of developing a dependence upon or addiction to stimulants and depressants. Although the church cannot take a legalistic approach to such things as caffeine or wine (1 Tim. 4:4-5; 5:23), God's people must not abuse the gifts of God (1 Cor. 6:13). The man of God must remember the injunction of 1 Cor. 10:31, 'Whether, then, you eat or drink, whatever you do, do all for the glory of God.'

Fifthly, there should definitely be a caution concerning excessive weight gain. The pastorate is a sedentary job except for the two to three hours per week spent in the pulpit. Studying, counseling, sitting in various meetings, do not require physical exertion. The transfixed seat is conducive to the accumulation of weight. Ministerial fat and ministerial usefulness are usually mutually exclusive. Excessive weight gain has so many negative ramifications. It produces sluggishness. It cripples the conscience with guilt. How can the man of God preach about the disciplines of the Christian life, if he himself is undisciplined at the dinner table? The blubber over the belt does not lie, and it testifies to a watching congregation. This in turn may break his grip on their consciences regarding undisciplined areas of their lives. 'Hey, if Pastor Jones can obviously indulge in extra calories, then why can't I indulge in ...?'

Sixthly, beware of the 'no day off' and a 'no vacation' pattern of life. A diligent pastor knows that if there were ten days in a week, he could fill each day from sunrise to sundown with meaningful ministerial activities. It is not a matter of how much work there is to do, but it is a matter of God's divine pattern of life (Gen. 2:2-3; Exod. 20:8-11). It is also a matter of falsely considering himself so important in the kingdom that he doesn't think he can get away with his family for a vacation without the kingdom collapsing. Elderships must be insistent on this point concerning full-time elders who carry a multitude of pastoral responsibilities. There ought to be sufficient vacation time and even study leaves. Pastors are not iron men!

Seventhly, beware of a stubborn refusal to listen to others who see the signs of emotional and physical weariness in the pastor. Often times wives have insight that husbands do not have, and they can see physical or emotional abnormalities, which he does not see. Others, who know the pastor and his personality and patterns, may identify warning signs. The pastor must give heed to those around him, lest he be like the fool of Proverbs, and not the wise man. 'He is on the path of life who heeds instruction, But he who forsakes reproof goes astray' (Prov. 10:17; see also Prov. 12:1, 15; 15:5, 10). 'He whose ear listens to the life-giving reproof will dwell among the wise' (Prov. 15:31; see also Prov. 19:20).

Not only is one's physical constitution vitally important for ministerial effectiveness, but emotional health cannot be discounted. There are many men in ministry who are so melancholic that they are difficult to be around. They so easily engage in a bitter criticism of their circumstances that one must conclude that the difficulties are always at the forefront of their minds. How torturous it is to sit under a melancholy ministry! When the emotional health is not holistically sound, the ministry is in grave danger of being lopsided regarding the emotional ruts of the pastor.

Therefore, it is necessary that men of God give heed to some caveats. They must beware of unnaturalness and ministerial stoicism. The pastor's people must see him laugh, they must see him cry, they must see that he feels deeply about his wife, his children and them. They need to see what redeemed humanity really is, not a pseudo-spirituality. He must also beware of social isolationism. There used to be an old piece of counsel, the author saw it in a pastoral theology book which he will not quote, that a pastor must not have any close friends in the congregation. This is not only unnatural, it is unhealthy. God's creatures are social creatures and they need friends. The Lord Jesus appointed seventy disciples, and those seventy were not on the same level as the twelve. But even the twelve were not on the same level as the three, Peter, James and John. If it is wrong to have a small circle of friends within the congregation, then the Lord was wrong. Of course nobody is advocating an exclusivistic mentality, and one must be on guard concerning the appearance of an undue favoritism, but by all means pastors must not be socially isolated people. It is emotionally unhealthy to be so.

Another area where there must be due caution is taking on too many responsibilities. The Pastor is always being asked to do this or that, and part of his calling is to serve the people. But in order to guard his emotional well-being, he must include 'no' in his vocabulary. If he is always saying 'yes' to every request and responsibility, he may experience burn-out (to use an overused phrase) or fall into various manifestations of stress. Although this is true in all ministries, it is especially true of church planting pastors. It is obvious that there is much to be done and not many to do the work. It is better to have ministries go undone than nearly to kill oneself attempting to make sure that everything is done.

A wholesome domestic climate becomes vital for maintaining emotional health and stability. Just as domestic unrest can magnify ministerial difficulties, so a domestic haven can cure many pastoral ills. To have a loving wife and precious children does the soul much good.The kids may still bicker occasionally and the pastor's wife may not always have dinner right on time, yet the home can still be a haven. It is in the realism of domestic life that the pastor cultivates the ability not to take himself too seriously. Wives and kids are great reality checks and so are fellow-elders who know where the warts are. Some brethren take themselves so seriously that they think the kingdom stands or falls on their next sermon. Although the pastor is a man of God, he is not a demagogue. He is still fallen, with foibles and failures, and quirks and tics. Learning not to take himself too seriously will be medicine to the emotions when he encounters the thorns in the flesh and the dark providences in the ministry.[91]

Finally, there must be a pattern of wholesome diversions. For some it may be chess, for others it may be gardening, working on an old car, target shooting, chasing a golf ball, or listening to Pavarotti. Whatever it is, it must be a relaxing diversion. If golf drives the pastor crazy, and he is tempted to lose his temper over double bogeys then, for his soul's sake and emotional well-being, he should choose something else. The activity must be something that is planned on a regular basis, and that is looked to with anticipation.

As a general rule, sustained effectiveness in pastoral ministry will be realized in direct proportion to the health and vigor of the redeemed humanity of the man of God. The man of God must be in a right relationship with God spiritually, intellectually, physically and emotionally. He must be one who is growing in his acquaintance with God and His ways. He must be maturing in his perception of the truth and how it relates to all of life. He must also actively maintain his physical and emotional health. It is only as the man of God pursues these areas that he will maintain effectiveness in the ministry.

4

THE MAN OF GOD IN RELATIONSHIP TO HIS CONGREGATION

In an effective ministry, the relationship between the man of God and his people will be central. The man of God must have love for his people. He must be free from all fear of men, that is, he must be a man of holy boldness. He must have the respect and confidence of his people. Where these things are operative there will be a climate conducive to a fruitful ministry.

The man of God must experience a growing measure of unfeigned love to his people

If the man of God is to be effective in pastoral ministry, he must not only be in a right relationship to God in the totality of his redeemed humanity, he must also be in a right relationship to his people. The axiom here is simple and straightforward: he must experience a growing measure of unfeigned love for his people. The words are chosen carefully, and deserve fuller explication.

Unfeigned love is that gracious and principled disposition of goodwill which desires and practically seeks the good of its object at personal cost. This is not a precise, technical definition, rather it is a working one, seeking to describe the kind of love necessary for pastoral ministry. First of all, it is *gracious*, that is, it is a fruit of grace (Gal. 5:22; 1 Cor. 13). This type of love does not grow in native Adamic soil, rather it grows out of Divine grace operative in the soul. Secondly, it is *principled.* Principled love is the opposite of whimsical or impulsive. It is an internal conviction that is steadfast. Just as the rails guide the train, keeping it in bounds, heading in the right direction, so principle likewise is the internal rail which governs, directs and keeps love within bounds. Thirdly, it is a *disposition*, that is, a characteristic attitude, the predominant bent of one's mind and heart.

This kind of love has action to it, as the definition reveals. *It desires and seeks the good of its objects at personal cost*. 'Love does not seek its own' (1 Cor. 13:5). 'Love does no wrong to a neighbor' (Rom. 13:10). Edwards in his series of sermons on 1 Corinthians 13 states:

> We ought to seek the spiritual good of others; and if we have a Christian spirit, we shall desire and seek their spiritual welfare and happiness, their salvation from hell, and that they might glorify and enjoy God forever. And the same spirit will dispose us to desire and seek the temporal prosperity of others.[92]

The truest demonstration of this kind of love is when it is at personal cost. In fact, it is when it is at personal cost, that one is assured that it is in conformity with God's love (John 3:16; Eph. 5:25f.). Edwards again notes:

> Christianity restores an excellent enlargement, and extensiveness, and liberality to the soul, and again possesses it with that divine love or charity that we read of in the text, whereby it again embraces its fellow-creatures, and is devoted to and swallowed up in the Creator. And thus charity, which is the sum of the Christian spirit, so partakes of the glorious fulness of the Divine nature.[93]

The quality of this love is *unfeigned*. It follows the New Testament pattern of 'love without hypocrisy [*anupokritos*]' (see 1 Pet. 1:22; 2 Cor. 6:6; Rom. 12:9). Too many pastors engage in a professional love, a mere ministerial act, which makes them appear soft and sentimental. If a man of God must put on a ministerial face, then his love is hypocritical. Effective pastoral ministry must be fueled by a love that is unfeigned, and it can be unfeigned only if it is a gracious and principled disposition.

The measure of this love is *growing* (1 Thess. 4:9-10; Phil. 1:9-11). Once the honeymoon is over, and the people see the pastor's warts and he sees theirs, the only glue that will keep shepherd and flock together, through thick and thin, is an expanding, abounding, growing love. This is the kind of love all married people must experience after they have seen what he/she really looks like in the morning, how they are when things really go wrong, and the irritating nuances of personality and habits finally register. If a newly married couple never get beyond those minor foibles, then their love never grows. So it is with pastor and congregation.

The objects of this love are *the people within the flock and the unsaved within his influence*. The man of God will have an affectionate unfeigned love for the people that God 'purchased with His own blood' (Acts 20:28). Those members who constitute the flock he is over will be the objects of this love. Furthermore, he will be moved with this kind of love towards the children and regular, yet unconverted attenders. This is the kind of love Paul expressed in Romans 9:1-3 and 2 Timothy 2:10. It should be a growing reality in life and ministry, to have the heart greatly enlarged towards the congregation. Such a heart longs for their good, that is, their welfare, and their salvation.

Be assured, this is no mere 'given' for the pastorate. Nor is it optional. It is vital! The importance of having a growing measure of unfeigned love cannot be overemphasized. If the man of God does not have this kind of love operating in his ministry, then he is under the condemnation of the Apostle in 1 Corinthians 13:1-3. The church is filled with enough noisy gongs and clanging cymbals! Pulpits all over are occupied with 'superstar' preachers and theologians, who have a great grasp on knowledge, and yet they are nothing!

Not only does 1 Corinthians 13:1-3 demand this kind of love in the ministry, evangelical law keeping also demands it. Paul says that love is the fulfillment of the law (Rom. 13:8-10). If the pastor seeks to walk in holiness before God, motivated by love for Him, he must love his neighbors! He must seek their good! John asks, 'Whoever has the world's goods, and sees his brother in need and closes his heart against him, how does the love of God abide in him' (1 John 3:17)?

It could be said that 1 Corinthians 13 and evangelical law keeping require this love of all Christians. That is certainly true, but if the man of God is to be one who excels in personal piety, how much more ought he to excel in these duties?

There is another facet that cannot be missed, and that is the pastoral office makes this demand of love in a unique way. God's servants are to shepherd the flock with a willing eagerness (1 Pet. 5:1-3). They are to follow the Lord Jesus in His example (1 John 2:6; Matt. 10:26), and He laid down His life for the sheep (John 10:11) and for His friends (John 15:13). Jesus was filled with compassion for the people who were like sheep without a shepherd (Matt. 9:36). He wept over the unbelieving and obdurate inhabitants of Jerusalem (Luke 19:41). He is the perfect, loving Shepherd.

Yet too many have been hardened because of a distorted Calvinism, or frequent rejections. But should Christ's under-shepherds love less than the One who made the decree? Should they love less than the One who was rejected by His own creation? They should be like their Master, who was moved with compassion as He looked on the multitudes, was beseeched by lepers, and called upon by desperate fathers. As He ministered to those in need, 'His heart was open and readily responded to the delights of human association and bound itself to others in happy fellowship.'[94] If the one in pastoral ministry does not know that compassion and delight, he might simply be a hireling.

Another element of pastoral ministry that makes growing, unfeigned love an indispensable reality is the relationship between assured love and the open ear. If the man of God is to preach effectively to his people (and if he loves them, he will desire for them to benefit from effective preaching!), then they must know that the pastor loves them. When the congregation knows the pastor loves them, he has access to an open ear. Baxter, that sagacious pastor who still has so much to teach this present generation, instructs at this very point.

> The whole of our ministry must be carried on in tender love to our people. We must let them see that nothing pleaseth us but what profiteth them; and that what doeth them good doth us good; and that nothing troubleth us more than their hurt. We must feel toward our people, as a father toward his children; yea, the tenderest love of a mother must not surpass ours. We must even travail in birth, till Christ be formed in them. They should see that we care for no outward

> thing, neither wealth, nor liberty, nor honour, nor life, in comparison of their salvation; but could even be content, with Moses, to have our names blotted out of the book of life, i.e., to be removed from the number of the living: rather than they should not be found in the Lamb's book of life. Thus should we, as John, be ready to 'lay down our lives for the brethren', and with Paul, not count our lives dear to us, so we may 'finish our course with joy, and the ministry which we received of the Lord Jesus'. *When the people see that you unfeignedly love them, they will hear anything and bear anything from you....* We ourselves will take all things well from one that we know doth entirely love us. We will put up with a blow that is given us in love, sooner than with a foul word that is spoken to us in malice or anger.... Oh, therefore see that you feel a tender love to your people in your breasts, and let them perceive it in your speeches, and see it in your conduct. Let them see you spend, and are spent, for their sakes; and that all you do is for them and not for any private ends of your own.[95]

This principle of unfeigned, increasing love also has some very important pragmatic ramifications. This kind of love in the heart of the man of God will exert influence in both the preparation and delivery of sermons. In preparation there will be a holy obligation, not only before God, but for the sake of the people, to deal faithfully with every text of Scripture. No effort will seem beyond reason when gripped by the fact that he is preparing their spiritual food. That same diligence will carry over into the actual sermon outline. Love for the people compels him to make the sermon logical, structurally clear and lucid.

As the sermon is delivered, and love for the people pulsates in his heart, he will strive to rivet the Word to their consciences. The faces of men and women and boys and girls, whom he has loved and spent time with in times of joy and grief, and labored over in prayer, will compel a certain kind of sanctified pleading. He will have a holy drive to make sure that they don't leave without the Word lodged in their hearts, doing its work. Oh, how the blood-earnestness of preachers gushes forth when their hearts are aflame with the truth of God and love for his people! The pathos and persuasion is unmistakable. Lloyd-Jones's words are convicting:

> A special word must be given also though in a sense we have been covering it, to the element of pathos. If I had to plead guilty of one thing more than any other I would have to confess that this perhaps is what is lacking in my own ministry. This should arise partly from a love for the people. Richard Cecil, an Anglican preacher in London towards the end of the eighteenth and beginning of the nineteenth century said something which should make us all think. 'To love to preach is one thing, to love those to whom we preach is quite another.' The trouble with some of us is that we love preaching, but are not always careful to make sure we love the people to whom we are actually preaching.[96]

What a rebuke to the 'take or leave it' preaching of today. How many times has it been heard or read, 'my job is just to serve the meal, I can't make anyone eat.' What this translates into is a cool, talking head communicator who is more concerned about his eloquence and sermonic polish than the souls of men. If a man of God is going to be in right relation to his people before the God he serves, unfeigned love must make its mark.

The observation of anyone with any pulpit experience is that this love wanes from time to time, and either through neglect of the preacher or hardness of heart on the part of the people, men of God sometimes find themselves quietly drifting away from this love. Therefore, pastors are in need of practical suggestions for the nurture and manifestation of this pastoral love. Very simply, the place to start is in the prayer closet, where *he cries out for this kind of love*. If the fruit of the Spirit is love (Gal. 5:22), and the filling of the Spirit is something one must cry out for (Luke 11:13), then the man of God must not neglect praying to God for the Spirit in such a way that he will increase his love for his people. If he is not praying frequently for this, it may be an indicator that he is negligent of this kind of love.

Another suggestion is that he deliberately and periodically meditates upon those truths calculated to produce this love. For instance, he should spend time meditating on the flock's worth before God. This is God's flock (1 Pet. 5:2), He purchased it with His own blood (Acts 20:28), and they are precious to Him! Baxter, in top form, drives this home with these words,

> Oh, then, let us hear these arguments of Christ, whenever we feel ourselves grow dull and careless: 'Did I die for these souls, and wilt not thou look after them? Were they worth my blood, and are they not worth thy labor? Did I come down from heaven to earth, "to seek and to save that which was lost"; and wilt thou not go to the next door, or street, or village, to seek them? How small is thy condescension and labour compared to mine! I debased myself to this, but it is thy honour to be so employed. Have I done and suffered so much for their salvation, and was I willing to make thee a fellow-worker with me, and wilt thou refuse to do that little which lieth upon thy hands?' Every time we look upon our congregations, let us believingly remember that they are the purchase of Christ's blood, and therefore should be regarded by us with the deepest interest and most tender affection. Oh, think what a confusion it will be to a negligent minister, at the last day, to have this blood of the Son of God pleaded him; and for Christ to say, 'It was the purchase of my blood of which thou didst make so light, and dost thou think to be saved by it thyself?' O brethren, seeing Christ will bring his blood to plead with us, let it plead us to our duty, lest it plead us to damnation.[97]

Another truth that the Spirit can use to stir the heart with pastoral love is the worth of just one soul. Jesus clearly taught that one soul is worth more than all the possessions in the world (Mark 8:36). As the minister looks into the faces of his congregation (and he should look right at them!), as he recalls their faces in prayer, as he speaks with them face to face, he should remember, that the one before him is made in the image of God, he or she has a never-dying soul, which one day will enjoy the bliss of heaven or the agonies of hell.

It is for souls such as these that Christ suffered and died. The quotation from Baxter should remind its readers how much Christ Himself poured out on their behalf. The prophet Isaiah states that, 'He rendered Himself as a guilt offering' (Isa. 53:10). The same prophet also says that it was the Father who 'crush[ed] Him, putting Him to grief' (Isa. 53:10). The cry of dereliction, 'My God, my God, why have You forsaken Me?' ought to stir the souls of preachers with a love for souls.

Those people whom God has placed under the pastor's charge are either redeemed and precious in the sight of God, or they are lost and face an eternity of torment in hell. If the true state of men does not move him with a Christlike, pastoral love, then he ought to get out of the ministry and sell insurance or used cars. These are the truths which every pastor must spend time meditating on in order to produce this kind of love and kindle it afresh over and over again.

As to the actual manifestation of this love, the pastor must manifest it both in and out of the pulpit. His words must express affection. As a pastor he must not be afraid of counter-cultural language that reflects a Christian pathos and affection. The Apostles are the models, and their language was filled with joy, love, yearning, tears, brokenness and frankness. Paul expresses to Timothy his yearning to see him, recalling Timothy's tears (2 Tim. 1:4). The pastor who is too 'macho' to give another man in the assembly a hug and tell him that he loves him is so 'macho' that he has ceased to be apostolic.[98]

Affection must not be in word only, it must be in deed (1 John 3:18). One concrete demonstration of pastoral love is maintaining a high standard of pulpit ministry. The congregation will know whether or not their pastor labored for them that week. Make no mistake about it, if there is a commitment to a Colossians 1:28-29 ministry, it will take agonizing labor (*kopiō agōnizomenos*). Like Paul, the man of God should show that 'I will most gladly spend and be expended for your souls' (2 Cor. 12:15).

Watch out though, lest in a false piety, those who love to study say, 'I show my people I love them by sweat in the study' but then neglect them outside of that realm. Furthermore, the pastor must take the initiative with his people, being sensitive to their individual needs. Some people will have no reservations about interrupting the pastor in his study, or during the dinner hour. Most, however, will be so sensitive to their pastor's time in the study and with his family that they would never dream of calling or dropping by with a problem. Therefore, the man of God must take the initiative with them, doing his best to be sensitive to their needs. He must make phone calls, write cards and letters, make inquiries and find other means of keeping in touch with his people.

Finally, in demonstrating pastoral love and affection, he must have an affectionate relationship with the children in the congregation, even as Christ had. Jesus had such a relationship with the children around Him that when He called one of them into the midst of a group of adults, they had no qualms about obeying His request (Mark 10:13-16; Matt. 18:1-6). Children did not feel threatened around Jesus. Pastors must emulate this, for he who lays his hand upon a child's head, lays his hand on his mother's heart.[99]

In interviewing a family who had been at Trinity for about 25 years, the writer asked the four girls who had all grown up under Pastor Martin's ministry, 'In the light of Pastor Martin's intense and strong preaching, have you ever felt aloof or afraid of him?' All four girls laughed, 'Afraid of Pastor Martin! Never!' What followed was a barrage of stories of how Pastor Martin had jumped in wading pools filled with greenish-yellowish water, with his clothes on; or how he had clowned around as an 'uninvited' guest at a five year old's birthday party. With such a vivid example there are many who could testify that their response towards the children in their congregations has been enriched because of Pastor Martin.

If one is to have an effective pastoral ministry, he must be growing in unfeigned love towards his people. It is vital for his work among God's flock. In nurturing this unfeigned pastoral love and affection, he must continually ask God for fresh supplies of it; he must continually meditate on truths which are conducive to the production and kindling of this love. In manifesting this unfeigned love, he must show it in his high standard of pulpit ministry. He must take the initiative with the saints, being sensitive to their needs. He must also be warm and affectionate with the children in his congregation.

The man of God must experience an increasing liberation from the fear of men. (He must grow in the grace of holy boldness.)

If pastoral ministry is to be effective, the man of God must not only be growing in unfeigned love, but he must also be liberated from the fear of men. There is a complexity here which the Bible sets clearly before God's servants. First of all, every one of God's servants is a social creature (Gen. 2:18), who was made for social interaction. If he is a normal human being, he wants to be liked and loved by those around him. The difficulty begins to emerge when he considers that man, by nature, squashes the truth of God (Rom. 1:18), hates the law of God (Rom. 8:7) and loves darkness rather than light (John 3:19). The difficulty comes to full bloom when one considers that the natural man attacks the messenger through whom the truth comes before he ever directly attacks the truth. Jesus reminds His disciples that since the world hated Him, it would hate them too (John 15:18-27). This is nothing new: the people fought against Jeremiah (Jer. 1:17-19; 19:14 – 20:2), and in the words of Amos, 'They hate him who reproves in the gate, and they abhor him who speaks with integrity' (Amos 5:10). The Apostles frequently faced this reproach (e.g., Gal. 4:16).

Herein lies the conflict: The pastor loves the people, and his desire is to be loved in return, but many times his calling to be faithful will create just the opposite response. If he bends in his faithfulness to maintain his lovableness, he will undermine his effectiveness in pastoral ministry. This is not a contradiction to the first point concerning unfeigned love, it is the height of proving unfeigned love. A man who acquiesces to people's wants and desires instead of standing firm in God's truth does not have a genuine love that is looking out for their best interest.

Biblical examples of holy boldness abound. Paul, after a stinging rebuke to the Galatians states in Galatians 1:10, 'For am I now seeking the favor of men, or of God? Or am I striving to please men? If I were still trying to please men, I would not be a bond-servant of Christ.' Paul likewise says to the Thessalonians, 'but just as we have been approved by God to be entrusted with the gospel, so we speak, not as pleasing men but God, who examines our hearts' (1 Thess. 2:4). He also asks that the Ephesians would pray for his holy boldness in preaching the gospel (Eph. 6:19).

Young Elihu was no stranger to holy boldness. Hear his words,

> I too will answer my share, I also will tell my opinion. For I am full of words; the spirit within me constrains me. Behold, my belly is like unvented wine, like new wineskins it is about to burst. Let me

> speak that I may get relief; let me open my lips and answer. Let me now be partial to no one; nor flatter any man. For I do not know how to flatter, else my Maker would soon take me away (Job 32:17-22).

Elihu is a paradigm for holy boldness in that he is about to burst with what he has to say. He is committed to giving no flattery whatsoever, knowing that he must answer to God for his speech.

Examples can be multiplied of men who were as fearless as lions in the face of opposition. Moses, Elijah, Jeremiah, Daniel and others flood into the mind as one remembers their holy boldness, their deep convictions and their utter liberation from the fear of men. Whatever examples we may recall, none surpasses that of our Lord, who was the perfect example of holy boldness. He spoke the truth in such a way that even His enemies recognized that He spoke from God (Mark 12:14). Jesus pulled no punches with sinners (e.g., the woman at the well, John 4:15-18; and the rich young ruler, Matt. 19:16-26), or with the religious establishment (e.g., Matt. 23:1-36).

This grace of holy boldness is a vital necessity. The pastor will inevitably grow in his knowledge of his people, and with that increasing knowledge will come an increased awareness of their personal issues. In his efforts to win their confidence and approval, he may be subtly gripped by a fear of offending. This fear may hinder him in his preparation and especially in his delivery. This fear of men will cut the nerve of effective preaching, as well as circumventing the power of the Word in their lives. The man of God cannot be bought by smiles nor shut up with frowns. Proverbs 29:25 should be emblazoned above every pastor's desk and pulpit, 'The fear of man brings a snare, but he who trusts in the LORD will be exalted.'

Bridges set forth this truth with power and beauty:

> For what can be more degrading to our Divine commission, than that we should fear the face of men? What unmindfulness does it argue of our Master's presence and authority, and our high responsibilities, as 'set forth for the defense of the Gospel!' The independence that disregards alike the praise and the censure of man, is indispensable for the integrity of the Christian Ministry....

> But the question is not, how our people may be pleased; but how they may be warned, instructed, and saved. We would indeed strongly rebuke that modesty, which makes us ashamed of our grand message; or that tremulous timidity, which seems to imply, that we are only half-believers in our grand commission. To keep offensive doctrines out of view, or to apologize for the occasional mention of them, or to be over-cautious respecting the rudeness if disquieting the conscience with unwelcome truth; to compromise with the world; to connive at fashionable sins; or to be silent, where the cause of God demands an open confession- this is not the spirit that honors our Master, and which He 'delighteth to honour'.[100]

Holy boldness is a grace in which the man of God must grow. That grace is initially implanted within him at conversion, when he is fundamentally liberated from the fear of men. He is not ashamed of Christ (Matt. 10:32), he makes open confession with his mouth (Rom. 10:9-10), and God has put His fear in his heart (Jer. 32:39-40). Nevertheless, he must cultivate this grace if he is to be the man God has called him to be. The first conscientious area where this boldness must be cultivated is in his walk before God as a Christian man.

Boldness in his walk before God as a Christian man begins by maintaining a good conscience before God and man. Having that gut-level determination to maintain a good conscience with God keeps one's perspective radically God-centered, so that even in the face of opposition, one remains true to God. Paul, in a hostile environment, looked intently on the enemies of the gospel and affirmed he had no controversy with God (Acts 23:1, see also 24:16). The Apostle was willing to live with contention between him and others, if it meant a clean conscience with God. He would not live, looking over his shoulder, hearing footsteps. Indeed, 'The wicked flee when no one is pursuing, but the righteous are bold as a lion' (Prov. 28:1).

There is nothing to stir up the spirit of holy boldness like looking to good models (Phil. 3:17; 2 Tim. 3:10; Heb. 13:7). As he reads the Scriptures he is stirred by the holy boldness of prophets, apostles and the Lord Jesus. He is challenged again and again to boldness by such examples as Shadrach, Meshach and Abednego.

It is this same dynamic that is picked up from good biographies. How many of God's people have been stirred by Luther before the Diet of Worms, or Calvin taking his stand in front of the Lord's Table against the Libertines, or Knox before the Queen? These great moments in history of Spirit-wrought courage stir the soul to a greater boldness. Gardiner Spring captures one such moment in the life of Samuel Davies:

> That distinguished American preacher, Samuel Davies, then President of the College of New Jersey, when on a visit to England, in behalf of the college, was invited to preach before George III. His youthful queen was sitting by his side; and so enchanted were they by the preacher's eloquence, that the king expressed his admiration in no measured terms, and so audibly and rudely as to draw the attention of his audience, and interrupt. The preacher made a sudden and solemn pause in his discourse, looked around upon the audience, and fixing his piercing eyes upon the monarch, said, 'When the lion roars, the beasts of the forest tremble; when Jehovah speaks, let the kings of the earth keep silence before Him!'[101]

The second area where the grace of holy boldness must be conscientiously cultivated is in the man of God's posture before God as a minister. He must stir himself up afresh with the reality that it is by the will of God he has been put to this glorious task (Rom. 1:1, 5; 1 Cor. 1:1; 2 Cor. 1:1; Acts 20:28). If it is God who called him, it is to God that he shall give an account. The man who is called by God is not bullied by the ecclesiastical power brokers, nor moulded by the expectations of a congregation. His marching orders come from on high, his calling and commission is not from man, but from God (Gal. 1:1). Therefore, in the discharge of his duties, with this in the forefront of his mind he must act accordingly.

The eye of God is also upon him in the discharge of this task, 'we speak in Christ in the sight of God' (2 Cor. 2:17). This was Paul's banner that seemed to wave over his every move. It was God that Paul sought to please, knowing that this same God would test his heart (1 Thess. 2:4). Paul, in turn, with a good conscience, could solemnly charge Timothy 'in the presence of God and of

Christ Jesus, who is to judge the living and the dead, and by His appearing and His kingdom' (2 Tim. 4:1). It is as the man of God lives and moves, conscientiously in His presence, that he has this holy boldness. The congregation may not know if he pulls a punch, but the all-watching eye of God sees, and therefore, he must live and minister conscientiously *coram Deo*.

Finally, the reality that one day, in the court of heaven, all ministers of the gospel will give an account to Almighty God and He in turn will judge their faithfulness with the truth, ought increasingly to cultivate a holy boldness. Who shall be feared? God or man? Who will be behind that bench on the great day? God or man? In this day of men-pleasers, may true ministers of the gospel be consumed with the reality of appearing before the judgment seat of Christ! May they remember, that they are the watchmen on the wall (Ezek. 3:17-21). They will either be clean of the blood of men, or will be stained (Acts 20:26). How Christ's servants in gospel ministry ought to meditate on the appearing of the Chief Shepherd (1 Pet. 5:4) and of giving an account (Heb. 13:17), which will be according to a stricter standard of judgment (Jas. 3:1). What sort of men ought pastors to be in light of such sobering reality?

In our current saccharine ministerial culture, there are those who would decry such an approach to ministry, claiming that such boldness will make preachers hard, caustic and insensitive. To be sure, many in the name of truth have become so, but what is to be made of that objection? First of all, it simply is not true in the biblical examples cited. The same Apostle who said he sought to please God and receive His approval alone (1 Thess. 2:4), within the same chapter uses language of the deepest warmth and affection. 'We proved to be gentle among you, as a nursing [mother] tenderly cares for her children' (1 Thess. 2:7), 'being affectionately desirous of you' (1 Thess. 2:8), 'like a father with his children' (2:11). With the Galatians, Paul can use strong language, 'O foolish Galatians! Who bewitched you?' (Gal. 3:1). Bold language indeed! Did it turn Paul into a crusty, caustic, acid-tongued preacher? 'My little children, with whom I am again in labor until Christ be formed in you' (Gal. 4:19). Never!

The Lord Himself, the boldest of all preachers, never became hardened and insensitive. The same preacher who denounced the cities for unbelief (Matt. 11:20-4), wept over their unbelief (Matt. 23:37-9). Within the economy of grace, the same Spirit who gives holy boldness to a heart, has put unquenchable love in the heart (Rom. 5:5). Jesus was the perfect representation of this. The man of God, in lesser degree, operates within the same orbit of Spirit-filled life.

Another objection to this kind of preaching is that it tends to alienate people. They will hear it once and then never again. This is the major objection which the author hears in relation to this kind of preaching from church planting colleagues and peers outside Reformed circles. If preaching is biblical, then it will most definitely alienate some people. In fact, if it is the true aroma of Christ, it will be to some an aroma of life unto life, but to others it will be the aroma of death unto death (2 Cor. 2:14-16). But let every preacher or would-be preacher come to the realization that they have no right to try to change the aroma of the message! To try to change the aroma to make it pleasing to all is to destroy and nullify the message of the cross (1 Cor. 1:17)! The preacher can't hide the smell if he is faithful! Maurice Roberts gives a balanced and thoughtful statement, when he says,

> It must be a sign that reformed preachers are rendering acceptable service when they are resented and resisted by the carnal in their congregation. This is not meant as a defence of ministerial indiscretion but an a encouragement to ministerial faithfulness. A young preacher is apt to blame it all on himself when the principal men and women of a congregation are aroused against him. It may indeed be that he is partly to blame. But the greatest sin might rather be in those who rise up against him because his application of God's Word is all too true. Religious sinners, when cut close to the bone, can react with incredible fury and they can spit fire at the hand which wields the sword in the pulpit.[102]

Who will be alienated by faithful, biblical preaching? The enemies of truth will always take offense. Those who want to be autonomous in their reasoning and in their morals will never bow under the scepter of the Word. Nor will they acknowledge that this is the problem; they will always blame the preacher. Others may temporarily be alienated, but as the Spirit works the Word into their hearts and minds, they often end up becoming good friends and supporters of the ministry. As the Proverbs declare, 'He who rebukes a man will afterward find favor, than he who flatters with the tongue' (Prov. 28:23). If a man or woman is serious about their soul, they will eventually love the faithful proclamation and application of the Word.

Those the man of God is trying to reach will often recoil in anger (Acts 7:54). The natural man is at enmity with God and hates His law (Rom. 8:7). If the lost are enemies of God and hate His holy law, then what can be said about a ministry when unregenerate men love the preaching? It is amazing when lost relatives or friends talk about the church they attend and how much they love the pastor and his preaching. There must be something fundamentally wrong when the unregenerate love the preaching and fail to see their sin and need. To be sure, there have been lost people who have come into biblically faithful assemblies and have been drawn to the preaching, not because of the saccharine approach, but because the Spirit of God was opening their heart. But mark it well, they know through the preaching that they are sinners and only Christ can save! If a lost person can sit under preaching without learning their true condition and the only remedy, then the preacher may be a hireling and not one sent by God!

Growing in the grace of holy boldness and being liberated from the fear of men is an essential ingredient in effective pastoral preaching. This grace, which is cultivated and strengthened in a variety of ways, does not calcify the preacher, but rather frees him to love as he ought to love. And although some will be alienated, others will be filled with love and gratitude for a man who will stand for truth and the good of their souls.

The man of God must earn and experience the increasing respect and confidence of his people

The essential elements of effective pastoral ministry and

especially pastoral preaching are being examined. The first essential element of the life of the man of God is his life in relationship to God. The second essential element of the life of the man of God is his relationship to his people. The man of God must be experiencing a growing measure of unfeigned love for his people. He must also be experiencing increased liberation from the fear of men and the cultivation of the grace of holy boldness. Next, he must earn and experience increased respect and confidence from his people.

Grace cannot confer respect and confidence. Although Christians operate within the arena of grace, when it comes to respect and confidence, it can be rightly spoken of in terms of 'earning' it. This respect and confidence, unlike grace, must be earned, but it, also unlike grace, is never immune from being lost. On the other hand, there is a measure of respect that naturally accompanies the office of overseer itself. Nevertheless, no man must ever be satisfied with an external nod of respect because he bears the title 'pastor'. Rather, he must strive to win his people's confidence and respect for greater influence and effectiveness in his ministry with them.

It is sufficiently clear from the biblical requirements for the office of elder that the man of God must be a man who is respectable. 'An overseer must be above reproach' (1 Tim. 3:2). 'The overseer must be as God's steward above reproach' (Titus 1:7). 'Let no one *look down* on your youthfulness' (1 Tim. 4:12). 'Your progress will be evident to all' (1 Tim. 4:15). 'In all things show yourself an example of good deeds' (Titus 2:7). 'Let no one *disregard* you' (Titus 2:15). 'Commending ourselves to every man's conscience in the sight of God' (2 Cor. 4:2). The testimony is clear: the man of God must conduct himself in such a way that he earns the respect of those who know him and wins the confidence of those who are under him. As far as this aspect of respect and confidence goes, it is easier to delineate the areas of crucial concern, than to give steps on how to win confidence and respect. If a man is faithful in his duties and avoids those areas, he will, in all probability, have the respect of his people.

The man of God must avoid *ministerial laziness* or *sloth*. The pastoral office is by necessity an office filled with the mental and spiritual 'sweat of the brow'. Paul speaks of it as 'labor to exhaustion' (***kopiaō***). Paul views the ministry in terms of 'soldiering', 'farming', 'shepherding', 'running' and 'boxing' (1 Cor. 9:6-14, 24-7). Not only is there a tremendous breadth to the work of the ministry, there is almost a limitless depth to the work. Laziness in the pastor will kill people's confidence in their pastor. They will view him as being on welfare and abusing the system at that!

God's people know their own Bibles well enough to know that idleness and laziness are to be met with hunger pains (2 Thess. 3:6-12)! They know of Paul's excellent reputation of being a hard worker (2 Thess. 3:6-12; Acts 20:34-5; 1 Thess. 2:8-9). Since the typical pastor has no time cards, and many can work at home, laziness can be a temptation to the pastor and a curse to the people. 'Woe, shepherds of Israel who have been feeding themselves! Should not the shepherds feed the flock? You eat the fat and clothe yourselves with the wool, you slaughter the fat without feeding the flock' (Ezek. 34:2-3).

Laziness in sermon preparation will erode people's respect and confidence in the man of God. The fruit of his labor ought to reveal the sweat of his labor, and the astute will know that the sermon didn't appear overnight, but there was real work put into it on their behalf. But they will also know when they are getting scraps and leftovers. They will resent it; and they should. The difference between pulpit excellence and mediocrity is hard work over the long haul. The man who is not willing to work to exhaustion in exegesis, outlining, illustration and application, ought to get out of the ministry. If he won't get out of the ministry, then his congregation ought to help him out.

> O that men should dare, by their laziness, to 'quench the Spirit', and then pretend the Spirit for the doing of it! O outrageous, shameful and unnatural deed! God hath required us, that we be 'not slothful in business,' but 'fervent in spirit, serving the Lord'. Such we must provoke our hearers to be, and such we must be ourselves.... Take heed to yourselves, lest you are weak through your own negligence, and lest you mar the work of God by your weakness.[103]

Laziness not only shows up in sermon preparation, but also in necessary diaconal duties. In a young or struggling work, many of the mundane duties will fall on the man of God. In fact, God may providentially bring these opportunities in order to use them as building blocks for trust and confidence. Therefore, it is absolutely necessary for the man of God to exhibit a Pauline work ethic (1 Thess. 2:9; 2 Thess. 3:8; Acts 20:34-5) and a Christlike attitude of service (John 13). Whether it be cleaning up after some event or hanging dry-wall, the pastor had better not be lazy or avoid the work, but rather get in and do the best he can. If he is aloof from the mundane (i.e., lazy), he will cause his people to get the impression that pastors are 'too good' (i.e., lazy) for that kind of work.

Another 'confidence killer' is *self-defensiveness*. There is something very unbecoming about a man of God who is always defending himself. Whenever one makes an observation, raises a question or offers a rebuke, if walls of defense immediately go up, it erodes respect. Remember, 'reproofs for discipline are the way of life' (Prov. 6:23). 'Do not reprove a scoffer, or he will hate you. Reprove a wise man, and he will love you. Give instruction to a wise man, and he will be still wiser. Teach a righteous man, and he will increase his learning' (Prov. 9:8-9). 'The way of a fool is right in his own eyes, But a wise man is he who listens to counsel' (Prov. 12:15).

Covetousness also will undermine people's confidence and respect. First of all, this characteristic excludes one from pastoral office (Titus 1:7; 1 Pet. 5:2) and eternal life (1 Tim. 6:9-11). Even if this is not a life-dominating sin, any trace of it will infect the people with the idea that the man of God is nothing but a hireling, who is trying to have a life of relative ease at their expense (John 10:12). He must be on guard about this appearance. A few practical suggestions for avoiding any appearance of covetousness: Do not be a fashion hound; do not be addicted to new cars or unduly expensive cars; do not agitate discussion about salary and benefits;[104] do not complain about the parsonage, the car, or other material items.

The man of God must be like Samuel before the people of

Israel, 'Whose ox have I taken, or whose donkey have I taken, or whom have I defrauded? Whom have I oppressed, or from whose hand have I taken a bribe to blind my eyes with it' (1 Sam. 12:3). The people responded, 'You have not defrauded us or oppressed us or taken anything from any man's hand' (12:4). Likewise, with Paul, the man of God should be able to say, 'I have coveted no one's silver or gold or clothes' (Acts 20:33). Let every minister of the gospel be determined never to be grouped together with such men like Achan, Gehazi, Judas or Demas, who stand out as monuments who declare: 'Beware of covetousness'.

The fourth area of concern deals with *sexual impurity*. This area is a peculiar temptation for pastors because they are often the objects of pointed Satanic attacks. If the devil can shoot a captain, then the troops are scattered and distracted. Baxter's insight on this point is unsurpassed,

> Take heed to yourselves, because the tempter will more ply you with his temptations than other men. If you will be the leaders against the prince of darkness, he will spare you no further than God restraineth him... As wise and learned as you are, take heed to yourselves, lest he outwit you. The devil is a greater scholar than you, and a nimbler disputant... Take heed to yourselves, because there are many eyes upon you, and there will be many to observe your falls.[105]

Pastors find themselves in a particular place of temptation. There is the sickening, yet real sin of 'preacher worship' due to the high profile of the pastoral office. This may tragically be wed to the pride of the preacher. Add to this the fact that the pastor has access to his people at virtually any time. Furthermore, he has access to the affections of people at the deepest levels. Things which people would never share with others, they will share with their pastor. This access to their affections and burdens is not evil in itself, in fact, it is good and healthy. However, this easy access can quickly turn into fuel for a fatal fire. If one is burned with this fire, he and a multitude of others will bear the scars for life! Men of God must do everything in their power to avoid and overcome this temptation.

This begins by maintaining vigorous spiritual health in general.

'Keep watching and praying that you may not enter temptation' (Matt. 26:41). John Owen states it well when he says, 'Without sincerity and diligence in a universality of obedience, there is no mortification of any one perplexing lust to be obtained.'[106] Owen goes on to exhort his readers with these words, 'If we will do any thing, we must do all things. So, then, it is not only an intense opposition to this or that peculiar lust, but a universal humble frame and temper of heart, with watchfulness over every evil and for the performance of every duty, that is accepted.'[107] If the man of God loses the perspective of a universal holiness within the framework of vigorous spiritual health, he will begin cutting corners here and there, and it is in the cutting of the corners with apparently unrelated sins, that he lays the foundation for sexual immorality. Not many see the connection between compromising conscience on paying taxes and sexual immorality, but it is there!

Not only must he be vigorous in his spiritual health in general, he must also maintain good marital relations with his wife in all areas. His wife must be his closest friend and confidant. The current notion that men must have a group of men with whom they are closer than even their own wives is an unhealthy perversion of the marital union. The man of God and his wife must be communicators who can be open and honest with one another in such a way that they support each other in the battle of life and ministry. Furthermore, within a healthy marital relationship, there must also be a good sexual relationship. Solomon's admonition is especially relevant to the pastor.

> Drink water from your own cistern, and fresh water from your own well. Should your springs be dispersed abroad, streams of water in the streets? Let them be yours alone and not for strangers with you. Let your fountain be blessed, and rejoice in the wife of your youth. As a loving hind and a graceful doe, let her breasts satisfy you at all times; be exhilarated always with her love. For why should you, my son, be exhilarated with an adulteress, and embrace the bosom of a foreigner? (Prov. 5:15-20).

Beyond a well-rounded marriage built on trust, openness, communication and healthy sexual relations, there is the need for cultivating preventive disciplines. Paul exhorts Timothy to treat younger women as sisters and older women as mothers (1 Tim. 5:2). This is a good reminder. Also, as a general rule, the pastor should never enter a home when a woman is alone. Nor should he counsel alone if his study is at home. A wife, children or even a faithful deacon, on the premises, is a good precautionary measure. Window shades should be open, and visibility from without should be maintained at all times. The pastor should also never physically touch a woman in private. All physical contact should be in view of others. He should also beware eye contact which is flirtatious or inquisitive (Prov. 6:25).

Finally, as a preventive discipline, the man of God should load his conscience with the warnings of Scripture and the issues at stake. Owen also gives this advice, when he says, 'Load thy conscience with the guilt of it.'[108] First, there is the holy Law of God. The seventh commandment forbids adultery (Exod. 20:14). It is such a heinous sin that God continually illustrates spiritual apostasy in terms of adultery. Next, bring the nature of the sin into the light of the gospel, thinking deeply upon the abundant mercy and grace God has shown in the gospel. Meditate upon His love and faithfulness. Ponder afresh the greatness of forgiveness and salvation. Owen's words are priceless, 'If this make it not sink in some measure and melt (i.e., bringing the lust to the gospel mercy of God) I fear thy case is dangerous.'[109] Consider the threats against adulterers (1 Cor. 6:9-10; Gal. 5:19-21; Eph. 5:3-5). Consider the danger of tasting that forbidden fruit and then being enslaved and hardened, entering the road to apostasy (Heb. 3:12-14). Meditate upon the terrifying words, 'Depart from me you worker of iniquity!' Cling to God's promises to supply His people with grace to fight the good fight.[110]

Not only does the conscience need to be loaded with the warnings and promises of Scripture, but it also needs to be loaded with the issues at stake. Randy Alcorn gives a number of consequences to sexual impurity:[111]

* Grieving the Lord who redeemed us, thus displeasing the One whose opinion matters most.

* Dragging Christ's precious name in the mud, giving the enemies of God an occasion to blaspheme.
* Having to face the Lord Jesus at His judgment seat, being accountable for the sin and its consequences.
* Experiencing severe Divine discipline.
* Adding my name to the list of disgraced leaders, held in contempt by the church and world.
* Causing untold suffering to those around me, in the congregation and others, much like Achan.
* Loss of respect from my precious wife.
* Loss of trust from my life partner.
* Untold hurt to my precious children.
* Betrayal of my office, and total loss of credibility in ministry, nullifying all labor.
* Shame to my family (the cruel comments which would come to my wife and children).
* A bloodied conscience, and a sin which would ever be before me.
* Disqualified from the calling and ministry I love.
* Years of training, education, experience, all wasted for a moment of pleasure.
* Irretrievable damage to my witness, especially among loved ones.
* Being a stumbling block for the gospel to those in my community.
* Possible physical consequences (gonorrhea, herpes, AIDS, the infection of my spouse, etc.)

The consequences are painful just to think about! If the mere thinking on these things brings pain, what would be the reality of it! A man who loses his moral integrity loses all respect and confidence. Make no mistake about it, falling into sexual immorality is to ruin one's life and ministry.

Another 'confidence killer' is *domestic incompetence*. Domestic competence is obviously a qualification for the eldership (1 Tim. 3:4-5; Titus 1:6). The man of God must take care of his domestic surroundings. He should beware an overgrown lawn and a messy house. He should beware a bossy domineering wife, a broken, down-trodden wife, unruly children, crushed children. He must be real and transparent, not trying to be something he is not. And he must not overreact to the goldfish bowl syndrome in such a way that he hides problems. There must be a domestic competence which could be held up as an example to those watching. If it is not there, the respect with people is lost, and their confidence in him diminishes.

'Confidence killer' number six is *inconsistency in general*. The man of God is called to be a model of good works, integrity, seriousness, speech, conduct, love, faith and purity (Titus 2:7; 1 Tim. 4:12). While the man of God should avoid what Spurgeon calls 'ministerial starch', he should also make sure that, in the midst of his being real, he doesn't become inconsistent. Some must merely watch those fun games and sports times where competition is present. There is something about competition which makes some more aggressive, and they can find themselves behaving unbecomingly. When old friends come to minister or visit, the pastor must watch his speech and conduct, lest in a moment of 'letting loose' he gets too loose. He must be cheerful.

> I commend cheerfulness to all who would win souls; not levity and frothiness, but a genial, happy spirit. There are more flies caught with honey than with vinegar, and there will be more souls led to heaven by a man who wears heaven in his face than by one who bears Tartarus in his looks.[112]

While cheerful, he must not become trivial, superficial or carnal.

If the man of God becomes trivial, superficial or carnal, people will see a gross inconsistency in his life. If they hear inappropriate speech or conduct, it will erode respect and confidence. What the man of God is in the pulpit must be verified by what he is out of the pulpit. To be sure, he may act or say things out of the pulpit, which he would not say in it. But his people will know whether that intensity in the pulpit is real or feigned by what they see in him when he is out of the pulpit. Spurgeon notes, 'Many young men have ruined themselves in the pulpit by being indiscreet in the parlour, and have lost all hope of doing good by their stupidity or frivolity in company.'[113]

Finally, *slovenliness or social boorishness* must be avoided. The man of God must be sensitive to such matters as clothing, grooming, laughter, manners and mannerisms. He must not lead the fashion parade, but he also ought not bring up the rear. He should be well groomed and have good hygiene. There is something about bad breath which detracts from pastoral authority and wisdom. Body odor, while it may cut down on time in counseling, may also cut back respect. Boisterous laughter, domineering conversation and the rest make a man socially undesirable. 'A man has no more right at the table to eat all than to talk all.'[114]

Effective ministry means earning the respect and confidence of the people. It is part of the requirement for the office and must be guarded at all times. Confidence killers such as laziness, self-defensiveness, covetousness, sexual impurity, domestic incompetence, a general inconsistency and slovenliness in appearance and behavior must be avoided like the plague. It will take longer to earn the confidence of some than others, because of personalities or past experiences. But if the man of God is faithful, those confidences will be gained. It must also be remembered, that confidence earned over a long period of time may be lost in a moment or eroded over a long period of time. Therefore, the man in ministry must protect what he has by grace built up.

5

THE MAN OF GOD IN RELATION TO HIMSELF AND HIS FAMILY

The axiom governing this section of the life of the man of God in the pastoral office is: *As a general rule, sustained effectiveness in pastoral ministry will be realized in direct proportion to the health and vigor of the redeemed humanity of the man of God.* This axiom has been explored in how it unfolds in the life of the man of God in relationship to God and in relationship to his people. Now it is explored in relationship to himself. As a man in relationship to himself, the pastor must seek to gain and maintain an increasingly realistic understanding and acceptance of his own unique and present identity as a man and as a servant of God.

Notice that this understanding is to be 'gained and maintained'. As has already been noted, there is a necessary measure of accurate self-assessment at the beginning of his ministry. This was examined under the call to the ministry. He must also be aware that with the passing of time he is changing with respect to what he is as a man and as a servant of God. It is within that context of change that he must maintain an accurate understanding of himself. His understanding must be realistic. He must avoid an idealistic or visionary view of himself. On the other hand, he must not in false humility have an inaccurately low view of himself. It must simply be realistic. The realism, of course, takes into account his uniqueness as a human being individually created by God. This extends to who he is both in his redeemed humanity as a man and also as a servant of God with reference to present age, gifts and experience.

Many in the ministry suffer from an artificiality, which is not necessarily ill-motivated, but rather emerges from an unrealistic perspective of what they are and need to be in the pastoral ministry. The ministry suffers under such pretensions. Yet the Bible itself never leads God's servants into these faulty notions: rather just the opposite is true. For instance, the passage which has been called into service a number of times already, Romans 12:3, states, 'For through the grace given to me I say to every man among you not to think more highly of himself than he ought to think; but to think so as to have sound judgment, as God has allotted to each a measure of faith.' This is Paul's call to sober, realistic self-assessment. Professor Murray's words are instructive:

> If we consider ourselves to possess gifts we do not have, then we have an inflated notion of our place and function; we sin by esteeming ourselves beyond what we are. But if we underestimate, then we are refusing to acknowledge God's grace and we fail to exercise that which God has dispensed for our own sanctification and that of others. The positive injunction is the reproof of a false humility which equally with over self-esteem fails to assess the grace of God and the vocation which distinguishing distribution of grace assigns to each.[115]

Jesus's parable of the talents (Matt. 25:14ff.) conveys the same truth. One is given five talents, the other two, the other one. In the giving of the talents, there is a realistic expectation of return or productivity. In the arena of ministry, this is sovereignly governed by the way in which God put a man together in his mother's womb (Ps. 139:13-17) and how He gifted him at the new birth. If God made him a five talent man, then he must evaluate that and function accordingly. If God made him, to use car imagery, a mechanically sound, efficient four-cylinder Honda, then he ought to function as the best, mechanically sound four-cylinder Honda he can be, and not bemoan the fact that he is not an eight-cylinder Jaguar. Proverbs 27:8 conveys the truth, 'Like a bird that wanders from her nest, so is a man who wanders from his home.'

> Not less senseless and dangerous is it lightly to leave the place, society, or calling, which Divine Providence has marked out. Here man is 'in God's precincts, and so under God's protection'; and if he will be content to remain in his place, God will bless him with the rich gain of 'godly contentment' (1 Tim. 6:6). But the man wandering from his place is 'the rolling stone, that gathers no moss'. He is always restless, as if he had a windmill in his head. Every new crotchet puts him into a new course. His want of fixed principles and

> employment exposes him to perpetual temptation. Always wanting to be something or somewhere different to what and where he is, he only changes imaginary for real troubles. Full of wisdom is it to know and keep our place. The soul, the body, the family, the society– all have a claim upon us. This feverish excitement of idleness is the symptom of disease, wholly opposed to religion, the bane of both our comfort and usefulness.[116]

As men of God come to this critical truth which impinges so much on their effectiveness, they must remember that there exists in the wisdom and sovereignty of God a great diversity of legitimate preaching styles and effectiveness. The Holy Spirit has sovereignly gifted each pastor with a unique blend of giftedness, ministries and effects (1 Cor. 12:4-7). Paul applied this principle to himself and Apollos (1 Cor. 3:4-7). God made all His servants differently, and His servants must understand this and accept it. Much damage can be done to a man's ministry if he is discontent with who he is and tries to be someone else. In order to avoid this trap, one should be careful when he reads the biographies of great preachers of the past, realizing that they were unique men. He should also avoid picking up all of his formative influences from only one source. Paul reminds the Corinthians that 'All things belong to you, whether Paul or Apollos or Cephas or the world or life or death or things present or things to come; all things belong to you, and you belong to Christ; and Christ belongs to God' (1 Cor. 3:21-3). In other words, he must glean what he can for his own edification and improvement within the context of who God made him and how He gifted him.

> If there is any maxim which you might inscribe on your seal-ring and your pen, it is this, Be yourself. As Kant says, every man has his own way of preserving his health, so we may assert that every true servant of the gospel has his own way of being a preacher; and I pray that you may never fall among a people so untutored or so straightened as to be willing to receive the truth only by one sort of conduit. Every genuine preacher becomes such, under God, in a way of his own, and by a secret discipline. But after having reached a certain measure of success, it will require much humility, much knowledge of the world, and much liberality of judgment, to preserve

him from erecting his own methods into a standard for even all the world.[117]

The Holy Spirit is not the author or owner of the unnatural and affected. If the man of God fails to accept his own unique identity, he cannot expect the sovereign Spirit to bless his efforts. This however does not mean that he fatalistically accepts his weaknesses and does not try to overcome them. If the preacher mumbles, or leaves the last syllable off every word, or uses poor grammar, he should not say, 'Well, that is how God made me.' Rather as a workman who is diligently laboring in order not to be ashamed (2 Tim. 2:15), he take pains to make progress (1 Tim. 4:15). If he is a four-cylinder Honda Civic, then he must make every effort to stay tuned in order to achieve maximum performance. It is unacceptable to say, 'Well it is just a Chevette, I won't change the oil, adjust the timing or keep it aligned.'

It is not being implied that the man of God will not or ought not be influenced by the imitative element of preaching. If one man excels in vividness or clarity or simplicity, then the other man should do everything he can to learn those principles which make the one the effective preacher that he is. It is a matter of 'he who walks with wise men will be wise' (Prov. 13:20). There are some biblical principles which are seen in certain men, which should by all means be imitated. Great preachers give birth to a school of preaching. In fact, that is what this current project is all about: learning from Pastor Albert N Martin those principles and truths which have shaped him into the preacher that he is. But here is the crux of the issue, whatever he learns from Pastor Martin and others and begins to embody in his own ministry must have his own fingerprints all over it! No one wants clones of Albert N Martin, but if he can learn the truths and principles which have shaped Pastor Martin into the effective preacher that he is, and in turn practice them within his own uniqueness, it would enhance the effectiveness of his ministry.

Men of God who have recognized and accepted their own identity will glean and learn as much as they can, but never stop being themselves. A vital ministry is that in which the man of

God ministers to his people as the man God made him! The true people of God and even discerning unbelievers will generally be suspicious of the forced and the unnatural. So, let every man of God learn and grow and improve, but let him do it in such a way that what he learns and how he improves are embodied in who and what he is. There is great liberty and freedom in accepting his unique identity, and allowing his ministry to flow from the real person. It is as he experiences that liberty that he will see genuine Spirit-wrought effectiveness in his labors.

The axiom for this fourth vital element of effective ministry is the man of God must attain, maintain and manifest an exemplary biblical standard of domestic competence. 'Attain, maintain and manifest' are calculated to underscore the fact that these issues are neither static or secret. As the family grows in size and as his wife and children pass through various stages of growth and development the competence of the man of God must parallel those changes. The word 'exemplary' underscores that the man of God must be a standard bearer in this area. Finally, the term 'biblical' emphasizes the fact that the man of God must educate his conscience in these matters by the Word of God. Neither tradition nor culture sets the standard, but the Word of God alone.

Domestic competence in the life of the man of God is a necessity. It is a necessity first of all because it is a general Christian duty. Such familiar texts as Ephesians 5:25ff; 1 Peter 3:7; Ephesians 6:4 and 1 Timothy 5:8 support this affirmation beyond question. The Bible sets forth a high domestic standard which should be obeyed by all Christians. A husband who loves his wife as Christ loves the church, a wife who submits to her husband, and children who obey their parents should mark the Christian home. Everyone knows that there are no Christian homes where these things are perfected, but these foundational biblical principles should mark the tone and direction of any home which would call itself 'Christian'.

Secondly, this domestic competence is an explicit requirement for the office of an elder (1 Tim. 3:1-7; Titus 1:6, 8). Many of the requirements for the office of elder are seen as general mandates for all believers. However, when these issues are brought into the arena of the office of overseer, they bear a non-negotiable quality, so that if they are not conformed to, the lack of conformity disqualifies a man from office. In the domestic realm, the elder must be one who 'manages his own household well, keeping his children in subjection with all dignity' (1 Tim. 3:4). The connection of this requirement to the office of overseer is manifest when Paul says parenthetically, 'for if a man does not know how to manage his own household, how will he take care of the church of God' (1 Tim. 3:5)?

This requirement of domestic competence specifies that the children must be submissive and respectful. Geoffrey Wilson notes, 'Thus the good pastor will be a man whose "gravity" or calm dignity will secure the respect and ready obedience of his children.'[118] Included in this requirement of a well-managed household would also be a wife who conforms to the standards of godly submission (Eph. 5:25ff.). Furthermore, the man of God must exhibit fatherly balance between kindness and gentleness and authority and discipline (Eph. 6:4; Col. 3:21). Although there are many factors and variables which come into play in this requirement which are beyond the scope of this section, it must be affirmed that domestic competence is a necessity in the life of the man of God because Scripture demands it.

Thirdly, domestic competence is a necessity because the man of God occupies the position as an example to his flock (Titus 2:10; Phil. 2:14-15; 1 Pet. 5:1-3; 1 Tim. 4:12; Titus 2:7; Matt. 10:25; 23:3, 15). In the present day there is a strong reaction, warranted in many ways, to the goldfish bowl syndrome of the pastor's family. The kids are expected to be perfect, the wife should be seraphic and the husband should the quintessence of all desirable traits of godly manhood. This kind of expectation for a pastor and his family is not only unrealistic, it is harmful. However, in reaction to the goldfish bowl syndrome, let no man throw the goldfish out with the water! All must make the distinction between those things which are normal and human and those things which are rebellious. A child picking his nose is not cause for the elders to call a special meeting. A child swearing at his parents is. Perfection is not the standard, but there is nonetheless a standard. There must be domestic competence, control and structure. A pastor should be able to say, 'My family is a good model for the members of the congregation to follow.'

Finally, the particular circumstances of this current generation make domestic competence a necessity as well. No longer are well-ordered families the norm; rather the stridently abusive and the dysfunctional litter the domestic landscape. The stereotype is warranted (Titus 1:12).[119] In contemporary culture, Christian families must not be conformed to the world, rather the church must have transformed families, families that swim salmon-like against the current (Rom. 12:1-2). The ministry of the local church must help rescue the families who are casualties in the societal breakdown, and if the pastor is among the wounded, he will bear no mantle of credibility to minister to those around him. The peculiar circumstances of the family in this generation, therefore, make it necessary that a pastor and his family maintain domestic competence and integrity.

Just as there is a critical necessity for domestic competence, so there are peculiar ministerial temptations which may lead to domestic incompetence. Although most would like to believe that all pastors' families are solid models of domestic health and stability, too many times the family falls into temptations which are unique to the man of God and his family. One of those temptations is the propensity to rationalize domestic failures in the light of ministerial duties. In other words, the minister who neglects his wife or children and fails as husband and father may rationalize his failure by pointing to his enormous responsibilities as a pastor. A broken promise to a child is not acceptable because an 'emergency' visit needed to be made to a whining sheep.[120]

There is also a temptation to be insensitive to the special pressure upon his wife and children because he is a pastor. A wife may feel tremendous emotional pressures. These pressures may be the normal attendant pressures which any wife in the ministry may feel, or they may be pressures aggravated by a negligent husband. Obviously the pastor's wife is restrained in many ways in her ability to seek counsel from others. (It would usually be unwise to talk to church members about such problems.) It is possible that these emotional pressures, unless understood and addressed by the husband, could lead to emotional and sexual vulnerability or outright abandonment. It does happen. Every man of God must be on guard for his wife's emotional health and well-being. Too many pastors, being task-driven men, ride roughshod over their wives and that takes an emotional toll. Many pastors desperately need the admonition of 1 Peter 3:7 pressed upon them again and again, 'You husbands in the same way, live with your wives in an understanding way, as with someone weaker, since she is a woman; and show her honor as a fellow heir of the grace of life, so that your prayers [and it might be added, "ministry"] won't be hindered.'

The pastor's wife also faces physical pressures. With the demands of hospitality that are duly expected from a pastor and his wife, there will come physical weariness because of the extra requirements in the household. Here the man of God can alleviate pressure by giving a hand in the cleaning or other domestic duties. He can also be sensitive to her weariness by not putting additional physical demands on her. After her long day of cleaning the house and taking care of the kids, he should be sensitive to her tired frame.

It should be noted that he must also beware the temptation to submit to the unreasonable demands of a wife not fully sympathetic to his calling. Loving firmness may be required in the training of a wife whose husband is in ministry. Perhaps she has not learned to guard that time of sermon preparation, or has not yet learned to discern genuine emergencies from things that can wait. In his efforts to be loving and sensitive, let him not in turn give in imprudently to the undiscerning demands of an unsympathetic wife. In the light of this, let single men who are looking at the ministry be ever so careful in the choosing of a life partner. Many men have had the joy of ministry drained right out of them because of a nagging, unsympathetic, demanding wife who would not bend with the demands of ministry.

The pastor's wife has a difficult calling, too. In the light of these added difficulties and temptations, the pastor must constantly be asking himself whether or not he has so conducted himself that his wife knows him to be what others tell her he is. When others tell her, 'Oh, I thank God for your husband, he labors for us in prayer, he is always there with a word of wise counsel, he is so wonderful.' Does she think, 'Oh brother! I wish he cared about me like that!' Or can she say with deep conviction, 'If you only knew the half. He is indeed a man of God!' Ministry marriages are special targets for Satan's attacks, and pastors must be on guard and nourish their wives, emotionally, physically and spiritually. Confession and repentance should be frequent. Let the man of God strive to live before his wife with integrity and godliness and patience. For many, God has provided a wonderful helper. Let them guard that precious deposit in the light of an unusually difficult calling.

The pastor's children are also vulnerable to special temptations. There are two direct temptations which are unique to the pastor's kids. The first is that there may be inordinate attention heaped on the children by virtue of Dad's position. This must be monitored because it could cause pride in the children. They could end up thinking highly of themselves because daddy is the pastor. Even young children have been known to exploit their position. A pastor's kids might suffer from 'big-shot*itis*' because of their father's position and profile. Pastors must do everything they can to neutralize the inflated views their kids may get of themselves. The Proverbs may come in very handy here, especially those which deal with pride and humility.

There are other pressures which may come indirectly to a pastor's children. There may be the temptation to bitterness and resentment because of the demands of the office. Plans have to be scrapped from time to time, because the man of God can't schedule deaths or serious crises. This can create a sense of bitterness in his kids. In order to ward off this resentment, which is common among pastors' kids, he must make it clear to his children that when an emergency comes up, he doesn't like being pulled away from them. Guard certain times with the family. Instruct the congregation not to call during certain times, for instance, from 5:00-7:30 p.m. The pastor's kids must see him make strong efforts to protect his plans with them. One thing that the author has implemented personally is to take each of his children out to lunch every other week. That is special time. If someone calls to set an appointment on the day he has scheduled to have lunch with one of his children, he tells them that he has a previous engagement. The pastor must not put his kids in a position where they fill out a visitors card on the Lord's Day and tick the box 'I would like a visit from the pastor'.

Another peculiar temptation is for the pastor's children to have resentment because of wrong motives of discipline. Discipline must be governed by the glory of God and the children's good. The man of God must make sure that he doesn't discipline them because 'Daddy is the pastor'. No special discipline should be applied because of his ministerial standing! His children will resent his office if they believe that his office has been a factor in disciplining them.

Resentment also might come because of an unrealistic standard of expectation of them as preacher's kids. The pastor must remind his people that they must not lay on his children a standard which God has not laid on those children. His children are children, not half angel, half human. Pastors' kids pick their noses and have bodily functions just like every other kid. Although high standards of domestic competence are upheld, everyone also needs to be realistic and know that only sinners live in a pastor's home!

Finally, there is a temptation for his kids to frame a wrong conception of daddy as a man of God professionally but not in reality. Much could be said here, but let it suffice to say that his kids must see his faith in action. Of course, they will hear him offer the public prayer with fervency, and see him preach with passion, but what will they see at home? What do they see in family worship? Do they see a father who has a vibrant love for the Word in the pulpit, but a half-hearted love for the Word in family worship? Do they see his zeal for Christ and His Word at home? If they do not, they will gain the impression that daddy is only a professional Christian.

Practical counsel for the maintenance of domestic competency

(1) *The man of God must pray in and periodically refresh his convictions of the unyielding necessity for exemplary domestic competence.*

He should make 1 Timothy 3 and Titus 1 his constant companions. He needs to set time aside to load his conscience with the reality that if he fails as a husband and father, he forfeits the ministry and much more.

(2) *The man of God should seek the periodic assessment of his domestic life by competent observers.*

His fellow elders should be able to speak frankly with him about his family. He should not be defensive, but open to honest assessment.

(3) *The man of God should seek the periodic assessment of his domestic life by his wife and children.*

He ought to ask his wife if there were anything she could change in him, what it would be. After her three-hour discourse, they then should go over the things which can be worked on. Let the kids do the same.

(4) *The man of God must bind himself to some inescapable pressure in this area of domestic competence.*

Pastor Martin has vowed with his wife that if she ever saw anything in his life which he was unwilling to repent of, she should go over his head, straight to the elders. For the sake of her husband and the sake of the congregation, she should do it. So many pastors in this day have put themselves beyond such an inescapable pressure; friends, wife, children and others have kept their mouths shut while they watched a man of God lose his grip on his integrity and purity. If only he had had a chain bound around his conscience, whispering in the midst of temptation that his wife would not be silent, it might well have been enough to rescue him. Let every man of God take his calling to domestic competence seriously, realizing that it is a critical factor in effective ministry, and that without it, there will simply be no ministry.

6

THE MAN OF GOD IN RELATION TO THE MANAGEMENT OF HIS TIME AND MANIFOLD RESPONSIBILITIES

The pastoral office is one that requires incredible self-discipline and self-mastery. As a result, the man of God must have control of himself, his time and his manifold responsibilities. Self-control is one of the fruits of the Spirit of Galatians 5:23 and one of the faith-virtues of 2 Peter 1:5-7. It is not only a Christian grace, but also a moral quality required for an overseer (Titus 1:8). The man of God must have self-mastery in the daily race of the Christian life, which includes his passions (1 Cor. 9:25; 7:9).

Therefore, he must acquire and maintain a clear understanding of and a conscientious commitment to his God-given ministerial duties. It is Christ alone who has the right to dictate the duties of the office which He has conceived and instituted. Ecclesiastical tradition, ministerial fads, congregational expectations and the carnal inclinations of remaining sin do not set the standard of duties. The Head of the Church, through His Word, lays those down and the pastor must be intimately knowledgeable of them. An overview of these ministerial duties are: the disciplines essential to the maintenance of a vital and growing piety (Acts 20:28; 1 Tim. 4:7, 16); the disciplines essential to the maintenance of intellectual vigor and balance (Jer. 3:15; Titus 1:9); the disciplines essential for adequate preparation for public ministries (2 Tim. 2:15); the disciplines essential for the demands of individual care of needy sheep (Acts 20:28; Col. 1:27); the disciplines essential to the wise administration of the life of the people of God (1 Tim. 3:5; 1 Pet. 5:2); and the disciplines essential to the maintenance of good emotional and physical health (1 Tim. 4:8, 5:23; Mark 6:31-2).

Not only must the man of God know what the Word of God

requires of him as a minister, he must also acquire and maintain a clear understanding of a conscientious commitment to his God-given general or ordinary responsibilities. Being a good husband takes time and planning. Being a father is a time-consuming responsibility, especially as children grow.[121] He also has the joyful responsibility of maintaining friendships through phone calls and letters. He is a son and has relatives, and thus extended family obligations. Finally, but not exhaustively, he is a citizen and a neighbor. All of these general responsibilities take time and effort.

As a result of ministerial and general duties, the man of God ought carefully to establish a structured schedule which reflects a commitment to fulfill all of these responsibilities before God. The life of the man of God demands that he be a wise steward of his time. Sloth or disorganization is inexcusable in the ministry. If he is to have an effective ministry, he must master himself, his time and his duties. This grace of self-control will work itself out in the pastor's daily schedule. Weakness in this grace will cripple a man's ministry and bloody his conscience.

The schedule itself ought to be realistic. There are only 24 hours in each day, and part of that time has to be consumed with sleeping, eating and exercising. God remembers that His people are but dust (Ps. 103:13-14). God commands the preservation of life (see the Westminster Larger Catechism on the sixth commandment), and He also demands that His servants evaluate themselves realistically. If this be so, then one must not make a schedule for Superman, but for oneself. Although the ministry can be a hiding place for sluggards (who will sooner or later be found out), it can also be an early grave for men driven by God-given responsibility. So let each take care that schedules are realistic, taking into account all that God has given him to do. This means he must be willing and able to say the word 'no'. It means he must be able to distinguish true emergencies in the life of the congregation from the bleating of an over-demanding sheep. It means taking time to blow his nose and go to his kids' birthday parties and take his wife out to dinner. It means self-control in setting priorities.

The schedule should also be comprehensive. God has given

His servants all the time they need to fulfill all the duties He has given to them. He has not necessarily given them time to fulfill all the desires of all the people all the time. The schedule should comprehensively entail general and ministerial duties. It should also be tenaciously pursued. That which has been carefully and prayerfully planned, should not be at the whim of others or even of the pastor's own flesh. With a US Marine mentality, he must pursue the duties and not be at the mercy of his own laziness or the clamoring of others. This grace of self-denial is critical in order to stay on schedule. 'No more practical instrument will attend ministers in cultivating the gardens of the Lord than self-denial. No grace is more Christlike. No cloak is so becoming to servants in his house.'[122]

Now it must quickly be added that this schedule must be reasonably flexible. It is not the law of the Medes and Persians. The Proverbs are helpful here. Proverbs 16:3, 'Commit your works to the LORD and your plans will be established.' So far, so good. The man of God makes his schedule, he plans his work, he commits it to God. He establishes those plans. Nevertheless, 'The mind of a man plans his way, but the LORD directs his steps' (Prov. 16:9). Yes, man plans, but God is sovereign. This flexibility is rooted in his understanding of God's sovereign providence (Prov. 19:21, 20:24). It is illustrated in the perfect example: the Lord Jesus Christ. Jesus made a plan to get away and rest (Mark 6:30-1), but the crowds followed, and Jesus altered His plan out of compassion (Mark 6:33-44). However, this flexibility did not always mark Jesus' ministry (Mark 1:35-9). Flexibility, therefore, must be reasonable.

In order to implement these truths practically the man of God must first master himself (Gal. 5:23; 1 Cor. 9:27). His life must be under the control of Christ and His lordship, so that he is not 'mastered by anything' (1 Cor. 6:12). He must also master his own home (1 Tim. 3:4-5). This subject has already been discussed. He must master his phone. The phone is a wonderful servant, but a tyrannical master. He must set hours for incoming calls, he should use his answering machine and keep tight reins on the phone. He must master his calendar. (Before he masters his calendar, he must be committed to using one!) He must master his television and newspaper. An inordinate amount of time can be wasted in front of a television or a newspaper, not to mention the fact that these things can be instruments to feed carnality which can sap spiritual vigor.[123] We must master our pillow and blanket. The Proverbs warn about the sluggard, and all would do well to take heed. A zealous and earnest man is not one who sleeps late into the morning! He must master his legitimate avocations (i.e., recreations, hobbies, etc.). Again, he cannot afford to be so absorbed in golf or fishing that they begin to control him and make demands of his time. In this battle of self-control, he should secure the cooperation of his wife, children, fellow elders, flock and friends. They can help guard his time and keep him on track in following his schedule.

Slothfulness kills an earnest ministry. It is the self-control of a Spirit-filled life which permeates a ministry with effectiveness. May it please the Head of the Church to protect those who are in earnest, filled with zeal, passion and self-control. May it please Him to raise up more like them. May the Head of the Church also do for this present generation of preachers what he did many generations ago, by bringing many to repentance and a fresh resolve. In His kindness their words have been preserved for following generations:

> *We have been selfish.* We have shrunk from toil, difficulty and endurance, counting not only our lives dear unto us, but even our temporal ease and comfort. We have sought to please ourselves, instead of obeying Romans 15:2: 'Let every one of us please his neighbor for his edification.' We have not borne, 'one another's burdens, and so fulfill the law of Christ' (Gal. 6:2). We have been worldly and covetous. We have not presented ourselves to God as 'living sacrifices', laying ourselves, our lives, our substance, our time, our strength, our faculties – our all – upon His altar. We seem altogether to have lost sight of this self-sacrificing principle on which even as Christians, but much more as ministers, we are called upon to act. We have had little idea of anything like sacrifice at all. Up to the point where a sacrifice was demanded, we may have been willing to go, but there we stood; counting it unnecessary, perhaps calling it imprudent and unadvised, to proceed further. Yet ought not the life

of every Christian, especially of every minister, to be a life of self-sacrifice and self-denial throughout, even as was the life of Him who 'pleased not Himself'?

We have been slothful. We have been sparing of our toil. We have not endured hardness as good soldiers of Jesus Christ. Even when we have been instant in season, we have not been so out of season; neither have we sought to gather up the fragments of our time, that not a moment might be thrown idly or unprofitably away. Precious hours and days have been wasted in sloth, in company, in pleasure, in idle or desultory reading, that might have been devoted to the closet, the study, the pulpit or the meeting! Indolence, self-indulgence, fickleness, flesh-pleasing, have eaten like a canker into our ministry, arresting the blessing and marring the success.

It cannot be said of us, 'For My name's sake thou has labored, and hast not fainted' (Rev. 2:3). Alas! We have fainted, or at least grown 'weary in well-doing'. We have not made conscience of our work. We have not dealt honestly with the church to which we pledged the vows of ordination. We have dealt deceitfully with God, whose servants we profess to be. We have manifested but little of the unwearied, self-denying love with which, as shepherds, we ought to have watched over the flocks committed to our care. We have fed ourselves, and not the flock.[124]

Conclusion

Renewing passionate, powerful, God-owned biblical preaching begins with a genuine call of God to the ministry, and a commensurate health and vigor of life in the man of God. Where the call is genuine and the life is holy, there is the soil for preaching which glorifies God, converts sinners and builds up the saints. May God grant the church a renewal of these truths in our time.

PART THREE:

THE PREACHING MINISTRY OF THE MAN OF GOD[125]

7

A BIBLICAL THEOLOGY OF PREACHING

Passionate, powerful, God-owned biblical preaching begins with a genuine call of God to the pastoral ministry. That seed of the call grows in the rich, deep soil of genuine godliness. It is the health and vigor of the man of God in the totality of his redeemed humanity which gives his preaching credibility and power. However, this must be qualified by saying that it is not merely a genuine call and a godly life which makes for God-owned preaching, it is also the thorough possession of a biblical theology of preaching. The theology of preaching must be part of the preacher. It must thoroughly course through his veins and be the undergirding of his ministry. John Stott recognized this when he stated,

> In a world which seems either unwilling or unable to listen, how can we be persuaded to go on preaching, and learn to do so effectively? The essential secret is not mastering certain techniques *but being mastered by certain convictions*. In other words, theology is more important than methodology. By stating the matter thus bluntly, I am not despising homiletics as a topic for study in seminaries, but rather affirming that homiletics belongs properly to the department of practical theology and cannot be taught without a solid theological foundation. To be sure, there are principles of preaching to be learned, and a practice to be developed, but it is easy to put too much confidence in these. Technique can only make us orators; if we want to be preachers, theology is what we need. *If our theology is right, then we have all the basic insights we need into what we ought to be doing, and the incentives we need to induce us to do it faithfully* (Italics are added).[126]

A biblical theology of preaching must begin and end with God (Rom. 11:36). His glory is the great end of preaching. Cotton Mather said, 'The great design and intention of the office of a

Christian preacher is to restore the throne and dominion of God in the souls of men.'[127] The man of God must be convinced that biblical preaching is ordained by God as His appointed means of glorifying Himself through saving sinners and building up the saints (1 Cor. 1:17 – 2:5). 'God uses contemporary preaching to bring His salvation to people today, to build His church, to bring in His kingdom. In short, contemporary *biblical preaching is nothing less than a redemptive event*' (Italics added).[128]

God-owned biblical preaching, which reaches people with the truth can be pictured as a convergence of two forces, one from above, one from underneath. The force from above is the unction of the Spirit, the felt power of the truth, which comes mightily on the man of God when preaching. The force erupting from underneath is the man of God's own biblical theology of preaching, which is always beneath him, but in the act of preaching, combined with the force from above, serves to propel the man of God in such a way that preaching becomes 'truth on fire'. Without a sufficient theology of preaching, the pastor's preaching ministry will lack power! He must know what he is there to do.

The view of preaching which is assumed here is unashamedly Reformed and experimental. The deep conviction is that the kind of preaching most owned by God and used for the conversion of sinners and the edification of the saints is Reformed and experimental. Reformed, experimental preaching is nothing less than biblical preaching. While it is truly biblical exposition, there are some distinctives to this kind of preaching. The term 'Reformed' designates two aspects of this kind of preaching. First, there is the historical aspect. Reformed preaching is preaching which stands in the glorious traditions of Reformers and Puritans and their heirs; which in turn is nothing less at its root than apostolic preaching. The second aspect of Reformed preaching is content. The great truths of the Reformation, namely a radically God-centered worldview, the centrality of Christ and the supremacy of His Word and the sovereignty of grace and the life of faith saturate the content of this kind of preaching. It is preaching which is first and foremost concerned with the ultimate *solus* of the Reformation: *Soli Deo gloria*, 'to God alone be the glory'.

This kind of preaching is also 'experimental'. The term may be used interchangeably with 'experiential' to mean 'something experienced'. Dr. Joel Beeke defines 'experimental preaching' as

> That which addresses the vital matters of Christian experience. It is preaching that stresses the need to know the truth of God by experience. It is discriminating preaching; defining the differences between the Christian and non-Christian, pressing home the promises of forgiveness and eternal life to those who believe and promises of wrath and judgment on those who are unconverted. It sets forth Christ as the One who saves sinners, and who must be experienced personally. It is applicatory preaching, which seeks to apply the truth of God's Word to every aspect of life. The goal of experimental preaching is to promote a religion which is power and not mere form (2 Tim. 2:5). Experimental preaching is earnest about salvation and damnation. It extols the glory of God and paints the horrors of separation. It teaches the marks and fruits of grace and exposes false professors.[129]

It is this kind of preaching which is assumed throughout Pastor Martin's seven axioms on preaching. These seven axioms apply to all of the different kinds of sermons, whether textual, consecutive expository, or topical expository. Each axiom is based on elements of preaching: proclamation, explanation and application. Each axiom is concerned with describing a certain aspect of effective pastoral preaching. These axioms, although not exhaustive, will give a well-rounded theology of preaching.

8

PREACHING THE WORD

(1) The proclamation, explanation, and application of scriptural truths must constitute the heart and soul of all preaching.

The foundation for this axiom rests in the function of Scripture itself, the nature of the ministerial and preaching office, and the explicit commands of God's Word. First, the function of Scripture demands that it and it alone must constitute the heart and soul of all preaching because of the way in which Scripture functions in the saving purposes of God. The Scriptures are the instrument by which men are born again. The Word of God begets the divine life in the soul. 'By willing He gave birth to us by the Word of Truth' (Jas. 1:18, author's translation). Stephen Charnock notes, 'From this passage, it is very obvious that the gospel is the instrument whereby God brings the soul forth in a new birth.'[130] Charnock goes on to say with a burning eloquence, 'The word is the chariot of the Spirit; the Spirit the guider of the Word; there is a gospel which comes in word, and there is a gospel which comes in power, 1 Thessalonians 1:5.'[131] Again, the Scripture makes this clear, 'For you have been born again not of seed which is perishable but imperishable, that is, through the living and enduring Word of God' (1 Pet. 1:23).

Not only are the Scriptures used by God in the begetting of divine life in the soul, they are also used to nurture that life. No one ever outgrows the Scriptures. Just as God uses them as the seed in the new birth, so He uses them as the milk and meat in the new life. Our Lord Jesus reveals this when He prays, 'Sanctify them in the truth, Your Word is truth' (John 17:17). Calvin in commenting on this text, says, 'Christ expressly says that the truth by which God sanctifies His sons exists nowhere but in the Word.'[132] The Apostle Paul sets forth the same when he states, 'All Scripture is inspired by God and profitable for teaching, for reproof, for correction, for training in righteousness; that the man of God may be adequate, equipped for every good work.' The interesting elements to note in 2 Timothy 3:16-17 are the ontological statement, what God's Word is ('God-breathed') and the functional statement, what it does ('is profitable for ...') and the obvious connection with what should be done with it, 'preach the Word' (2 Tim. 4:2). Robert Godfrey's comments are valuable,

> The force and clarity of the Apostle's teaching here are striking. In spite of the rich oral teaching Timothy had, he is to preach the Scriptures because those Scriptures give him clearly all that he needs for wisdom and preparation to instruct the people of God in faith and all good works. The Scripture makes him wise for salvation, and equips him with everything he needs for doing every good work required of the preacher of God. The sufficiency and clarity of the Word are taught in this one section of Scripture over and over again.[133]

In the saving purposes of God, His truth as inscripturated in the Bible stands as the supreme instrument of regeneration and sanctification. 'For it is not an idle word for you; indeed it is your life' (Deut. 32:47). What should make up the heart and soul of all preaching? If it is understood that the great goal of preaching is the glory of God in and through the conversion of sinners and the edification of the saints, then it must be said, without compromise, the Word of God alone will constitute preaching because the Word of God is the instrument by which God saves and sanctifies sinners!

> The God of heaven is the God of Truth; truth is infinitely dear to his pure and holy mind. He is its great assertor and guardian; nor will he be respected, loved and obeyed, and this earth filled with his glory until it is flooded with his truth, as the waters cover the sea. The Scriptures instruct us that truth is the great instrumentality by which his purposes of mercy are accomplished, the wisely selected means by which he operates, a means well adapted to the end; nay, the necessary and indispensable means, because truth alone presents the only objects of all that variety of right thoughts and holy affections and emotions which constitute true religion. The pulpit has no other instrumentality.[134]

The proclamation, explanation and application of scriptural truths must constitute the heart and soul of all preaching because Scripture itself is the means by which God regenerates and sanctifies. However, there is another reason scriptural truth must be the heart and soul of preaching: the nature of the ministerial and preaching office. A survey of the descriptive words used in the New Testament reflects the simple fact that the minister is one under authority. He does not come with his own message, in his own authority; rather he comes with another's word in his mouth and another's banner over his head. Paul says he is a herald (e.g., 2 Tim. 1:11, *kērux*). The 'herald', as has already been noted, is one who proclaims the message of another. Paul says he is an ambassador (e.g., 2 Cor. 5:20). An ambassador never gives his own ideas, nor does he have the power to act on his own, he is a man sent by another. The same could be said of a steward (1 Cor. 4:1), an overseer (1 Pet. 5:1) and even a ruler (Heb. 13:7, 17). All these words reveal that the minister is speaking and acting on behalf of another, but only within the specified boundaries that have been established.

What is it that defines the authority of the minister in light of these descriptive terms? Simply, it is the Word of God. The herald proclaims the Word of God (2 Tim. 4:2); the ambassador offers the terms of the gospel (2 Cor. 5:20); the steward has responsibility for the 'mysteries of God' (1 Cor. 4:1). An overseer and ruler uses the scepter of the Word as a servant-leader under the Chief Overseer (1 Pet. 5:1-4; Heb. 13:7). With this in view, it must be affirmed that all preaching must have as its heart and soul the Word of the One who sends His messengers.

> Although the Spirit's speaking is by no means limited to preachers (think of parents, teachers, friends, and neighbors through whom the Spirit speaks today), contemporary preachers have a special responsibility to proclaim the word of the Lord. No less than their biblical counterparts, contemporary preachers are called to be channels of the word of God. The metaphors of herald and ambassador apply as much to them as they did to the apostles. This high view of preaching came to clear expression in the Reformed Second Helvetic Confession of 1566: *Praedicatio verbi Dei est verbum Dei* (the preaching of the word of God is the word of God).[135]

Finally, the explicit and implicit commands of Scripture demand that Scripture alone be the heart and soul of all preaching. The prophet Balaam, who everywhere else is instructive in the negative, is positively instructive on this point. The angel of the LORD tells Balaam, 'you shall speak only the word which I tell you' (Num. 22:35). Balaam, in turn, tells Balak, 'Behold, I have come now to you! Am I able to speak anything at all? The word that God puts in my mouth, that I shall speak' (22:38). After frustrating Balak, Balaam reminds him, 'Though Balak were to give me this house full of silver and gold, I could not do anything contrary to the command of the LORD, either good or bad, of my own accord. What the LORD speaks, that I will speak' (Num. 24:13).

Our Lord Jesus, in the great commission, commands His disciples to 'teach them to observe all that I commanded you' (Matt. 28:19). The Apostle Paul exhorts Timothy to be one who makes a straight cut through the Word of Truth (2 Tim. 2:15). As mentioned earlier, it is the same God-breathed Word that he is to preach (2 Tim. 3:16 – 4:4). Whether it be Old Testament or New Testament, the servants of God had no right to speak anything except the Word of the living God. Let all true servants of Christ who would dare to say, 'I am called of God', plant their flag on this hill, willing to fight and die there! They cannot, they must not, they dare not proclaim anything else except the Word of God alone!

> The Bible is unique and indispensable for preaching because it provides the definitive *interpretation* of God's acts in history; the Bible is the source for contemporary preaching because it alone provides the normative *proclamation* of God's acts of redemption and the response he requires. The Bible itself, therefore, can be seen as preaching: authoritative proclamation for future generations of God's good news of salvation. As such the Bible is the only normative source for contemporary preaching.[136]

In working this axiom out, there are a number of corollary truths about the sermon itself which will determine if it has as its heart and soul the Word of God. The biblical sermon, that is, the sermon which has the Bible as its heart and soul, will be *thoroughly exegetical* in its raw materials. In order for a sermon to be thoroughly exegetical, it requires that good exegesis be done by the preacher in the study. Exegesis is the historical, grammatical, lexical, syntactical and canonical analysis of a given text in its original language, drawing out of the text itself the meaning of the author. The doctrine of verbal, plenary inspiration compels those who handle the Word to assert that careful exegesis forms the raw material of any biblical sermon.

Exegesis has fallen on hard times in the pastorate. Many seminaries are lowering their language requirements, some have even dropped them altogether. Many pastors do not use their Hebrew and Greek texts with enough frequency to maintain any efficiency. This is indeed criminal! As a man of God called to labor in the Word of God, the preacher must do everything he can to be an expert in the Book! Luther used to tell his students, 'Keep hard at the languages, for grammar is the sheath in which the Sword of the Spirit rests.' B B Warfield expressed similar convictions when he wrote,

> The minister must learn the code in which the gospel message is written. He must be able to de-code it; to de-code it for himself. No trusting the de-coding to another! This is the message of salvation, and he is the channel by which it is conveyed to men. He cannot take it second-hand. He must get it for himself, and convey it first-handed to those entrusted to his care. He must, in other words, know the languages in which the gospel is written; and he must be skilled in drawing out from the documents the exact meaning.[137]

Above every pastor's desk there ought to be the words of Warfield engraved in stone: 'What we need in our pulpits is scholar-saints become preachers.'[138]

Obviously the average pastor will never have time to become an accomplished lexicographer, or even a first class linguist. Nevertheless, if the man has had the privilege of training in languages, he ought to use it so that his sermons will be exegetically sound. If he does not want to be ashamed for the way he handled God's Word, then let him sweat over the text, with grammars and lexicons open, striving to give his people his best. If he wants confidence in his preaching, that what he is saying is true to the Word, then let him sweat over the text. If he is to be able to refute the gainsayer, then let him sweat over the text, mastering to the best of his ability the nuances of the original. Rigorous exegesis will keep him honest with every text; toppling initial impressions of texts, traditional or dogmatic uses of texts, fanciful allegorizing or spiritualizing of texts and the clever and forced accommodation of texts. Rigorous exegesis will keep him disciplined in the Word for a variety of tasks, not the least of which will be preaching. Even for those who have not had the benefit of formal training, the ready availability of help today means that sloppy exegesis is inexcusable.

The biblical sermon will be *predominantly biblical* in its overall substance. A biblical sermon is not simply an exegetically sound sermon, there is more to it than that. John Piper notes, 'I say that good preaching is "saturated with Scripture" and not "based on Scripture" because Scripture is more (not less) than the basis for good preaching. Preaching that proclaims God's supremacy does not begin with Scripture as a basis and then wander off to other things. It oozes Scripture.'[139] Biblical sermons should be marked by quotations of biblical texts, biblical illustrations and allusions. Biblical sermons should be like John Bunyan, of whom it was said, 'Prick him anywhere and he bleeds bibline.' It is at this point where the church so desperately needs reformation in this day.

Dabney once again hits the mark with these penetrating words:

> Whenever the pulpit is evangelical, the piety of the people is in some degree healthy; a perversion of the pulpit is surely followed by spiritual apostasy in the Church. And it is exceedingly instructive to note, that there are three stages through which preaching has repeatedly passed with the same results. The first is that in which scriptural truth is faithfully presented in scriptural garb – that is to say, not only are all the doctrines asserted which truly belong to the revealed system of redemption, but they are presented in that dress and connection in which the Holy Spirit has presented them, without seeking any other from human science. This state of the pulpit marks the golden age of the Church. The second stage is a transition stage. In this the doctrines taught are still those of the Scriptures, but their relations are moulded into conformity with the prevalent human

> dialectics. God's truth is now shorn of a part of its power over the soul. The third stage is then near, in which not only are the methods and explanations conformed to the philosophy of the day, but the doctrines themselves contradict the truth of the Word.[140]

Let every preacher examine the sermons he has preached in the last year, and ask himself with judgment day honesty, 'Are my sermons predominantly biblical in their overall structure? Do they ooze Scripture? Am I in Dabney's first stage, or have I drifted away?' If Evangelical and Reformed men believe our bibliology, if they have a high theology of preaching, then they must preach sermons which are exegetically sound and thoroughly drenched in the Bible itself.

The biblical sermon must be *theologically harmonious* in its statements of truth. This really is an apostolic injunction for preachers. 'Retain the standard of sound words which you have heard from me' (2 Tim. 1:13). The body of Christian truth fits a pattern or standard, which is harmonious and congruent, forming a unity. It is this reality which gives birth to systematic theology. Biblical sermons therefore must be harmonious with that system of divine truth which is based on biblical and historical theology, and has come to fruition in systematic theology.[141]

The pastor must be a theologian. He must have a systematic theology. Spurgeon noted that 'Verbiage is too often the fig-leaf which does duty as a covering for theological ignorance.'[142] How can a man deal with difficult texts which touch on the theological issues of historic Christianity without having a systematic theology helping him to navigate the waters of the delicate interplay of divine sovereignty and human responsibility? The arrogant preacher who claims he only has a biblical theology, and whatever the texts says that he will preach, will soon find out that his congregation is smarter than he thinks, because they will see the glaring inconsistencies, incongruities and lack of coherence in what they hear. Martyn Lloyd-Jones has words of wisdom on this subject.

> If then I say that preaching must be theological and yet that it is not lecturing on theology, what is the relationship between preaching

> and theology? I would put it like this, that the preacher must have a grasp, a good grasp, of the whole biblical message, which of course is a unity. In other words the preacher should be well versed in biblical theology which leads on to a systematic theology. To me there is nothing more important in a preacher than that he should have a systematic theology, that he should know it and be well grounded in it. This systematic theology, this body of truth which is derived from Scripture, should always be present as a background and as a controlling influence in his preaching. Each message, which arises out of a particular text or statement of Scripture, must always be a part or an aspect of this total body of truth. It is never something in isolation, never separate or apart. The doctrine in a particular text, we must always remember, is a part of this greater whole – Truth or the Faith. That is the meaning of the phrase, 'comparing Scripture with Scripture'. We must not deal with any text in isolation; all our preparation of a sermon should be controlled by this background of systematic theology.[143]

The biblical sermon will be *intensely practical* in its overall thrust. It appears today that there is a false dichotomy in preaching between the doctrinal and the practical. It is assumed that if a sermon is to be doctrinal, it certainly cannot be practical, and if practical it will certainly avoid doctrine. This is not only a false dichotomy, it is a diabolical one. The same God-breathed Scripture which is profitable for doctrine, is also profitable for reproof, correction and for training in righteousness (2 Tim. 3:16). These are the same Scriptures which must be preached, in season and out of season; and in that preaching, which is certainly doctrinal, there will be rebukes, exhortations and instructions (2 Tim. 4:2). It is obvious from Paul's words that he saw no disjunction between the doctrinal and practical. In fact, the doctrinal is always the foundation for the practical. To put it another way, the indicatives of Scripture lead to the imperatives of Scripture.

Much of the hard work of preaching rests right here: if biblical preaching is intensely practical preaching, then it is more than merely informational preaching. If a man has a grasp of theology, informational preaching comes easy, but bringing practical application of theology to bear on the minds and hearts is hard work. If biblical preaching is intensely practical preaching, then it is more than just exclusively emotional preaching. Although preachers should raise the affections of their hearers with the truth, they are not merely trying to pull heart strings and get some tears. If they are seeking to move people to action with truth, which is practical preaching, then they must labor to this end. Dabney observes,

> Music and the imitative arts are designed primarily to gratify the taste. Their immediate aim is at the sentimental affections of the soul. But the immediate end of eloquence is to produce in the hearers some practical volition.[144]

When the congregation comes away from the sermon they should have been moved to some affection, they should have had some information imparted to them, but they also should go away having some area of thought, word, deed or affection challenged and given a clear path of repentance, faith and obedience. Obviously the implication of a sermon being intensely practical is very broad, and the spectrum of what constitutes 'practical' is almost limitless, but suffice it to say that most people know when the truth has been preached in such a way that it was brought home with relevant application.

The final corollary truth to the first axiom is that the biblical sermon will be *pervasively evangelical* in its overall climate and flavor. There is a glory in the Scriptures which makes the Law, the prophets, and covenant history shine with brilliance, and that glory is the glory of the only begotten Son of God. He is Scripture's grand theme, as He Himself taught (Luke 24:45-8). It is not that every sermon must be explicitly about the person and work of Christ, but rather there must be an evangelical aroma to every sermon. The gospel must be marbled throughout a sermon in such a way that the Christ of the gospel is present. Jay Adams is quite correct when he states,

> If you preach a sermon that would be acceptable to the members of a Jewish synagogue or to a Unitarian congregation, there is something radically wrong with it. Preaching, when it is truly Christian, is distinctive. And what makes it distinctive is the all-pervading

> presence of a saving and sanctifying Christ. Jesus Christ must be the heart of every sermon you preach. That is just as true of edificational preaching as it is of evangelistic preaching.[145]

Paul is so vitally clear on this whole subject of Christ-centered preaching. Let every preacher spend hours of exegetical, contemplative and prayerful time in 1 Corinthians 1:17 – 2:5. 'We preach Christ crucified', 'I determined to know nothing among you except Jesus Christ and Him crucified.' This is the same apostle who declared 'the whole purpose of God' (Acts 20:27). For Paul there was no contradiction between preaching the whole counsel of God and 'we proclaim Him' (Col. 1:28). For Paul, Christ was the beginning, middle and end of the whole counsel of God (1 Cor. 15:3-4; Eph. 1:10, 3:8-9).

Thomas Murphy, whose entire section on this subject is worth reading again and again, brings it into focus with unusual clarity and balance.

> A sermon which does not in some way contain the salvation of Christ cannot with any propriety be called a gospel sermon. It may be so impressive as to awaken deep interest, or so beautiful as to please, or even such a high moral tone as to cultivate and refine, but it is not the gospel, for the publishing of which all preaching was appointed.
>
> It is not meant that the death of Jesus in the place of sinful men should be the announced subject of every sermon, nor even that His name should be in every point that is handled; this might not always be possible, nor would it always be best. But what is meant is, that the salvation of Christ should be the drift, the center, the substance, the aim – should give tone and direction and impulse to every discourse. This can be done in perfect consistency with keeping up a proper variety and interest. The whole Word of God leads to Christ and centers in Him, but that through thousands of different avenues.[146]

To preach with a pervasively evangelical climate and flavor is to avoid legalistic and moralistic preaching. Legalistic preaching is preaching the imperatives (the commands) of Scripture apart from the redemptive realities which should underlie all Christian ethics. Legalism is naked Law, apart from Christ, who is the goal of the Law (Rom. 10:4). Moralistic preaching is taking the examples of Scripture, e.g., Joseph, David, Daniel, and setting them forth *strictly* as good role models, apart from their redemptive-historical roles.[147] Of course the men and women of the Bible are examples to us (this is the point of Heb. 11:3 – 12:1, and is specifically stated in Rom. 15:4; 1 Cor. 10:6, 11; Jas. 5:10). However, the words of Bishop Horne, as quoted by Bridges, set a balanced tone:

> To preach practical sermons, as they are called – i.e., sermons upon virtues and vices – without inculcating those great Scripture truths of redemption and grace, and which alone can excite and enable us to forsake sin, and follow after righteousness; what is it, but to put together wheels, and set the hands of a watch, forgetting the spring, which is to make them all go.[148]

The proclamation, explanation, and application of scriptural truths must constitute the heart and soul of all preaching. The Word of God alone is the instrument of regeneration and sanctification. Therefore, biblical preaching must be exegetical in its raw material; it must ooze the Bible through and through because it is saturated with it; it must be theologically consistent and harmonious, intensely practical and pervasively evangelical. When Scripture is preached with these competent parts, the sermon is well on its way to becoming a God-owned redemptive event, whereby He is glorified and good is done to the souls of men.

9

PREACHING TO THE NEEDS OF THE CONGREGATION

(2) **The proclamation, explanation and application of scriptural truths which are most needed by the pastor's regular hearers must constitute his constant goal.**

At first this axiom seems to have little to do with an actual theology of preaching. However, upon deeper examination it is revealed that this axiom contains a vital element which is often overlooked in preaching. This axiom is far from the current interest in scratching people where they itch, rather it is grounded on three biblical bases: (1) the nature of preaching in relationship to the prophetic office of Christ; (2) the implications of the pastoral office; (3) the pattern of biblical preaching itself.

One of the glorious truths of the church of Jesus Christ is His glorious presence among His assembled body. In Revelation 1–3 Jesus is seen in the midst of the lampstands (i.e., the churches) and He addresses each one, specifically and individually, through the appointed messenger of each congregation. The glorified Christ walks among His churches, exercising His office of prophet, priest and king. It is as prophet that He addresses His people.

> His prophetic role is the most prominent of all especially as it affects the churches. His voice is as the sound of many waters. All truth is mediated through Him and from Him must come the living message to all the churches. His encouragements, instructions and reproofs proceed through the messengers designated as seven stars in His right hand.[149]

The prophetic office of Christ is exercised through His appointed ministers in the churches. R B Kuiper concurs, 'The work of a prophet is to deliver messages from God to men. Therefore those who proclaim the Word of God represent Christ as prophet.'[150]

Christ, as the great Head of the Church, seeks to nurture and nourish His bride (Eph. 5:29), which means that as her prophet, He brings her those specific words of encouragement, rebuke and challenge, as she has need. This is illustrated in each message to each church in Revelation 2–3. In light of these biblical realities, pastors must be sensitive to the needs of the congregation. If the pastor is to be the representative of Christ as prophet to a local assembly, then he must preach those scriptural truths which are most needed by his regular hearers.

The second biblical basis for the axiom is the implications of the pastoral office. The pastor is a shepherd who is to shepherd the flock of God (Acts 20:28; 1 Pet. 5:2-3). As a good shepherd, modeled for all in Psalm 23 and John 10, we see that the shepherd is always aware of the present state of the flock. If the sheep need medicine, the sensitive shepherd does not press forward with his plans of giving regular food. If the sheep are hungry and waiting to be fed, the sensitive shepherd does not take out the medicine and give it as if it were food. If the sheep need mending, the sensitive shepherd does not administer the rod of correction. Furthermore, there is the metaphor of a father (1 Thess. 2:11; 1 Tim. 3:5). A good father knows the present condition of the household and is sensitive to the genuine needs of the family. The wise governor (see Heb. 13:17) knows the state of the commonwealth, and acts accordingly.

The third biblical basis is the pattern of biblical preaching itself. The recorded sermons of both Old and New Testament were occasional, that is, they were addressed for a particular occasion or situation. Isaiah's message was different from Ezekiel's, and so on. The New Testament epistles bear witness to the same truth. The letter of 1 Thessalonians would have been completely inadequate for the Galatian churches. The Galatians needed strong medicine to combat heresy, while the Thessalonians needed encouragement and confirmation. The Corinthians needed everything from rebuke to having their questions answered.

These three bases of biblical evidence demonstrate that God-owned pastoral preaching must be those biblical truths which the congregation needs most. Again, this is not the 'scratch me where

I itch' syndrome of modern evangelicalism. It is however, a sensitivity to the uniqueness of each congregation and the particular stage of life it is in as a body. This does not deny the fact that there are perennial truths which are universally beneficial, but it does call for pastoral sensitivity. The question which now arises is what principles govern the pastor in his selection of sermon material? How does he know what he should preach?

There is one fundamental principle followed by some general guidelines for the wise selection of sermon material. The fundamental principle operative in a wise selection of material is that there is a constant and delicate interplay between the natural and supernatural. The theological term for this interplay is 'confluence', the convergence of the divine and human, the natural and the supernatural. The man of God lives not as merely a spirit-being, nor as merely matter in motion, but he is body and soul; he is spiritual and natural; there are the elements of the mystical and the rational. This reality is spoken of in Scripture in such texts as Philippians 2:12-13, 'work out your salvation with fear and trembling; for it is God who is at work in you, both to will and to work for His good pleasure', and Colossians 1:29, 'and for this purpose also I labor, striving according to His power, which mightily works within me'. Both texts show that the pastor's activity is not all human, nor all divine and spiritual, but rather there is an interplay which he must be aware of, even though he may be ignorant of the mechanics involved.

Knowing that this interplay exists, the pastor should beware of the iron-clad rule makers. There are some who under the subject of choosing sermon material would deny one was preaching the whole counsel of God if he did not do consecutive, expository messages through the books of the Bible. Others, such as that great preacher, Charles Haddon Spurgeon, laid down some iron-clad rules in the opposite direction. He told his students, 'Wait for that elect word, even if you wait till within an hour of the service. This may not be understood by cool, calculating men, who are not moved by impulses as we are, but to some of us these things are a law in our hearts against which we dare not offend. We tarry at Jerusalem till power is given.'[151]

The Doctor gives some much needed balance:

> What, then, does one say about this? All I can say is that it seems to me to be quite wrong to be rigid in the matter, and to lay down any hard and fast rule. I cannot see why the Spirit should not guide a man to preach a series of sermons on a passage or a book of the Bible as well as lead him to one text only. Why not? What is important – and here I am with Spurgeon whole-heartedly – is that we must preserve and safeguard 'the freedom of the Spirit'. We must not be in control in this matter; we must not decide in cold blood, as it were, what we are going to do, and map out a programme, and so on.... So, having asserted that we are subject to the Spirit, and that we must be careful to make sure that we really are subject to Him, I argue that he may lead us at one time to preach on odd texts and at another time to preach a series of sermons. I would humbly claim that I have known this many times in my experience.[152]

Pastor Martin humorously relays the agony he suffered as a young itinerant preacher while he waited for those elect texts. Anyone in the ministry for any amount of time resonates with that sense of frustration, bathed in prayer of course, as he flips to passage after passage, waiting for a hand to reach out and grab his collar. After a period of time has gone by, and no hand pulls his eyes to a text, he resorts to going over old sermon notes, and then wonders how he ever preached a sermon from those pathetic notes. In Pastor Martin's experience, he finally got fed up with the frustration and confusion and determined that he would no longer subject himself to such agony. Where is the freedom? It comes in not listening to the iron-clad rule makers, but rather recognizing that interplay between the mental and spiritual.

The pastor can be guilty of being an enthusiast (used in the older sense of the word), expecting a divine revelation. If he is given to subjective impressions, and has a dreadful fear of violating the will of God, he can create undue anxiety and even internal agony for himself. On the other hand, if he rules out providential guidance, and has no sensitivity to God's dealing with him and his congregation, then he may be so rationalistic that he cuts that dynamic nerve which creates the interplay between the divine and human. He can also be too stubbornly (even rationalistically and legalistically) inflexible with his own plans. As he maintains the interplay as the operative principle, he is free to move to other guidelines for wise sermon material selections.

The first general guideline is that he seeks to be consistently prayerful for divine guidance. In a sense, this prayerfulness is an inner disposition of the soul. He needs to be seeking wisdom (Jas. 1:5) for his preaching menus. He needs to ask God to grant him His Spirit (Luke 11:13), confessing his own inadequacy (2 Cor. 2:16). He must trust that He will lead him (Prov. 3:4-5), and that since he has asked, God will grant it to him (Jas. 4:4).

The second general guideline is that he must seek to be aware of the needs and present capacity of the flock. 'To shepherd the church of God' (Acts 20:28) requires that he knows them and where they are in their struggles, their questions, and even in their sins and weaknesses. It is Prov. 27:23 that exhorts to this wisdom as well, 'Know well the condition of your flocks, and pay attention to your herds.' William Gurnall noted, 'The preacher must read and study his people as diligently as any book in his study, and as he finds them, dispense like a faithful steward unto them.'[153] Baxter also stated along this line,

> I confess, I think NECESSITY should be the great disposer of a minister's course of study and labour.... I confess, necessity hath been the conductor of my studies and life. It chooseth what book I shall read, and tells me when, and how long. It chooseth my text, and makes my sermon, both for matter and manner, so far as I can keep out my own corruption.[154]

As has already been noted, it was the need of the hour that shaped the epistles of the New Testament. Good pastors, making wise sermon choices, need to be apprised of what is happening in their congregations and what has been their history. There may be general needs which have been shaped by antinomianism or dispensationalism. This will direct him to the book or passage he must preach in order to neutralize the negative effects of prior teaching. Perhaps there has been an unhealthy hyper-Calvinism, or excessive duty apart from the indicatives of the gospel. These, too, can be neutralized by teaching certain portions of the Word of God. In the life of a congregation there will arise certain difficulties or trials, such as a death of a precious saint or young child. These must be addressed from the Word of God to the bleeding and aching hearts of the people. If the pastor avoids these things, he may be guilty of a shameful irrelevance.

If certain national events occur, it would generally be irresponsible for the pastor to ignore them. If the minds of his congregation are riveted on the death of a president, a princess, or the destruction of a space shuttle, then he will not most likely win their hearts and minds if he tells them, 'Last Lord's Day we were in 2 Chronicles 6, today turn to 2 Chronicles 7.' Pastor Martin has exemplified this sensitivity, giving outstanding demonstrations of this by preaching occasional sermons on each of the three events mentioned above and more. When President Kennedy was assassinated the country was in shock. Pastor Martin took that event which had gripped the nation and put it into the perspective of Divine Sovereignty. When the Challenger Space Shuttle exploded in mid-air, he brought a relevant message to bear on what God might be saying to America. More recently, when Magic Johnson announced he had AIDS and Princess Diana was killed in a car crash, he brought some pointed biblical truths out of those situations.

There will also be times when God is dealing with His servant's own heart and mind. As he reads the Word, as he reads good books by proven guides, he will find 'fire being shut up in his bones'. A certain truth or duty may stir his own soul. There may be times of unusual blessing and experience of redemptive privileges or even dark nights of the soul; what the Puritans called desertion. All of these experiences and more may go into that providential mix which leads the man of God to a particular book or subject. The prince of the Puritans, John Owen, expresses his own experience of this,

> [T]he thoughts here communicated were originally private meditations for my own use, in a season wherein I was every way unable to do anything for the edification of others, and far from the expectation that ever I should be so able any more in this world. Receiving, as I thought, some benefit and satisfaction in the exercise

> of my own meditations therein, when God graciously pleased to restore a little strength unto me, I insisted on the same subject in the instruction of a private congregation. And this I did, partly out of a sense of the advantage I have received myself by being conversant in them, and partly from an apprehension that the duties directed and pressed unto in the whole discourse were seasonable, from all sorts of present circumstances, to be declared and urged in the minds and consciences of professors; for leaving other unto the choice of their own methods and designs, I acknowledge that these are the two things whereby I regulate my work in the whole course of my ministry. To impart those truths of whose power I hope I *have had* in some measure a *real experience*, and to press those duties which *present occasions, temptations, and other circumstances, do render necessary* to be attended unto in a peculiar manner, are the things which I would principally apply myself unto in the work of teaching others; for as in the work of the ministry in general, the whole counsel of God concerning the salvation of the church by Jesus Christ is to be declared, so in particular we are not to fight uncertainly, as men beating the air, nor shoot our arrows at random, without a scope and design (italics added).[155]

In addition to being aware of God's dealings with his own soul, the man of God must seek after sensitivity to his own present development as a preacher. The man of God not only grows in grace, but also in gift and ability. Just as certain vocalists and musicians recognize that some pieces and roles are beyond their abilities, certainly preachers ought to recognize that certain series and books are beyond them. Many have noted that lengthy consecutive expository series, fashioned in the likeness of a Martyn Lloyd-Jones or a James Montgomery Boice, have given a congregation a great distaste for such preaching because the gifts and ability were not commensurate with the fashioned series. The opinion of certain modern homileticians that a series must not exceed twelve weeks is certainly rejected, but it must be acknowledged that not everyone is gifted to preach through Romans in ten years. Nor is everyone equipped to teach Revelation, Ezekiel, Job or the Song of Songs without bringing some damage to his listeners. Being sensitive to where the man of God is as a preacher, and at what level his gifts are operating are vital in making decisions about sermon material.

The pastor must seek to be sensitive to the reaction of the flock of God. Although he is not a man-pleaser, the pastor must not ignore feedback from the godly and mature in the congregation. If one ventures out on a verse by verse exposition of the Proverbs (not recommended!), and one of the wise men in the congregation, who exemplifies the wisdom of the Proverbs, comes and says, 'Pastor, this repetitive yet practical series is indeed imparting wisdom but also testing our perseverance, please change direction', this is not the voice of carnality, but sensitivity. This is not compromising boldness, but rather it is simply listening to people with an open ear and heart. There is a sense in which the pastor's service must be acceptable to the saints (Rom. 15:30-1).

The proclamation, explanation and application of scriptural truths which are most needed by the pastor's regular hearers must constitute his constant goal. This is supported by the nature of the preaching office and Christ's office as prophet. It is also supported by the clear implications of the pastoral office and the pattern of biblical preaching itself. This demands that he give attention to wise selection of sermon material. Such wisdom comes from recognizing the interplay between the natural and supernatural and following some general guidelines. As this axiom is practiced, it will provide the sermon material for truly experiential preaching. If this axiom is followed, preaching which is irrelevant, purely didactic and non-applicatory will not find its way into the pulpit, rather there will be a dynamic experiential nature to the preaching which will be owned by God to build up His saints and convert sinners.

10

PREACHING WITH CLARITY

(3) **The proclamation, explanation and application of scriptural truths with perspicuity of form and structure must constitute the man of God's conscious endeavor.**

If preaching is to be used by God to build up saints and convert sinners; if much good is to be done by the sermon; then it must be understood. It will only be understood if it is clear in form and structure. Obviously the work of the Holy Spirit in enlightenment is a sovereign work (Eph. 1:18-19; 1 Cor. 2:6-16). But the raw material that the Spirit uses is the sermon and it must have form and structure. There must be divisions of headings, arrangement of thought and progression, linked by the obvious relationship of the same. There must be perspicuity, that is, clarity, transparency, lucidity. Paul, in a discussion on tongues, puts the principle this way, 'Yet even lifeless things, either flute or harp, in producing a sound, if they do not produce a distinction in the tones, how will it be known what is played on the flute or on the harp? For if the bugle produces an indistinct sound, who will prepare himself for battle' (1 Cor. 14:7-8)?

This perspicuity of form and structure must be a continuous and conscious effort. Whether a man is naturally endowed with an analytical, logically precise mind which thinks in lucid divisions, arrangements and relationships, or he has had training which has facilitated such thinking patterns, or if he has a mind which is like a can of alphabet soup, there must be labor in this area! What may be clear to him may not come across clearly to the congregation. He has lived with the exegesis, the outlining, the commentaries; his mind is marinated in these things. The congregation is coming to it fresh, with no frame of reference, and therefore it must be clear. Clarity demands work. John Broadus brings home the importance of this issue.

> The effective arrangement of the materials in a discourse is scarcely less important than their intrinsic interest and force. This is a distinct part of the speaker's work, and should be contemplated and handled as something apart from invention on the one hand and from style on the other, albeit closely connected with both. In fact, the task calls for a specific talent. Some men exhibit from the very outset a power of constructing discourses which is quite out of proportion to their general abilities; and other men find nothing so difficult to acquire or exercise as skill in arrangement. And here, as in everything else that demands specific talent, there is need of special training and practice.
>
> In this respect the speaker is an architect. Out of the gathered materials he is to build a structure, and a structure suited to its specific design. The same, or nearly the same materials may be made into a dwelling, a jail, a factory or a church. But how different the plan of the building according to its design, and how important that it be built with special reference to the design. In like manner, substantially the same materials may be wrought into a story, a dialogue, an essay, or a speech; and several speeches on the same subject, and embodying much the same thoughts, may make a very different impression according to the plan of each. . .
>
> 'Good thoughts,' says Pascal, 'are abundant. The art of organizing them is not so common.... I will not go so far as to say that a discourse without order can produce no effect, for I cannot say that an undisciplined force is an absolute nullity.... But we may affirm in general, that other things being equal, the power of discourse is proportional to the order which reigns it in, and that a discourse without order is comparatively feeble. A discourse has all power of which it is susceptible, only when the parts proceeding from the same design are intimately united, exactly adjusted, when they mutually aid and sustain one another like the stones of an arch.'[156]

This element of clarity of form and structure cannot be overstated. It is rigorously asserted that, for the sake of the preacher himself and his listeners, he must labor and sweat to attain perspicuity of form and structure. First, the importance of clarity for the preacher himself is demonstrated. If the man of God labors in clarity and form, he will grow in the discipline of clear, orderly and detailed preparation of the sermon. His study habits will be greatly helped. This discipline will enhance the ability to think through the texts logically, analytically and thoroughly. Broadus again notes:

> One has not really studied a subject when he has simply thought it over in a desultory fashion, however long-continued and vigorous the thinking may have been. The attempt to arrange his thoughts upon it suggests other thoughts, and can alone give him just views of the subject as a whole. Good arrangement assists in working out the details, whether this be done mentally or in writing. Each particular thought when looked at in its proper place, develops according to the situation, grows to its surroundings.[157]

Very simply, many pastors have not developed the discipline of clear, orderly and detailed study, thus it does not come out in the message. There will never be another Jonathan Edwards, but it is here that Edwards challenges pastors to be clearer thinkers and better investigators.

> My method of study, from my first beginning the work of the ministry, has been very much by writing; applying myself, in this way, to improve every important hint; pursuing the clue to the utmost, when anything in reading, meditation, or conversation, has been suggested to my mind, that seemed to promise light in any weighty point; thus penning what appeared to me my best thoughts, on innumerable subjects, for my own benefit. – The longer I prosecuted my studies in this method, the more habitual it became, and the more pleasant and profitable I found it.[158]

Beyond imparting discipline in the study, this seeking after clarity will also greatly assist the preacher's freedom in the actual delivery of the sermon. If the man of God cannot get the thoughts out of his head with ease, he will stumble through the exercise and fail to get anything into the listener's head, although much energy has been exerted. If the thoughts are clear, arranged orderly and properly related in the preacher's head, then they will come out in similar fashion. Broadus observes:

> One reason why some preachers find extemporaneous speaking so difficult is, that they do not arrange their sermons well. And not only to invention and memory, but to emotion also, is arrangement

> important. Whether in preparation or delivery of sermons, a man's feelings will flow naturally and freely, only when he has the stimulus, support, and satisfaction which comes from conscious order.[159]

This is one of the many areas where Pastor Martin excels. He consistently has a structural cohesiveness which makes his sermons exceptionally clear. This labor in the study manifests itself in the pulpit, not only in his clarity of form and structure, but also in the freedom with which he delivers the message. The author has arbitrarily chosen a sermon from Pastor Martin to illustrate the consistency of his practice.[160] This particular illustration of his clarity in form and structure comes from a closely detailed exposition of Ephesians 2:7. He explains the theme of 'bare bone of grace'. However, Paul does not present naked grace, but rather grace which is clothed in flesh and skin. The flesh and skin is the latter part of the verse, 'the surpassing riches of His grace in kindness toward us in Christ Jesus'. At the outset of the sermon, he announces his three points, and reiterates them in the process of the sermon. The result is a sermon which is easy to follow.

1. The measure of grace: the exceeding riches
2. The manner in which this grace operates: in kindness towards us
3. The sphere in which this grace operates: in Christ Jesus

Pastor Martin usually does red flag his points. This does help with clarity in preaching and listening. Although some advocate this and others avoid it, Bishop Ryle's wisdom wins the day:

> There is a morbid dread of 'firstly, secondly, and thirdly', in many quarters. The stream of fashion runs strongly against divisions, and I must frankly confess that a lively undivided sermon is much better than one divided in a dull, stupid, illogical way. Let every man be fully persuaded in his own mind. He that can preach sermons which strike and stick without divisions, by all means let him hold on his way and persevere. But let him not despise his neighbor who divides.[161]

Again Ryle says:

> By all means, let there be order – order, whether you bring out your 'firstly, secondly, or thirdly,' or not – order, whether your divisions are concealed or expressed – order so carefully arranged that your points and ideas shall follow one another in beautiful regularity, like regiments marching past the Queen on a review day in Windsor Park.[162]

From this order great benefit flows to the listener. This clarity in form and structure is a major factor in making what the preacher says intelligible. It is not the Holy Spirit's responsibility to take sermon globs and make them intelligible, it is the pastor's responsibility. Furthermore, it is a major factor in making what he says aesthetically pleasing. He is not laboring for oratorical floridity, but rather he is aiming at doing everything in his power to make the sermon pleasing to the senses. No amount of passion can cover chaos. Broadus emphasizes this when he states:

> 'Order is heaven's first law'. Even those phenomena in nature which seem most irregular, and those scenes which appear to be marked by the wildest variety, are pervaded by a subtle order, without which they would not please. Chaos might be terrible, but could never be beautiful. And discourses, which are pleasing but have no plan, will be found really to possess an order of their own, however unobtrusive or peculiar. An ill-arranged sermon may of course contain particular passages that are pleasing, but even these would appear to still greater advantage as parts of an orderly whole, and the general effect of that whole must be orderly incomparably better.[163]

Clarity in form and structure also has a morally persuasive dynamic to it. Moral persuasion is biblical (Acts 24:25, 26:28; 2 Cor. 5:11). This is the point of logical argumentation, which is so vivid in the whole book of Romans and other passages such as 1 Corinthians 15. Moral persuasiveness is not the same as emotional manipulation; rather it is the sanctified use of truth with all of its logic and rational properties, under the power of the Spirit, to sway the consciences and affections of those who hear. Broadus again points us to the truthfulness of this:

> He who wishes to break a hard rock with his sledge, does not hammer here and there over the surface, but multiplies his blows upon a certain point or along a certain line. They who lift up huge buildings apply their motive power systematically, at carefully chosen points. So [also] when motives are brought to bear upon the will. And the hearer's feelings will be much more powerfully and permanently excited, when appeals are made in some natural order.[164]

Finally, clarity in form and structure benefits the hearer in that it makes what was said intellectually retainable. If God's inspired Word resorts to mnemonic devices, such as Psalms 1 and 119 with their alphabetic poetry, then the man of God should not be ashamed to labor for a form and structure which is easily remembered. Alliteration is not a sin, as long as the goal is mnemonic aid and not a pedantic display of a clever mind. Spurgeon's humor and wisdom are well worth repeating:

> Let the good matter which you give them be very clearly arranged. There is a great deal in that. It is possible to heap up a vast mass of good things all in a muddle. Ever since I was sent to shop with a basket, and purchased a pound of tea, a quarter-of-a-pound of mustard, and three pounds of rice, and on my way home saw a pack of hounds and felt it necessary to follow them over hedge and ditch (as I always did when I was a boy) and found when I reached home that all the goods were amalgamated – tea, mustard, and rice – into one awful mess, I have understood the necessity of packing up my subjects in good stout parcels, bound round with the thread of my discourse; and this makes me keep to firstly, secondly, and thirdly, however unfashionable that method may now be. People will not drink your mustardy tea, nor will they enjoy muddled up sermons, in which you cannot tell head from tail, because they have neither, but are like Mr. Bright's Skye terrier, whose head and tail were both alike. Put the truth before men in a logical, orderly manner, so that they can easily remember it, and they will the more readily receive it.[165]

Clarity in form and structure will have a price. It will cost the labor of diligently remaining focused on the true, God-ordained ends of preaching, namely, the conversion of sinners and the edification of the saints. The price will be a resolute determination not to give in to the current ministerial fads. In the author's own experience, as computer and video technology have soared, many men are using multimedia presentations in their preaching, for outlines or illustrations. This certainly grabs the TV glutted culture, but it is nothing more than a fad which detracts from true God-owned preaching. It is tempting to want to be on the cutting edge of what's new, but the man of God must resist it, keeping his eyes on the goal of true biblical preaching.

There will also be the price of one's reputation. The preacher may notice certain gifts that he has in telling stories or using imagination in drawing mental pictures. He may have a penchant for technology. All these things could put him into the spotlight of his denomination. These things could get him speaking engagements at association meetings and other gatherings. But if he is to know nothing except Jesus Christ and Him crucified, then he must subject his peculiar gifts and abilities to the category of sanctified service, and accept the fact that although his congregation will love him and be blessed with his labor and God will be pleased with his labor, he may not gain a wider reputation. Many men have had to put to death carnal pride and say 'no' to reputation for the sake of keeping their preaching in line with its God-ordained goals. Many more men have been lured by the pursuit of a wider reputation and although popular in the conference and retreat circuits, have little lasting usefulness in the kingdom.

The price paid in this area will also entail the mortification of any carnal desire to attain elegance and a reputation for eloquence in preaching. John Flavel reminds his readers that the preaching of a crucified Christ must be accompanied by a crucified style.[166] If men are preaching Christ for Christ's sake then they will gladly forego any pretensions of being recognized for elegance and eloquence. Robert Murray McCheyne noted, 'I see a man cannot be a faithful minister, until he preaches Christ for Christ's sake – until he gives up striving to attract people to himself, and seeks only to attract them to Christ.'[167]

Another aspect of the price will be constantly ignoring those whose opinions, wishes and tastes pressure the pastor to change direction and give up on clear, plain biblical preaching. The consciences of some men cannot bear the sting of the ethical implications and spiritual applications of the truth, and they will make their voices heard. The pastor's fellow elders must be sold out to perspicuous biblical preaching, and they must form a united front. They must be like Paul and throw the approval of men to the wind (Gal. 1:10).

Finally, it will cost the agony and toil of incessant mental labor. Many who have entered the ministry find that there is sometimes a disparity between loving to study the Word and the necessary toil of putting it into a final homiletical form which is clear in both form and structure. The sweat that goes into hammering out that proposition or principle, or the time and energy in working out a clear outline, sometimes causes the preacher to be weary of the work. But if the commitment is to a clarity in preaching, then he must labor in the Word and teaching (1 Tim. 5:17), striving for that which is intelligible, aesthetically pleasing, morally persuasive and intellectually retainable.

Now that the case has been firmly made for clarity in form and structure, the essence of what constitutes this clarity must be unfolded. It is recognized that there is a legitimate diversity of organizational taste and inclination, as well as God-given ability. It has already been mentioned that some are naturally endowed with an analytical and logical mind, which categorizes and systematizes quite naturally. Others, by training and education, have acquired these facilities and are quite adept in the use of them. Others will always have great difficulty. But no matter what degree of competence is brought to the desk, there will always be arduous labor involved in attaining clarity of form and structure.

Of first importance is the order of the sermon itself. There must be a sequential progression of thought. A sense of unity must also be brought to the sermon. One of the problems with inexperienced preachers is that they often preach three to five sermons in one. There must be unity of theme and purpose. The sermon must be proportional, that is, it must have a sense of symmetry. Of course a preacher can be so symmetrical that he is paralyzed, but that is not the issue. The points must be proportional to one another.

Another ingredient is simplicity. The pastor is not attempting intricate and complex theological treatises, rather he is seeking to do good to the souls of men, and simplicity is a virtue. Finally, the form and structure must be complete. There can be no strings left dangling. Each of these elements come together to give the sermon clarity in form and structure.

This clarity needs to be cultivated. There is a great danger of attaining some ease with words! If a man preaches for five or ten years, he notices a facility in words. This facility can lead to a laziness. He can become a 'Bible talker'. He can be winsome and illustrative, and forget that he committed himself to the task of perspicuity. Therefore, he must maintain the conviction that the edification and salvation of his hearers demands it. If he is to cultivate this clarity, he needs to keep in front of him this conviction, and such texts as 1 Corinthians 14:8-9 'For if the bugle produces an indistinct sound, who will prepare himself for battle? So also you, unless you utter by the tongue speech that is clear, how will it be known what is spoken? For you will be speaking into the air.' And Acts 14:1-2, 'In Iconium they entered the synagogue of the Jews together, and spoke in such a manner that a large number of people believed, both of Jews and of Greeks. But the Jews who disbelieved stirred up the minds of the Gentiles and embittered them against the brethren.'

The pastor should be continually reading the proven guides on this subject, such as Spurgeon, Broadus, Dabney, Ryle and others, who wrote lasting works on homiletics. Exposure to good models is also necessary. Pastor Martin does indeed stand head and shoulders above most today in this category. A preacher should listen to good preaching, not only for edification, but for education. Securing the input of those who can be trusted, such as a wife, fellow elders, children and mature people in the congregation is also a good method by which to test himself. Asking the pertinent questions and being open is a place to start. These trusted people should be told the areas the preacher is looking to improve in, and then asked to evaluate those areas.

The man of God should be giving himself to constant labor in this area. It is labor which will be wonderfully apparent or woefully absent in the week in and week out preaching. If preaching is to be owned by God, the truth preached must be clear in form and structure. If the listeners reject the message, may they reject it because they too clearly understood and not because it seemed like a mass of unrelated titbits of truth.

11

PREACHING WITH APPLICATION

(4) **The proclamation, explanation and application of scriptural truths with specific reference to thinking, behavior patterns, affections, consciences and wills of the hearers must constitute the man of God's continuous practice.**

The heart of Reformed, experimental, biblical preaching is the application of the truth to the hearers.[168] Faithful, Christ-centered exposition, if it is to be genuinely biblical, must address the thinking, behavior patterns, affections, consciences and will of those who hear. John Angell James noted this well when he said,

> But though a careful analysis of the text should form the basis of almost all our sermons, there must be something more than mere exegesis, however clear, correct and instructive. We have to do not only with a dark intellect that needs to be informed, but with a hard heart that needs to be impressed, and a torpid conscience that needs to be awakened; we have to make our hearers feel that in the great business of religion, there is much to be done, as well as much to be known.[169]

This vital axiom is unfolded under four main heads: the description and definition of application in preaching; the demonstration of the scriptural basis of application in preaching; guidelines for cultivating aptitude in application; concluding observations and counsel concerning application in preaching.

The description and definition of application in preaching

> Application is the highway from the head to the heart. It is the bridge from correct notions of biblical truth to proper affections and right volition in the light of the truth established. Application is that aspect of your preaching in which your hearers are made to feel that you are not only, or merely, stating true and good things, but that you are

> proclaiming vital things to their hearts. If the truth is the nail, application is the hammer by which the truth is fastened in the hearts of your hearers.[170]

The graphic Old Testament account of Sisera, the commander of Jabin's army, is used effectively to illustrate this aspect of preaching. After being defeated in battle, Sisera flees to the tent of Jael, the wife of Heber, seeking refuge. Jael gives him some milk, covers him with a warm rug, and then dutifully pounds a tent peg through his temple, fastening his skull to the ground (Judg. 4:17ff.). 'He (the preacher) must employ the rhetoric which Jael used upon Sisera, putting his nail to the head of his auditor, and driving it sheer and clear through his brain.'[171] Most preaching today simply takes the tent peg and loosens the dandruff on Sisera's head, instead of fastening his skull to the ground. If preaching is to be searching and lively in application, it must go beyond shaking a few flakes loose, and get to the real business of fastening the truth firmly into the heads of the listeners. 'The general sermons, that are preached to everybody, in fact, are preached to nobody.'[172] The congregation must be made to *feel* the conviction of sin, deeply and firmly. They must be made to *feel* the consolation of precious and magnificent promises. They must be made to *feel* that Christ is for them, that His blood can cleanse their sins. The tent peg of truth must be driven home if they are to *discern feelingly*, with judgment day discrimination, whether or not they are among Christ's sheep. Nothing less than that constitutes biblical preaching.

> We must not expect our hearers to apply to themselves such unpalatable truths. So unnatural is this habit of personal application, that most will fit the doctrine to anyone but themselves; and their general and unmeaning commendation too plainly bespeaks the absence of personal interest and concern. *The preacher must make the application himself.* The 'goads and nails' must not be laid, as if the posts would knock them in; but 'fastened by the masters of the assemblies'. To insist therefore upon general truths without distributive application; or to give important directions without clearing the way for their improvement – this is not, according to the design of our Ministry, to lay the truth at every man's door, to press

> it upon every man's heart, and to 'give them their portion in due season'. That tone of preaching, that smooths down or qualifies revolting truths – that does not cause the hearers some uneasiness – that does not bear directly upon them as individuals, but feebly illustrates the living power of the word; nor will it ever 'compel sinners to come in' to the Gospel.... This palatable ministry, that blunts the edge of 'the sword of the Spirit', in order to avoid the reproach of the cross, brings upon the preacher a most tremendous responsibility.[173]

It is not being implied that God only applies the truth when the preacher does. It is understood that the sovereign Spirit alone knows the thoughts and conditions of each listener, and that He, as the Author of truth, can apply it in ways which are beyond the man of God. Thanks is given for this, and the man of God knows that it happens each Lord's Day. John Newton recognized this truth, and supplies some balance.

> It is true, the Lord can, and I hope he often does, make that preaching effectual to the conversion of sinners [I would add also the sanctification of His people], wherein little is expressly said to them, only the truths of the gospel are declared in their hearing; but he who knows the frame of the human heart, has provided us with a variety of the topics which have a moral suitableness to engage the faculties, affections, and consciences of sinners; so far at least to leave themselves condemned if they persist in their sins, and by which he often effects the purposes of his grace; though none of the means of grace by which he ordinarily works can produce a real change in the heart, unless accompanied with the efficacious power of his Spirit.[174]

The demonstration of the scriptural basis of application in preaching

The basis for application in preaching does not come primarily from the Puritans or the preachers of the Great Awakening, but rather from the pages of Holy Scripture itself. The passage that stands at the forefront is 2 Timothy 3:16–4:2:

> All Scripture is inspired by God and profitable for teaching, for reproof, for correction, for training in righteousness; so that the man of God may be adequate, equipped for every good work. I solemnly charge you in the presence of God and of Christ Jesus, who is to judge the living and the dead, and by His appearing and His kingdom: preach the word; be ready in season and out of season; reprove, rebuke, exhort, with great patience and instruction.

The inspired Word which is profitable for doctrine, is also profitable for reproof, correction and instruction in righteousness. But how does the inspired Word come to the hearts of men? It comes by means of preaching; serious and steady preaching. This preaching is to be characterized by reproof, rebuke and exhortation. Each of these are strong applicatory terms. Therefore, preaching which is not applicatory is not biblical preaching because it is not commensurate with the stated biblical purposes for which Scripture was given. Application belongs to the essence of preaching. 'Application forms the life and interest of preaching.'[175] With this statement many will disagree, but the biblical evidence is significant.[176]

The recorded sermons of the prophets, of the apostles, and of our Lord Himself demonstrate clearly that preaching was not merely serving up some truth to the listeners, that they might 'take it or leave it'. Rather it was characterized by pointed, lively and searching application. Consider Isaiah's sermon in Isaiah 1. It is a scathing rebuke of the Israelites' shallow religion. They had mastered the externals, but lacked genuine faith and piety. Isaiah pulls no punches as he points out specific sins, like a prosecuting attorney. The diagnosis is pointed and stinging, exposing sin after sin with vivid imagery. But then a gracious prescription for forgiveness is offered, not in merely general or vague terms, but rather in a direct offer with a specific response set before them. Reward and punishment are both laid out, not in ethereal terms but in concrete expressions designed to penetrate the heart.

This very pattern is followed by the Lord Jesus in His preaching to the Pharisees in Matthew 23. Certainly if anyone defines preaching it is our Lord, and He had no hesitation in direct, applicatory preaching. Conviction was His aim, and it was achieved. The forerunner of our Lord, John the Baptist, not only preached pointed, applicatory messages to the Scribes and Pharisees, and to the multitudes, but he even preached such sermons to Herod himself (Mark 6:17-18). The Apostle Peter's Pentecostal sermon was so pointed that his hearers were 'wounded in their consciences' and they specifically asked, 'what shall we do?' (Acts 2:37). 'Personal application formed the nerve of the preaching of the Jewish prophets, and of our Lord's public and individual addresses.'[177]

The exposure of sin and the prognosis for the impenitent are not the only forms of applicatory preaching. Just as there are conviction, reproof and rebuke, there are also consolation and comfort. The same Isaiah who scathed the Israelites in chapter 1 holds out the comfort of Jehovah in chapter 40. It is a kind and compassionate call; her warfare is ended; her iniquity is removed. Direct and vivid imagery convey the Lord's tender mercy, He will pick them up in His arms like a shepherd holding a little lamb. Our Lord Jesus often spoke consolatory words in His sermons. Consider His message to His own disciples in the upper room discourse (John 14-16). He understands their confusion; He gives them promises to sustain them; He is careful not to overload them; He gives them hope for the immediate future in the midst of soon approaching fear.

Experiential, applicatory preaching is not only established in Scripture by precept and example, it is also demonstrated throughout church history. The Puritans were masters of searching, applicatory preaching. 'It was observed of Philip Henry, that he did not shoot the arrow of the Word over the heads of his audience, in flourishes of affected rhetoric, nor under their feet by homely expressions, but to their hearts in close and lively application.'[178] This kind of preaching is described by the Puritan James Durham,

> Application is the life of preaching; and there is no less study, skill, wisdom, authority and plainness necessary in the applying of a point to the conscience of hearers, and in the pressing of it home, than is required in the opening of some profound truth: and therefore ministers should study the one as well as the other.[179]

The Westminster standards advocate this kind of preaching in both the *Directory of Public Worship* and the *Larger Catechism.*

> He [the preacher] is not to rest in general doctrine, although never so much cleared and confirmed, but to bring it home by special use, by application to his hearers: which albeit it prove a work of great difficulty to himself, requiring much prudence, zeal, and meditation, and to the natural and corrupt man will be very unpleasant; yet he is to endeavor to perform it in such a manner, *that his auditors [hearers] may feel the word of God* to be quick and powerful, and a discerner of the thoughts and intents of the heart; and that, if any unbeliever or ignorant person be present, he may have the secrets of his heart made manifest and give glory to God (Italics are added).[180]

Throughout the history of the church, movements of the Spirit of God in reformation and awakening have always been marked by searching, experimental, applicatory preaching. The Reformers were models not only of clear biblical exposition, but also of penetrating application. Calvin's sermons on Job make the case well. After explaining the text, Calvin actually spends most of his time in application. In fact, it seems almost as if Job is simply a picture of Calvin's hearers. After a mere ten lines of introduction, Calvin moves into application:

> By the way (as I have said) we have to behold, in what anguish mortal man is, when God shows Himself as his adversary party. *And it is greatly for our behoof to mind this lesson*, because we be over negligent, yea, and there are over few who think upon this kind of temptation (italics added).[181]

Calvin immediately presses the experience of Job on to the experience of his hearers. He appeals to times of adversity and suffering, and brings out how his hearers had failed to think of them as God's hand against His people. Not only does he chastise his hearers for neglecting to see God's hand in their adversities, he also helps to prepare them for such times. He later asserts,

> Therefore, let us mark that when God afflicts us in our bodies, we can well take patiently the miseries that He sends us: for, that is

nothing in comparison of the anguish which they endure, whom he makes to feel his wrath and vengeance.[182]

The First Great Awakening was marked by tremendous applicatory preaching. The sermons of Edwards and Whitefield are filled with personal application. One is made to feel as if he is the only one being addressed with each and every word designed just for him.[183] What was true of the First Great Awakening is exemplified in the Second Great Awakening; especially in the sermons of Asahel Nettleton. All these men, and those who held their convictions, were committed to the exposition of the Word, but they were also committed to the searching, pointed, personal, discriminating application of the truth. Where, throughout church history, has the Spirit of God used bland, cold, didactic preaching to awaken sinners and reform the church? Preaching that has been owned by God has seriously sought to unfold and apply the Word as closely as possible, in conviction and consolation. Bridges has aptly stated, 'Preaching, in order to be effective, must be reduced from vague generalities, to a tangible, individual character – coming home to every man's business, and even to his bosom.'[184]

There are those who object to this kind of preaching. The objection is usually stated like this: 'The work of application is the Holy Spirit's work. He alone can make the truth spiritually perceived, morally effective, and more extensive.' Unfortunately, applicatory preaching is often decried as legalism or moralism by those who promote a certain kind of Christ-centered preaching.[185] They warn that those who press application are 'taking God's work in our own hands here'.[186] Christ-centered preaching has already been advocated in a balanced way under Axiom One, Preaching the Word. To be sure, biblical preachers should denounce legalistic and moralistic preaching, but they must also denounce a preaching which neuters application for fear of being legalistic or moralistic. One can preach Christ (which is synonymous with preaching the whole counsel of God, Col. 1:28; Acts 20:27) and apply the truth with power. It is only when application has been made that it can be genuinely said that Christ has been preached to the hearts of men. To deal only in vague generalities and 'trust the Spirit' for the application is presumption.[187] The same Spirit who does indeed apply the truth effectually has also given a witness in Scripture and history of the kind of preaching He applies! 'Let not therefore the dreaded imputation of being thought moral preachers, deter us from inculcating the requirements, as well as illustrating the doctrines, of the Gospel.'[188]

Guidelines for cultivating aptitude in application

First, there must be continual engagement in the disciplines of personal piety. A thorough treatment of the life of the man of God has already been given. However, it is worth reiterating that the life of the man of God is the soil out which his preaching grows. 'The mouth speaks out that which fills the heart' (Matt. 12:34). Therefore, the preacher must continually be engaged in the practice of personal piety. Bridges states,

> It is experience alone that qualifies the Minister for usefulness, by enabling him to touch the tender strings of the heart, and to suit his instruction to the different cases, trials, and circumstances of his people. 'When he has', (as Witsius beautifully observes) 'not only heard something; but seen, and handled, and tasted of the word of life, and has been taught, not by mere speculation, but by actual experience, what he has thus found out; he safely inculcates, from the assured persuasions of his mind, and applies to every case, from his own knowledge of what is suitable to each.' [189]

Murphy also instructs along the same line:

> When the preacher delivers the message of God, he should never separate himself from his audience as if he were not addressed. He needs the communications of grace just as much as his congregation does. His own experience of wants, of sins, of trials and of blessings should be wrought into his discourses. His own faults should be kept in view, and rebuked as sharply as those of his audience. Diligently should he listen for the voice of God as addressed to his own particular case, and then reiterate that voice from the sacred desk. This rule, given by another, should ever be his guide: 'in your preparations for the pulpit endeavor to derive from the subject on which you are about

> to preach that spiritual benefit you wish your hearers to receive.'
>
> The soul of the minister will almost necessarily grow in grace under such a process. Its own great interests will not be neglected through exclusive care for others; its prevailing maladies will be detected; it will be kept alive, and the proper nourishment will be given it. When every sermon is faithfully brought home to the preacher's heart, he must advance in purity, vigor, in knowledge and in every other grace. Perhaps not perceptibly, but very surely, will he make progress from year to year.[190]

Secondly, if aptitude in application is to be cultivated, there must be continual engagement in pastoral intimacy. Paul has left an example of this pastoral intimacy and how it impacts application. The Corinthians were fraught with all kinds of problems and errors. It was Paul's pastoral antennae that picked up the signals and then addressed the issues at hand (1 Cor. 1:11). Paul believed in the necessity of pastoral intimacy for the sake of ministerial efficiency (1 Thess. 2:8-9). This kind of intimacy is not feigned out of necessity in order to perform a task. Rather, this kind of intimacy grows out of a genuine love for God's people and one's particular congregation. If the ministry of the Word is to make a lasting impact on God's people, the pastor must have his ears and eyes open to the congregation and he must be sensitive to their hearts. Within this context of pastoral intimacy, the pastor is not Sir Oracle, but rather a gentle shepherd who is observing and learning how he can better minister to the flock of God.

Thirdly, there must be continual engagement in intellectual industry. To a large degree, preaching is an imitative art. Therefore it is necessary that the man of God continually expose himself to various models who reflect diverse abilities and gifts in application. The imitative element of preaching is cumulative, and so a deliberate and careful exposure is necessary if the man of God is to grow and cultivate aptitude in application. This intellectual industry will take the shape of studying books and listening to sermon tapes. Reading the sermons of the Puritans, for instance, is like going to school with the masters of application. Carefully observing their 'uses' in the sermon may spawn ideas for a particular text, as well as demonstrate an example of a specific manner of applying truth to the conscience. Edwards, Whitefield, Davies, Nettleton and Spurgeon are all excellent examples to learn from, with plenty of sermons in print.

In terms of books and taped sermons by contemporaries, many are available.[191] For an intense example of searching, applicatory preaching on the subject of self-examination, the author recommends Pastor Martin's sermon series, 'Are You For Real? A Study in Self-Deception.'[192] In this series, Pastor Martin exemplifies pastoral concern for the state of the flock, using texts which deal with the marks of true conversion, as well as detailed expositions of Matthew 7:13-14, entering by the narrow gate and being on the straightened way. Although these sermons are suited to a specific congregation during a specific time, they serve as a model of applicatory preaching. Again, the lessons have far less to do with the manner of preaching than the actual principles which are employed. The actual practice of the principle will look different with every preacher, and the principles of earnest application must be studied, observed and worked out in each individual pulpit ministry.

Concluding observations and counsels concerning application in preaching

This aspect of sermon preparation must be a matter of earnest prayer. The promises God's people possess concerning prayer are immense. Jesus says, 'Keep on asking, and it will be given to you; keep on seeking and you will find; keep on knocking and it will be opened' (Matt. 7:7. Author's translation). Application takes wisdom and the skill of a surgeon. And there is the promise, 'If any of you lacks wisdom, let him ask of God, who gives to all generously and without reproach, and it will be given' (Jas. 1:5). When the pastor finds that his application is lacking, that there is no power, no unction, then he must ask himself if he has made it an issue of prayer. Does his Master want him to apply the truth with power? Does his Master desire good to be done to the souls of men? Is his Master willing to give great gifts of the Spirit and wisdom to accomplish the purpose? Has his Master cut off the means from the ends? As a pastor he must say, if his application is weak or non-existent, 'I have not because I ask not' (Jas. 4:3).

Remember and consider the real and diverse categories of people who are attending the ministry.[193] There are the general divisions, which are present in every service: the church and the world; the faithful and the hypocrites who are church members; the various stages of spiritual growth within the church. There are also chronological divisions. If the conviction is firmly in place that children should sit under the ministry of the Word with their parents, then frequent application should be made directly to the various ages of children. The little ones should be addressed in a manner fitting to them. The teenagers should likewise be addressed. This pattern should be kept in the forefront of the pastor's mind in the course of his preparation. There are also occupational differences which should be kept in mind. The man who applies the truth to a congregation of white-collar professionals in a manner fitting for steel workers, or vice versa, may find little reception.

When applications are hard in coming consult the proven masters. How many have wrestled through a text and found their well to be dry, and then turned to Matthew Henry or J C Ryle, and found gems of application? Calvin, Spurgeon, Edwards and the Puritans serve as some who have great applicatory insights into the Scriptures. Check the table of contents and the Scripture indices of the great masters.[194]

Do not expect a uniform density of application in every sermon. As the man of God expounds the Scripture, week after week, whether consecutive or by category, he will find that certain texts or subjects warrant more or less application. Freedom and freshness must attend each exposition, and the shape and purpose of the text will dictate how much application will be necessary.[195]

Avoid a stereotyped and predictable structure of application. Some apply right after thirty minutes of exposition. Others introduce application with the same words each week. Others make the same application each week! There ought to be freshness and variety in application. Avoid the same sentences, the same vocabulary and the same ruts which many will expect. Some sermons will almost require that application be made after each point or principle. Other sermons will require five or ten minutes of application at the end. There may even be times when a sermon begins with some penetrating applicatory thoughts or questions. The counsel here is simply avoid predictability and keep it fresh. Spurgeon, with his usual wit, makes the point.

> I sat last year about this time on the beach at Mentone by the Mediterranean Sea. The waves were very gently rising and falling, for there is little or no tide, and the wind is still. The waves crept up languidly one after another, and I took little heed of them, though they were just at my feet. Suddenly, as if seized with a new passion, the sea sent up one far-reaching billow, which drenched me thoroughly. Quiet as I had been before, you can readily conceive how quickly I was on my feet, and how speedily my day-dreaming ended. I observed to a ministering brother at my side, 'This shows us how to preach, to wake people up we must astonish them with something they were not looking for.' Brethren, take them unawares. Let your thunderbolt drop out of a clear sky. When all is calm and bright let the tempest rush up, and by contrast make its terrors all the greater.[196]

Make judicious use of searching questions in application. The use of questions can cause the congregation to reflect upon themselves in a powerful way. J C Ryle was a master of asking penetrating, self-examining questions. In a sermon entitled, 'Do You Pray?' he begins with these words, 'I offer you a question which deserves serious consideration... It is contained in three little words, – Do you pray?'[197] After each point he asks, 'Do you pray?' This is an effective method of application, which Pastor Martin uses frequently.[198]

Pray for and expect the aid of the Spirit in suggesting additional applications in the act of preaching. This is not reliance upon some form of special revelation, but rather the providential working of the Spirit through association and suggestion. This is part of what has been called 'unction' or the 'anointing.' Anyone familiar with extemporaneous preaching should be familiar with this peculiar work of the Spirit. If there is to be true Spirit-empowered preaching, then there must be earnest, prayerful, heart-felt dependence on the Spirit. Out of that dependence, there is the confidence that the Spirit will speak through the man of God in such a way that it exceeds anything he himself prepared in the study. Marcel speaks forcefully on this issue:

> *In us and in the Church* EVERYTHING *depends on the Spirit.* And since God, as a father who feeds his children, *gives the Holy Spirit to those who ask* (Luke 11:11-13), *everything depends, in the last analysis, on the preacher's, the believer's, and the Church's relationships with the Spirit.* Preaching, which is properly speaking, the word *preached*, depends entirely on the Spirit.... Preparation and even reaction constitute only a *preliminary* part of preaching. It means rather that the preacher, in church, is to yield himself a malleable and living organ for what Christ by the Spirit wills him to say to those who hear. If Christ is left free, He will constrain the preacher to add, delete, and modify (in form or even in content) such and such a portion of that which he had intended to say, but which *he cannot now say* (capitals and italics are his).[199]

Finally, there must be the willingness to pay the price of consistent, searching application. The accusations of brow-beating, scolding and oppressing will abound. The charge of not trusting the Spirit for the results will flourish. The rumors of being unloving and heartless will be spread far and wide. Others will say that Christ is not preached. The indictments that one is guilty of legalism and moralism will ever be present. If there is a commitment to preach searching, pointed, applicatory sermons, there must be a concomitant commitment to pay the price. Any man who has stood firm on these convictions has felt the sting of these accusations from people within and without the walls of the church. 'Nevertheless, the firm foundation of God stands, having this seal, "The Lord knows those who are His"' (2 Tim. 2:19). More times than not, there must be a simple resignation to the fact that the Lord on the Last Day will be the final arbiter.

12

PREACHING WITH ILLUMINATING DEVICES

(5) The proclamation, explanation and application of scriptural truths aided by legitimate and judicious illuminating devices must be the man of God's constant labor.

An illuminating device is a linguistic device used to explain, clarify or bring lucidity to the substance of a sermon. An illuminating device can be used in any portion of the sermon; that is in the proclamation, explanation or application of the sermon. Illuminating devices can be similes, metaphors, allegories, parables, illustrations, anecdotes or imaginative descriptions. However, they must be used legitimately. There is an illegitimate and injudicious use of illuminating devices. An illuminating device can take too much time, actually taking priority over the truth it is supposed to be illuminating. It could be indelicate, assaulting the sensitivities of the congregation. It could be too emotionally overpowering or manipulative. An illuminating device could even be a platform for one to put on display certain gifts.[200] 'To me, that kind of thing is only professionalism at its worst, it is, as I say, the art of the harlot, because it pays too much attention to, and is too much concerned about, enticing people.'[201]

A demonstration of the desirability of these devices

These devices are desirable in a biblical sermon. General revelation teaches that there are God-given laws of learning. One such law teaches that people learn by moving from the known to the unknown. They learn by associating that which they know with that which they do not know, so that they may gain new knowledge. In the proclamation, explanation and application of biblical truth, the Holy Spirit is the true Illuminator. However, He works by and with this natural law of learning, not against it.

Special revelation has also demonstrated the desirability of illuminating devices. The Bible continually records modes of preaching which use a variety of illuminating devices. Think of Jeremiah's object lessons: the ruined waistband (Jer. 13); the potter and the clay (Jer. 18); the basket of figs (Jer. 24). What would Hosea's message have been without the living illustration of Gomer? Who could imagine reading 'Isaiah's wild measure'[202] without his vivid imagery and metaphor? Then of course, the Lord Jesus was the greatest of all preachers and a master of illuminating the truth with the familiar. J C Ryle expresses the sentiment well,

> I need hardly remind you of the example of Him who 'spake as never man spake', our Lord and Savior Jesus Christ. Study the four Gospels, and mark what a wealth of illustration His sermons generally contain. How often you find figure upon figure, parable upon parable, in His discourses! There was nothing under His eyes apparently from which he did not draw lessons. The birds in the air, and the fish in the sea, the sheep, the goats, the cornfield, the vineyard, the ploughman, the sower, the reaper, the fisherman, the shepherd, the vine dresser, the woman kneading meal, the flowers, the grass, the bank, the wedding feast, the sepulcher, – all were made vehicles for conveying thoughts to the minds of hearers. What are such parables as the prodigal son, the good Samaritan, the ten virgins, the king who made a marriage for His son, the rich man and Lazarus, the laborers of the vineyard, and others, – what are all these but stirring stories that our Lord tells in order to convey some great truth to the souls of his hearers? Try to walk in His footsteps and follow His example.[203]

Beyond the pages of Scripture, there is the history of preaching itself which demonstrates the desirability of illuminating devices. The preaching of Whitefield and Edwards is saturated with illuminating devices. Who can forget Edwards's vivid metaphor, illuminating with power the truth of an angry God or a gentle Lamb? Who has not been touched by the down-to-earth devices of the Puritans? Who can fail to remember the outburst of soliloquy by Whitefield? The history of Christian preaching has supported the Arabian proverb, 'Most powerful is the speaker who can turn a man's ear into an eye.' Broadus captures the import of this truth:

> The importance of illustration in preaching is beyond expression. In numerous cases it is our best means of explaining religious truth, and often to the popular mind our only means of proving it.... Besides, for whatever purpose illustration may be specially employed, it often causes the truth to be remembered. Sometimes, indeed, even where its force as an explanation or proof was not at first fully apprehended, the illustration, particularly if it be a narrative, is retained in the mind until subsequent instruction or experience brings out the meaning.... The example of our Lord decides the whole question; and the illustrations which so abound in the record of His preaching ought to be heedfully studied by every preacher, as to their source, their aim, their style, and their relation to the other elements of His teaching. Among the Christian preachers of different ages who have been most remarkable for affluence and felicity in illustration, there may be mentioned Chrysostom, Jeremy Taylor, Christmas Evans, Chalmers, Guthrie, Spurgeon, Richard Fuller, and Beecher.[204]

An explanation of the manifold functions of these devices

The primary function of these devices is the clarifying of the truth, either in its explication or application. It is this primary function which governs the uses of illuminating devices. They must be used for the purpose of edification, by bringing lucidity to the truth. 'The illustration is meant to illustrate truth, not to show itself, not to call attention to itself; it is a means of leading, and helping people to see the truth that you are enunciating and proclaiming still more clearly.'[205]

In light of the primary function of illuminating devices, there are at least four other secondary functions for these devices. An illuminating device can be an excellent means of gaining or regaining attention. Ryle realistically notes,

> If you pause in your sermon and say, 'Now I will tell you a story', I engage that all who are not too fast asleep will prick up their ears and listen. People like similes, illustrations, and well-told stories, and will listen to them when they will attend to nothing else.[206]

Dr. Jay Adams well illustrates the power of a good illustration:

> The preacher was droning on about the Amalekites. And although he was only seven minutes into his sermon, all over the congregation heads began to nod, eyelids drooped, children began to squirm, and teenagers started passing notes. Then an amazing thing happened: suddenly, his audience snapped to attention. Young and old alike strained to hear. What had occurred? What was it that so abruptly transformed this apathetic group of parishioners into an alert, interested body? They came to life when they heard these words: 'Let me tell you about an experience that I had during the last war....' The preacher had begun to tell a story![207]

An illuminating device can also secondarily be used as a powerful means of making a surprise attack upon the consciences of men. The prophet Nathan used the illuminating device of a parable (although his listener did not recognize it as such at first). As the prophet winds the parable down, his listener, so caught up in the injustice just illustrated, condemns himself with his own sentiments about such a one who would commit such crimes (2 Sam. 12). Of course the listener was King David. The parable served as an effective tool of surprise attack on the conscience of this King. The parable went after his bloodied conscience.

The Lord Jesus also told a story about some wicked men who rented out a vineyard (Matt. 21:33ff.). As Jesus masterfully engaged His listeners in the details of the story, they were drawn to the obvious conclusion that these vine-growers deserved swift justice, saying, 'He will bring those wretches to a wretched end and will rent out the vineyard to other vine-growers who will pay the proceeds at the proper seasons' (Matt. 21:41). Then the story takes on a twist, from the listeners' perspective, as their consciences are stung by the words of the Master, 'Therefore, I say to you, the kingdom of God will be taken away from you and given to a people producing the fruit of it' (Matt. 21:43). Then they realized He was speaking about them (Matt. 21:45).

Illuminating devices also have an aesthetic value, making the sermon more interesting, more pleasurable and attractive. Spurgeon, who was a master of metaphor, and thus is always a pleasure to read, aptly comments:

> Windows greatly add to the pleasure and agreeableness of a habitation, and so do illustrations make a sermon pleasurable and interesting. A building without windows would be a prison rather than a house, for it would be quite dark, and no one would care to take it upon lease; and, in the same way, a discourse without a parable is prosy and dull, and involves a grievous weariness of the flesh.... Let us not deny then the salt of parable with the meat of doctrine. Our congregations hear us with pleasure when we give them a fair measure of imagery: when an anecdote is being told they rest, take breath, and give play to their imaginations, and thus prepare themselves for the sterner work which lies before them in listening to our profounder expositions.... No reason exists why the preaching of the gospel should be a miserable operation either to the speaker or to the hearers. Pleasantly profitable let all our sermons be.[208]

Finally, an illuminating device may be greatly effective in aiding the memory. The device only serves its purpose if it brings the mind back to the truth it illuminated. But how often does the mind backtrack and do that very thing! A personal anecdote at this point will demonstrate this. Pastor Martin was preaching a sermon on 'The God of Absolute Perfection'.[209] He said, after many minutes of theological reasoning and intense application,

> Let me illustrate. You've been thinking hard. Let your mind relax a minute with an illustration. Think back to the days when there were kings, when they had thrones that cut mustard, so that what they said went, or else. Imagine a certain part of the earth where there is a true monarchy. And upon the throne of that particular kingdom sits a man, who in his person is the epitome of what we would say is highly cultured, well developed, mature manhood. In his person, he is a handsome man. His body is strong and agile. His mind is quick. But coupled with a strong will and a strong body is a sensitive heart. He lives each day for the good of his subjects. When he goes to bed at night his mind was filled, not with how he could acquire more wealth and grandeur and more prestige, but how he could better administer the kingdom for the benefit of its subjects. He is that kind of a king.
>
> The announcement was made that he was going to visit one of the precincts in his kingdom. The day for his visit comes. The town crier had gone through the town, saying, 'Your good, your beneficent, your gracious, your handsome, able and loving King is coming.'

The King enters with all his entourage. The town people line the street, just for a chance to look upon him. They are amazed at his beauty, but also coupled with his beauty is that sensitive eye and obviously feeling heart. As he comes through the thronging crowd of that little hamlet, off a block away is a man bent over a grinding wheel sharpening his ax for tomorrow's toil. He is not deaf, he's not blind. Everyone else is looking for the opportunity to catch just a glance of the king, even if they cannot see him, just knowing who he is and what he has done for them, in protecting them, preserving them, providing for them, they blend their voices with those who are close enough to see him, 'Long live the King! Long live the King! God bless our King!' Then someone happens to see this man bent over his grinding stone with his ax, and they say,

'Hey! What is the matter with you? Don't you know the King has come?'

'Oh ya, I know he's here.'

'Well don't you have any concern?'

'Nah, the kings come and the kings go. I've gotta cut wood tomorrow. Leave me alone to grind my ax.'

Now how would you interpret such an action? How do you think the King would interpret it? How would any of the subjects who know the King interpret it? Would that be considered an innocent pastime, while the glorious King was passing through the village? Would that be an innocent diversion? How about it kids, would it? No. It would be positive wickedness. Do I need to draw out the application? I think you see it, don't you. You sit here this morning because God as King of the earth is a gracious God. He gives you life and breath and all things. Even though you are unconverted, He sustains your life.... Listen to me, I am saying to some of you this morning, Behold the living and true God! He made you, He sustains you, He'll judge you in the Last Day! And you sit there grinding your ax, impatient until the final 'Amen' is mentioned. You can't wait to get out of here! Oh my dear young man, young woman, awake to righteousness! The hour is coming when the King will say, 'Seize that man and consign him to death!'[210]

Every time the author thinks of that story, he vividly thinks of a little man hunched over a grinding wheel, with a casual notion about the great King. His mind then naturally goes back to the truth of God's great worth because of His absolute perfection.

> Finally, [illuminating devices] greatly assist the memory of the hearer in retaining the lesson of the sermon. Good anecdotes and illustrations are far more easily remembered than bright sayings, and trains of argument. It is not uncommon experience with preachers to find that their finest sentences and profoundest observation easily slip the memory, while some apparently trivial anecdote or illustration remains. If these can be made so apt as necessarily to recall the argument or train of thought, so much the better.[211]

Words of warning and caution concerning the abuse of these devices

The first danger really emerges from the very arguments in favor of using illuminating devices: their popularity, their ability to grab attention, and so on. It is the illustration's effectiveness that tempts the pastor to overload the sermon with too many of these devices. Too much by way of illuminating devices takes away from the exposition of the Word. To do anything which undermines or detracts from the Divine Word must certainly be a sin! It is the preaching of the Word, not the illuminating devices to throw light on the Word, which is the power of God unto salvation and edification. A well-trained congregation should find a sermon top-heavy with illustrations as distasteful as a cup of coffee with twelve tablespoons of sugar. Again, Spurgeon's wisdom requires attention:

> While we thus commend illustrations for necessary uses, it must be remembered that they are not the strength of a sermon any more than a window is the strength of a house; and for this reason, among others, they should be not too numerous. Too many openings for light may seriously detract from the stability of a building.[212]

The Doctor again:

> Illustrations are just servants, and you should use them sparsely and carefully. As the result of listening to preachers for many years, preaching myself, and discussing these matters, and considering them constantly, I am prepared to go so far as to say that if you use too many illustrations in your sermon your preaching will be ineffective.[213]

Avoid using illustrations simply for their own sake. A multitude of sermons have been produced because somebody heard a good illustration and needed a sermon to fit it! To follow Spurgeon's metaphor, nobody is silly enough to build a house for the sake of a window. Too many negative castigations cannot be heaped on the man who looks for texts to support a good story. The man of God is a preacher of the Word, not a storyteller. In fact, this axiom has been carefully worded, these devices are 'desirable', not necessary. Many sermons that have been mightily used by God have lacked interesting stories, clever metaphors and the like. The illuminating device is always the servant, never the master.

Furthermore, illuminating devices should not be used to clarify the obvious. It is an insult to use illustrative material for those truths which need no further light. Illuminating devices can bring freshness to old truths, but unless the congregation is filled with less than average minds, they need not be employed to describe the obvious. Neither should illuminating devices be used as a filler. People know when filler is being added. Filler cheapens the sermon and does not edify.

Some suggestions for cultivating skill in the use of these devices

The cultivation of illuminating skill must be a conscientious effort, both indirectly and directly. The indirect cultivation takes place through ordinary conversation, when one attempts simply to introduce more metaphors, similes and allegories into everyday language. Practice using more sense-oriented words. 'Language by its very nature is *sense-oriented.* Picture words (*green, flashing*), onomatopoeic words (*buzz, bang*), tactile terms (*prickly, soft*), olfactory words (*rancid, fragrance*), and terms that stimulate the taste buds (*sour, briny*) are words of this sort [italics are his].'[214] Practice metaphors and similes, even if it means sounding a little awkward at first. Practice looking at the world around you for illustrations.

Conversations with children provide a great platform for expanding as well as learning illuminating devices. Children are wonderfully uninhibited when they speak, and come up with many wonderful expressions. Likewise, when speaking to children, use many descriptive terms that lack the sophistication of a scholar, but nevertheless communicate. An example here would be Pastor Martin's explanation of conscience, which although directly addressed to the children, doubtlessly made an impression on the listening adults. Conscience was described as that little man or little woman inside, with the big, long finger, who says, 'This is right! That is wrong!'[215]

A further indirect avenue of cultivation is exposing oneself to much general material as a means of impression and acquisition. Read Spurgeon, but also realize that this is an area where we can learn from nature as well as grace. Here the gifted communicators who are masters of metaphor and storytelling should be listened to occasionally.[216] Living models should also be consulted and analyzed. Once again, Pastor Martin is a good example of gripping terminology, parables and metaphor.

Cultivation takes place within the context of sermon preparation itself. Once the sermon is fairly well formed, go over it and note places where these devices are most needed, and then work them in. For some this exercise will come with ease. For others it will be more difficult than exegesis. In addition to this, analyze statements, transitions, propositions, and so on, and seek to make them more catching, memorable, forceful or clear. Pastor Martin, times without number, exhibits a thoughtful labor over certain propositions or applicatory principles. His oft repeated line is, 'I have chosen my words carefully.'

Illuminating devices are valuable assets in the preaching of the Word. Although there must be a steady watch against a mentality which views illustrative material as primary, there must also be a steady watch against the reactionary position which is going to give the meat of the Word blood-rare. These devices must be used legitimately and judiciously, for the sake of clarity. These devices are to be used as servants of the Word, assisting in gaining attention, making surprise attacks on the conscience, adding a pleasurable element to the sermon and aiding the memory of God's people. This skill can be cultivated and improved, but always with perspective.

13

PREACHING WITH SIMPLICITY AND PLAINNESS

(6) The proclamation, explanation and application of scriptural truths with earthiness, simplicity and plainness of speech must constitute the man of God's continual labors.

This axiom has emblazoned over it 1 Corinthians 14:9, 'Unless you speak intelligible words with your tongue, how will anyone know what you are saying?' (NIV). This axiom goes beyond clarity in form and structure of the sermon and touches the actual substance of communication. The key words to this axiom are 'earthiness', 'simplicity', and 'plainness'. Bridges notes the importance of this continual labor when he states,

> Education has formed our minds into a mould so different, and given us a language so remote, from familiar usage, that there must be a great, and possibly an uncongenial, change in our flow of thought and composition; and yet without losing that vigour or liveliness, necessary to arrest attention.[217]

Earthiness is that which is simple and natural. Pulpit speech must not be ornate oratory; rather it should have an earthy quality to it. The origin of biblical preaching is heaven. The themes which are taken up in biblical preaching are heavenly themes. The goal of biblical preaching is to help people on their way to heaven. To be certain, there is a heavenly quality to God-owned preaching, but it is clothed in earthiness. The garb of the heavenly Word is this present world. The faithful preaching of the Word must be within the context of flat tyres, wars, social disruption, political corruption, unemployment, violence and poverty. A very real parallel to the earthiness of effective preaching is the incarnation of our Lord Jesus Christ. He became 'in-fleshed' (John 1:14), not only in a body prepared for Him, but also in a world that went about its ordinary, natural business. He was laid in a cow stall. There is no greater expression of earthiness than that. So it is in that sense that biblical preaching, which has an earthiness to it, is heaven coming down to earth.

Simplicity is that which is free from intricacy, complexity and all affectation. Simplicity in preaching is not simplistic preaching. Simplistic preaching should be avoided because it is shallow and banal. Simplicity, however, is the primary language of our Lord, the prophets and the apostles. Yes, there were times in which enigmatic statements were made, and parables used to conceal truth as acts of Divine judgment. Yet in the main, the inspired preachers used simple language. They used the 'tent' Hebrew and 'market-place' Greek of their day. They used the familiar. They never assumed too much.[218] They were simple. That great cloud of witnesses, who followed in the train of prophets, apostles and our Lord, exemplified the same principle.

> They preached simply. They rightly concluded that the very first qualification to be aimed at in a sermon is to be understood. They saw clearly that thousands of able and well-constructed sermons are utterly useless, because they are above the heads of the hearers. They strove to come down to the level of the people, and to speak what the poor could understand. To attain this they were not ashamed to crucify their style, and to sacrifice their reputation for learning.[219]

Plainness (Greek, *parrēsia*) is 'outspokenness, frankness, plainness of speech, that conceals nothing and passes over nothing'.[220] This word is often translated 'boldness' (Acts 4:13; 2 Cor. 3:12) due to the nature of straightforward, plain speech. Effective preaching must have the element of plainness. It must be void of murky images, long technical terms and cryptic allusions.

> It is not enough, then, to have a solid grasp on the meaning and purpose of a preaching portion, if, when you attempt to apply the message, you garble it by the language you use. One of the great language spoofs of all time is the sign that pointedly reads *Eschew Obfuscation.* It is a perfect example of what it forbids, with two obscure terms – one obsolescent, the other obtuse. Every preacher should post it in his study.[221]

Plainness in preaching is simply being consistent with the manner of God's communication through His holy Word. God condescended and used plain Hebrew and Greek. There was no 'Holy Ghost' language by which God spoke; rather He used the vulgar (i.e., common) language of common men. The Lord Jesus, in His earthly ministry, spoke with plainness. The prophets thundered with the same plainness, as did the apostles; and quite frankly, even used amazingly blunt, crude language. Anyone familiar with the prophets and apostles will recall many examples. This of course, is not a warrant for unnecessarily crude speech, but rather simply to illustrate that the prophets and apostles communicated in language that people understood. They were concerned about their audience's getting the message, not their being impressed with the preacher.

> Vanity will make a man speak and write learnedly; but piety only can prevail upon a good scholar to simplify his speech for the sake of the vulgar. Such a preacher, though his worth may be overlooked by the undiscerning now, will one day have a name above every name, whether it be philosopher, poet, orator, or whatever else is more revered among mankind.[222]

This kind of speech will cost much labor. It is hard work to accommodate our speech. Pastor Martin illustrates this kind of mental labor in speaking to a group in Sweden, where English is not their first language. Words are struggled for; sentences are laboriously shortened; illustrations are hammered out. Ryle emphasizes the nature of this labor:

> Let me add to all this one plain word of application. You will never attain simplicity in preaching without plenty of trouble. Pains and trouble, I say emphatically, pains and troubles. When Turner, the great painter, was asked by one how it was he mixed his colors so well, and what it was that made them so different from those of other artists: 'Mix them? Mix them? Mix them? Why, with brains, sir.' I am persuaded that, in preaching, little can be done except by trouble and by pains.[223]

Spurgeon emphasizes the motivation of this labor:

> Love for souls will operate in many ways upon our ministry. Among other things, it will make us very plain in our speech. We shall say to ourselves, 'No: I must not use that hard word, for that poor woman in the aisle would not understand me. I must not point out that recondite difficulty, for yonder trembling soul might be staggered by it and might not be relieved by my explanation.' ... If you love men better, you will love phrases less.... Love's manner of addressing men disregards all the dignities and the fineries of language, and only cares to impart its meaning, and infuse the blessing.[224]

There are some practical cautions in this area of earthiness, simplicity and plainness of speech in preaching. First, do not stereotype what this principle will mean in the real situations of preaching. There will be a variety of cultural circumstances, and this principle will work itself out in a variety of ways. For instance, preaching in a farming community with earthiness, simplicity and plainness will be very different from preaching in a university town with earthiness, simplicity and plainness. The principle remains, but the garb will change.

The second caution is that elegance should not be despised where it is warranted. Elegance is not always prohibited. There are situations where elegance, within the framework of the principle, is warranted. Whitefield preaching before Lady Huntingdon was different from Whitefield preaching before the miners.

The third caution is not to mistake earthiness, simplicity and plainness for coarse, simplistic and shallow preaching. God's service does not require or even allow coarseness or vulgarity (in the contemporary meaning of that word). Ryle, again with consummate wisdom, notes,

> Finally, let me observe, that it is not coarse or vulgar preaching that is needed. It is quite possible to be simple, and yet speak like a gentleman, and with the demeanor of a courteous and refined person. It is an utter mistake to imagine that uneducated and illiterate men and women prefer to be spoken to in an illiterate way, and by an uneducated person. To suppose that a lay-evangelist or Scripture-

> reader, who knows nothing of Latin or Greek, and is only familiar with his Bible, is more acceptable than an Oxford first-class man, or a Cambridge wrangler (if that first-class man knows how to preach), is a complete error. People only tolerate vulgarity and coarseness, as a rule, when they can get nothing else.[225]

Finally, in order to help the preacher grow in this difficult discipline, there must be exposure to those who model this. Whether sacred or secular, whether Spurgeon or *Reader's Digest*, the preacher should study the models of earthiness, simplicity and plainness. He should also read and re-read those sections in the standard pastoral works, which address this. Charles Bridges' chapter in *The Christian Ministry*, on 'Plainness in Preaching', J.C. Ryle's essay in *The Upper Room*, 'Simplicity in Preaching', and Spurgeon's *Lectures to My Students* should be visited annually to keep this truth in the forefront of his mind. As the Scriptures are read, let the man of God pray in the manner of Divine speech. As he is preparing his sermons, may he take a step back and ask, 'What can I do to make this proposition more plain? Will the children understand this point? What illustration, or words, can bring an earthiness to this head?' May this continual labor reflect his earnest desire to preach Christ for Christ's sake, to make Him known in plainness. 'It is too often, that preachers perplex those whom they should instruct. There is a great deal of difference between people admiring the preacher, and being edified by his sermons.'[226]

14

PREACHING AND THE CLOCK

(7) The proclamation, explanation and application of scriptural truths for a reasonable and appropriate length of time must be the man of God's constant practice.

How long one preaches is conditioned by many dynamics in the act of preaching itself. The measure of liberty, unction, fluidity of thought, and other factors impact the length of the sermon. However, as a general rule, the major factors which determine and regulate the length of the sermon are found not primarily in the pulpit, but rather in the study. The formal preparation of the sermon, not its actual delivery, is usually the most determinative factor.

There are some qualifications to this axiom which must be stated at the beginning. The first qualifying assertion is that there are no fixed time limits applying to all preachers in all circumstances. Since the Scriptures do not lay down any specific rules regarding the length of the sermon, there can be no absolute on the issue of time. Spurgeon comes precariously close to laying down the law on length, when he says,

> In order to maintain attention, *avoid being too long*. An old preacher used to say to a young man who preached an hour – 'My dear friend, I do not care what else you preach about, but I wish you would preach *about* forty minutes.' We ought seldom go much beyond that – forty minutes, or say, three-quarters of an hour. If a fellow cannot say all he has to say in that time, when will he say it?[227]

Instead of establishing a rule on the length, the rule should be 'Let all things be done for edification' (1 Cor. 14:26). At times a thirty minute sermon will serve the optimum edification for the people. At other times, to stop at thirty minutes would be nearly criminal regarding their edification. There is no fixed time limit for all preachers in all circumstances.

The second qualifying factor is that there are no fixed time limits for any one preacher at all times and in all circumstances. There will certainly be general patterns developed by each preacher. However, he ought to avoid being a 'thirty-five minute man', a 'fifty-two minute man', etc. For a preacher to be personally set on a certain time could quench the Spirit. The preacher should avoid a personal strait jacket of a set time.

The third qualifying factor regarding time in preaching is that if one has agreed to a certain time limit (this would especially apply when visiting other churches, conferences, etc.), it is unethical not to keep to it. 'He who walks with integrity, and works righteousness, and speaks truth in his heart ... Swears to his own hurt and does not change' (Ps. 15:2, 4b). If one cannot in good conscience agree to the terms set in any preaching opportunity, then he ought not to agree to it at all. It is unethical to agree to a time limit, and then go beyond it under the banner of unction.

Factors involved in determining the reasonable and appropriate length of time for any given sermon

Factors present in the preacher

> Again I would say that we must not be mechanical, or too rigid either way. What determines the length of the sermon? First and foremost, the preacher. Time is a very relative thing, is it not? Ten minutes from some men seems like an age, while an hour from another passes like a few minutes.[228]

The Doctor's point is well taken: each preacher has his own measure of gifting to hold attention. His vocal apparatus may only be strong enough to go thirty minutes, or be listened to for thirty minutes. His voice and body may be adequately animated to hold attention for a longer period of time, or he may have some degree of inadequacy which would curtail length of attention. If a man is not gifted to go forty-five minutes, but only thirty, he will create some resentment in the congregation if he insists on that added fifteen minutes. The preacher should seek godly counsel on his measure of gift to hold attention.[229]

There is also the measure of growth in him as a preacher. The man of God will grow in his study and preparation skills, including application and illustration. This factor is very critical. Spurgeon notes:

> If you ask me how you may shorten your sermons, I should say, study them better, Spend more time in the study that you may need less in the pulpit. We are generally longest when we have least to say. A man with a great deal of well-prepared matter will probably not exceed forty minutes; when he has less to say he will go on for fifty minutes, and when he has absolutely nothing to say he will need an hour to say it in.[230]

There is also the factor of the man of God's physical and mental strength. Preaching is not merely a cerebral and vocal exercise, but it requires the engagement of the whole man. As will be demonstrated in the 'Act of Preaching', every fiber of the pastor's humanity is required for the task. Since that is the case, there may be physical or mental limitations. Some may simply be physically unable to preach for fifty minutes with optimum vigor. Perhaps a good example of this is Calvin. Dr. Joel Beeke concludes that Calvin preached between thirty to forty minutes. He would often shorten his sermons, speaking more rapidly, when his asthmatic condition was bothering him. When he was physically able, without undue discomfort, he probably lengthened his sermons.[231]

Factors present in the hearers

The next factor to consider has to do with the listeners. Who is being addressed? If the audience is a group of pastors, then it is reasonable to assume that because of training and mental capacity, motivation and appetite (in the case of a conference), there would be a higher level of listening ability. If there are many young families with infants and nursing mothers, it is insensitive to go too long, trying the patience of little children and risking physical discomfort to the mother.

Another consideration is the general spiritual climate of those who are being addressed. Is there a great deal of spiritual immaturity (as described in 1 Cor. 3:1-2; Heb. 5:11-14)? Is it a congregation which has been used to twenty minutes of fluff? It would be unwise to try to bring a congregation to maturity and a deeper level of appreciation of biblical exposition by prolonged sermons. If the congregation has grown up under substantial and reasoned exposition, then it would be negligent to spend only twenty minutes in the pulpit. Each congregation will have its own spiritual factors, which must be taken into consideration.

What is the preacher's relationship with the people at that particular point in time? Is the preacher a newcomer trying to win the confidence of the people? Is he is a young man of relative inexperience? Has he been with the people from the beginning of the church, and seen their children born and their parents die? These factors are all important in determining the appropriate length in preaching. To ignore these facets of a relationship with a particular congregation is detrimental to that relationship, as well as to the success of the ministry of the Word.

Physical and natural circumstances will also be factors. The congregation is not an assembly of dis-embodied spirits. A hot building with poor ventilation requires shorter sermons. When the nursery is crowded with crying babies, consideration for those frazzled nursery workers is important. Once again, Spurgeon speaks to the issue.

> The subject will not complain of you, but the people will. In some country places, in the afternoon especially, the farmers have to milk their cows, and one farmer bitterly complained to me about a young man – I think from this College – 'Sir, he ought to have given over at four o'clock, but he kept right on till half-past, and there were all my cows waiting to be milked! *How would he have liked it if he had been a cow*?' There was a great deal of sense in that question. The Society for the Prevention of Cruelty to Animals ought to have prosecuted that young sinner. How can farmers hear to profit when they have cows-on-the-brain? The mother who feels morally certain during that extra ten minutes of your sermon that the baby is crying, or the fire is out, and she cannot and will not give her heart to your ministrations. You are keeping her ten minutes longer than she bargained for, and she looks upon it as a piece of injustice on your part.[232]

Factors present in the content of the sermon

There will be certain passages or subjects which will require a longer period of time for exposition. If minds are to be enlightened and judgments carried, a full three quarters of an hour may be required. It may well be unwise to take a passage or subject which will require a longer period of time for sound exposition, and then try to apply it with any effectiveness. In such a case the preacher realizes that at least thirty minutes of application will be necessary. It may well be the way of prudence simply to give one Lord's Day to the exposition of the subject or text and then save the entire application for the following Lord's Day. Examples could be multiplied, but it is important to remember that the variables are innumerable.

> As to the length of a sermon, it would be well for a pastor to get it understood that he may sometimes make the sermon very short, and sometimes quite long. There are subjects which can be made very interesting and instructive for twenty minutes, but to occupy thirty or forty minutes it would be necessary to introduce matter really foreign and such as will lessen the effect, or so to hammer out the style as will make it less impressive.[233]

Factors relative to the presence of God

Christ is always present with His people (Matt. 18:20). Unless the Spirit is grieved and the presence of Christ has left a church (Rev. 1:20; 2:1, 5), the people of God know, by faith, that He is in their midst. However, there are special times when the felt presence of Christ is more deeply known among His assembled church. During these times of an experiential, conscious drawing near of God, time becomes very relative. Timelessness is part of the age to come and when God draws near we get a sense of that timelessness. When unction comes upon preacher and congregation, the issue of the length of the sermon enters a dimension which is not necessarily subject to the ordinary rules of homiletics. When such an event occurs, both preacher and congregation will know by their lack of consciousness to time, that whatever time was spent in the preaching of the Word, was time well spent.

Practical Exhortations

If the preacher is going to err, he should err on the side of being too brief. It is far better to have some people comment about a sermon being too short than to have some complain about it being too long. When the food is served in right proportions, one is left with the palate satisfied and a pleasant sense of enjoyment. However, if the food keeps coming after the point of contentment, the stuffed, bloated feeling afterwards vitiates all prior enjoyment.

The pastor should not be over-sensitive to a malcontent minority of unspiritual people. Matthew 11:16-19 should remind God's servants that there are some people who will never be satisfied with a ministry.

> But to what shall I compare this generation? It is like children sitting in the market places who call out to the other children, and say: 'We played the flute for you, and you did not dance; we sang a dirge, and you did not mourn.'
>
> For John came neither eating nor drinking, and they say, 'He has a demon.'
>
> The Son of Man came eating and drinking, and they say, 'Behold, a gluttonous man and a drunkard, a friend of tax collectors and sinners!'
>
> Yet wisdom is vindicated by her deeds.

Some will perpetually complain about the 'long-winded' preacher. If the preacher does cut back on a sermon or two, this same complainer will suggest the preacher isn't doing his job, and perhaps needs his pay cut. They won't like 'the flute and dance' or the 'funeral dirge'. To put it plainly, their own carnal disposition would have set their very hearts against the ministry of John the Baptist and even of our Lord Himself! The old adage, 'Consider the source', is appropriate advice under this exhortation.

However, the pastor should not be over-influenced by the excessive enthusiasm of a hungry but insensitive minority. There will always be some who think that their pastor is the greatest preacher to ever live. Their admiration and comments about how much they wish he had preached for another half hour come from a hungry but insensitive heart. They aren't in the nursery with the crying babies; they don't know what it is like to have milk come in around nursing time; they might not know what it is to have a little one who is hungry and sleepy and has just reached the end of his little tether. Keep in mind that that enthusiastic person probably represents a pretty small minority.

Therefore, the man of God should master the time-saving devices: limiting parallel citations of Scripture; quoting the citations without having everyone turn to each one; being prepared to omit good, but secondary, material; sticking closely (not slavishly) to his notes in the exposition; having prepared summations and transitions at each point.

Practical problems

1) *What should be done if in the intermediate or advanced preparation things start to expand beyond the original plan to an unreasonable length?*

The first step if such a problem occurs, is to reform the goals for that particular sermon. Exercise the discipline of exclusion. A sermon may need to be streamlined and the more discursive elements, as good as they may be, may need to be edited out. A sermon may also need to be divided into two or more sermons. There may be times when the indulgence of the people is begged at the outset and a longer sermon is preached.

2) *What should be done if in the act of preaching things expand beyond what was expected?*

It is possible to bring the sermon to a close at the point where the preacher strikes fire. Often what causes the message to be longer is that a section may open up in delivery. Even though it may be untidy, it might be wise to end the sermon after that unexpectedly expanded section is preached. Another option may be to go ahead and preach, if one has a reasonable assurance that the people are willing and able to take more. If it is the older people and those with a number of children who are saying, 'Turn the hour glass over preacher', then one may proceed with caution.

Summary and Conclusion

Reformed, experiential preaching, which seeks to 'establish the throne of God in the souls of men', is the great need of the day. It begins with a genuine call of God on the life of a duly qualified and gifted man. The man who is called by God takes his calling with a seriousness which compels him to know what he is called to do. There is a compulsion to hammer out a biblical theology of preaching because that theology of preaching will guide and shape his ministry; that theology of preaching will be the undergirding of his ministry. The seven axioms which were unfolded, serve as guidelines to effective pastoral preaching within the framework of this theology. These axioms stated: (1) all effective pastoral preaching must be at its heart and soul scriptural; (2) effective pastoral preaching must be shaped by those truths which are most needed by the flock; (3) effective pastoral preaching must be clear in form and structure; (4) effective pastoral preaching must be applicatory in reference to the thinking, behavior patterns, affections, consciences and wills of the congregation; (5) effective pastoral preaching should be aided by legitimate and judicious illuminating devices; (6) effective pastoral preaching must be earthy, simple and plain; (7) effective pastoral preaching must also be done within a reasonable and appropriate length of time.

These axioms are primarily axioms to guide the man of God in the study. But anyone who has ever stood in a pulpit and declared the Word of God, knows that there is a world of difference between the sermon on paper and the sermon in delivery. Marcel states, 'To sound out the scriptures in the study, to prepare, to write, to reflect, to pray, on the one hand, and to preach, on the other, are distinct acts which employ the distinct and complementary interventions of the Spirit. One cannot replace the other.'[234] Martyn Lloyd-Jones gives the same reminder:

> He has to prepare a sermon.... This is where he begins. But let me remind you that this is only the first half, this is only the beginning. There is another side. What is that? Well, that is the actual preaching of this sermon which he has so prepared; and, as I hope to be able to show, though you may go into the pulpit with what you regard as an almost perfect sermon, you never know what is going to happen to it when you start preaching, if it is preaching worthy of the name.[235]

PART FOUR:

THE MAN OF GOD IN THE PULPIT: THE ACT OF PREACHING[236]

15

INTRODUCTION: PRELIMINARY CONSIDERATIONS

Foundational axiom: The ultimate end which all the elements of preaching must serve is the glory of God and the good of men in their salvation and edification.

Paul commands, 'Whether, then, you eat or drink or whatever you do, do all to the glory of God' (1 Cor. 10:31). If such mundane activities as eating and drinking are to be done to the glory of God, how much more should the proclamation of His holy Word be done to His glory? Peter, more focused on the act of preaching, says:

> Whoever speaks is to do so as one who is speaking the utterances of God; whoever serves as one who is serving by the strength which God supplies; so that in all things God may be glorified through Jesus Christ, to whom belongs the glory and dominion forever and ever (1 Pet. 4:11).

Paul, in the same vein, states:

> For the Son of God, Christ Jesus, who was preached among you by us – by me and Silvanus and Timothy – was not yes and no, but is yes in Him. For as many as are the promises of God, in Him they are yes; therefore also through Him is our Amen to the glory of God through us (2 Cor. 1:18-20).

The man of God should have a conscious passion and goal of glorifying God as he preaches His Word. It is axiomatic that the act of preaching must reflect God's character and even His own communicative patterns in Divine revelation if it is to glorify Him. Is God more glorified by distinct and articulate speech or by mumbling? Is God more glorified by a passionate and earnest proclamation of repentance and faith or by an indifferent, dull proclamation? Is God more glorified in one who is a visual distraction because of annoying habits and mannerisms, or in one who physically conducts himself with dignity and expresses himself in a manner which is congruent with the message? Since preaching has as its ultimate end the glory of God, the man of God must subject every element, even the delivery, to that great end.

The Apostle Paul not only preached Christ for the glory of God, he also strove to win men to Christ (1 Cor. 9:19-23). He was willing to do whatever it took, within the context of preaching, apart from sin and buffoonery, to win his audience to Christ. This is exemplified in Acts 14:1, 'they spoke in such a manner that a large number of people believed.'[237] This is the same author who has attributed conversions to the sovereign grace and power of God (Acts 2:39, 47, 13:48, 16:14). Here he acknowledges that a certain manner of preaching was used by God to bring salvation to men.

Furthermore, preaching and all its elements must be employed for the edification of the church (1 Cor. 14:1-5, 12, 15-19, 26f). To make the point, the question is simply asked, are there certain ways of speaking which are more likely to be used by God to edify His people? Or to ask it another way, are there certain patterns of speaking which will cause the congregation, saved and lost, to be distracted from the message and thus not be edified? The answers, from Scripture and human experience, are both 'yes'.

The man of God must assiduously seek with passion the glory of God and the good of men. In his seeking to do this, he will labor to bring every element of preaching into alignment with this goal. When this axiom is applied, it will immunize the man of God from false guilt connected with conscious efforts to cultivate an effective delivery. The preacher is not an actor, and perhaps he has been made to feel that any effort at improving voice or body in the pulpit is mere *theatricals*. *Theatricals* are certainly deplorable, but they are not the same as seeking to glorify God by improving delivery skills. Furthermore, this axiom will slay a sinful complacency and paralyzing fatalism which would hinder conscious efforts at cultivating an effective delivery. Many have imbibed the prevailing homiletical indifference to delivery. They have been told so many times to 'be natural', which means 'don't think about these things', that they have developed a complacent attitude which has prevented them from making any efforts in this area. This axiom frees pastors to realize that just as they strive to be better exegetes in the study, they can study to be better preachers in the pulpit.

Formative perspectives

A number of convictions and perspectives drive this section. Although it is recognized that the subject of the act of preaching is subjective in many ways, there is also the understanding that certain perspectives on this subject come from biblical norms and the tested and proven experience of many men of God throughout history. One should not hastily assume that because tastes and styles are soaked with relativity there are no normative perspectives on the subject. Rather, a number of issues demand that this subject be treated as a distinct and vital issue. Consider the following.

A sermon is either born or stillborn in the act of preaching. A sermon is conceived and gestated in the closet and study; the delivery room is the pulpit. The pastor comes to the pulpit pregnant with that which was conceived and gestated in the study and closet. When he begins to preach, that which was conceived will either be born healthy and vital, bringing blessing to the people, or it will be brought forth dead and lifeless, with no manifest fruition of the activity in the study. Men who have preached know when there is a live birth or a still-birth in the pulpit. Isn't this what Paul was talking about in 1 Corinthians 2:4? 'My message and my preaching were not in persuasive words of wisdom, but in demonstration of the Spirit and of power.' Paul was pregnant with the 'word of the cross' (1 Cor. 1:18, 22, 2:1). When he preached in Corinth, there was a vital, living message which was born. Broadus says, 'The preparation is not a speech until it is spoken.'[238]

The delicate interplay and interpenetration of the divine and the human is most prominent in the act of preaching. This interplay was explicated under the second axiom, when considering how to choose sermon material. There is no contradiction between human labor and the work of the Spirit (Phil. 2:12-13; Col. 1:29). The same principle is operative in the act of preaching, but in an enhanced and more prominent way. There are many elements in the act of preaching which can be observed and analyzed. This is so because preaching is a human activity of communication. However, there are other elements in preaching which are mysterious and go beyond the ability to scrutinize and analyze. This is so because preaching is also a divine activity of redemption and sanctification. Finally, the presence or absence of the Spirit's assistance is most evident in the act of preaching. The filling of the Spirit, especially in Acts, is often associated with speaking the Word of God (Acts 1:8, 2:4, 11, 4:8, 31, 6:8-10, 10:44). Spurgeon, who was so conscious of the work of the Spirit, told his students, 'The Spirit of God acts also as an anointing oil, and this relates to the entire delivery – not to the utterance merely from the mouth, but to the whole delivery of the discourse.'[239]

A man's most fundamental convictions regarding the nature of preaching, that is, his theology of preaching, will be most clearly revealed in the act of preaching. The convergence of two forces, the unction of the Holy Spirit and the preacher's own theology of preaching, come together in the act of preaching. The preacher's own spiritual state as a Christian will also greatly and constantly influence the quality of the act of preaching. What a man is as a Christian before God will ordinarily come out most clearly in the act of preaching.

If a sermon can be delivered still-born or alive in the act of preaching; if there is a delicate interplay between the human and divine which is most prominent in the act of preaching; if the presence or absence of the Spirit's assistance is most evident in the act of preaching; if a man's most fundamental convictions about preaching are most clearly revealed in the act of preaching; and if a man's spiritual state is a constant influence in the act of preaching, then those who preach must study the act of preaching, or the delivery of the sermon!

This section will cover the five components which constitute the act of preaching: (1) the preacher's relationship to God; (2) his relationship to himself; (3) to his hearers; (4) to his paper;

(5) and to his physical context. The goal of this section is to bring an awareness of the vital elements which impact the act of preaching. Some of these elements have already been covered under other sections, as they applied to the various subjects. These elements are now unfolded as they apply to the act of preaching. However, where there is overlap, they will be treated in a briefer manner since they have already been explicated elsewhere.

16

THE PREACHER IN RELATIONSHIP TO GOD IN THE ACT OF PREACHING

This first element is really an exhortation for preachers to cultivate the thoughts which ought to dominate their consciousness in the act of preaching. If a man's most fundamental convictions regarding preaching are clearly revealed in the act of preaching, then the cultivation of his thought processes is vital for the activity of the pulpit. 'I have set the LORD continually before me; Because He is at my right hand, I will not be shaken' (Ps. 16:8).

The man of God must cultivate the awareness of preaching as in the sight of God. This was Paul's awareness (2 Cor. 2:14-17; 12:19), and it gave him a sincerity[240] which was part of his mantle of credibility. This awareness creates the deepest seriousness in the man of God. He has an Audience of One. Everything must be real and genuine. This awareness definitely kept Paul from affectation. Cowper's lines are fitting:

In man or woman, but far most in man,
  And most of all in man that ministers
And serves the altar, in my soul I loathe
  All affectation. Tis my perfect scorn;
Object of my implacable disgust.
  What! will a man play tricks, will he indulge
A silly fond conceit of his fair form
  And just proportion, fashionable mien,
And pretty face, in the presence of his God?
  Or will he seek to dazzle me with tropes
As with the diamond on his lily hand,
  And play his brilliant parts before my eyes
When I am hungry for the bread of life?
  He mocks his Maker, prostitutes and shames
His noble office, and instead of truth,
  Displaying his own beauty, starves the flock!

Therefore, away! all attitude, and stare,
And start theatric, practiced at the mirror![241]

The man of God must cultivate the awareness of preaching as one on his way to the judgment of God. Again, Paul is the model. He did his best to maintain a good conscience before God and men, knowing he would one day be judged (Acts 24:14-16). Paul knew that the 'judgment' of others towards him meant nothing, and that even his own judgment of himself ultimately meant nothing, but the only judgment really and ultimately to matter was the Lord's (1 Cor. 4:1-5). The Apostle uses this awareness to motivate Timothy to preach the Word in season and out of season (2 Tim. 4:1-2). He also used it to motivate himself to complete his ministry with perseverance and integrity (2 Tim. 4:8). This awareness is also employed by the writer of Hebrews to motivate the members of the church to submission to their leaders (Heb. 13:17). The recognition that one day each one will stand naked before the God who sees all and knows all things is a sobering reality which should dominate the consciousness of the preacher, especially in the act of preaching.

If this awareness is cultivated, the man of God will be released from the crippling fear of men (1 Cor. 4:4; Gal. 1:10). If this awareness is cultivated, the man of God will not simply 'serve his time', but will rather serve God and His people (2 Cor. 4:5). If this awareness is cultivated, and dominates the consciousness of the preacher, there will be a marked urgency in his preaching (2 Cor. 5:11). The man of God will be very 'Baxterian', preaching as a dying man to dying men. This awareness will also be the fuel for a resolute singularity of purpose (2 Cor. 5:9-10). Other pursuits and interests will always run a distant second to that great purpose of preaching the whole counsel of God, before the face of God, preparing for the penetrating eye of God.

The man of God must cultivate the awareness that he is preaching as an appointed ambassador, herald and gift of the ascended Christ. This awareness gripped Paul (1 Tim. 1:12). It should captivate every true man of God. He is the preacher through whom the lost hear the voice of Christ (Rom. 10:14, 15). He is the ambassador who pleads for sinners to be reconciled to God (2 Cor. 5:19). He is a gift, a part of that fourfold ministry, for the edification of the body (Eph. 4:11). An event in Pastor Martin's ministry well illustrates this very awareness. He was preaching at a Christian college and noticed a young woman being disrespectful. He gave a slight rebuke and continued to preach. After the chapel service a young man approached him, obviously incensed over Pastor Martin's comment to the woman and said indignantly, 'Who do you think you are?'

Pastor Martin replied, 'It is not who I think I am. It is who I represent. I represent the King of kings, and when I am speaking as His ambassador, I demand respect for His name.'

Finally, the man of God must cultivate the awareness that preaching is a uniquely chosen and unchangeably relevant instrument of God. Once again, the issue of the theology of preaching is brought to the fore. Does the man of God know what he is doing when he is preaching? Is he aware of why he is preaching and not doing a skit or mime? The conscious awareness of preaching as the instrument of God in salvation and edification is vital in the act of preaching (1 Cor. 1:18, 21; Rom. 10:14, 15; John 10:16, 17:17). It is here where many men fail and become jokers, storytellers and used car salesmen in the pulpit. It is here where many men fail and then search for the latest gimmicks, seminars and books on how to scratch the moderns or post-moderns where they itch. Without sounding simplistic, nothing fuels the man of God in the pulpit more than knowing that what he is doing has been ordained and blessed by God to bring dead bones back to life (Ezek. 37).

What will be the results of such cultivation? A holy enthusiasm and expectancy will touch the pastor and the people, week after week. The confident expectation that God's Word will not return empty (Isa. 55:10-11) will keep the pastor and the congregation in a state of zeal and expectation. In this present day, many who have lost the enthusiasm and expectancy have sought for it in special vocalists, special programs, signs and wonders, and the list could go on. But isn't it a marvel that there have been long and fruitful ministries which have maintained such enthusiasm and expectancy by simply preaching the Word! Such cultivation will keep the preacher and the congregation fresh, and steered away from the dull, lifeless and passionless. Once one has drunk deeply at the well of God-owned preaching, he is never satisfied with anything else.

17

THE PREACHER IN RELATIONSHIP TO HIMSELF IN THE ACT OF PREACHING

Preaching engages the whole man. Preaching is not merely an intellectual and verbal activity. Preaching involves the man of God's mind, his will, his emotions, his mouth and the rest of his body. The comprehensive axiom which governs the use of all these faculties is 'Let all things be done for edification' (1 Cor. 14:26).

If the man of God is to be wholly engaged in the act of preaching, he must exercise self-control. If the man of God is going to be used for optimum edification, he must exercise self-control. Paul reminds the Corinthians, who were given to excesses (see 1 Cor. 12:2), 'the spirits of the prophets are subject to prophets' (1 Cor. 14:32).

> Unlike the diabolical inspirations of heathenism [12:2], the breathings of God's Spirit do not carry away the prophet without his consent or will, and therefore, 'he has not right to make inspiration a pretext for refusing to submit to the rules laid down by the apostles' (Godet). And this must be so for it would be the height of impiety to attribute the confusion which would result from a prophetic free-for-all to Him who is the God of peace.[242]

One of the fruits of the Spirit is self-control (*engkrateia*, Gal. 5:23). Paul notes that 'everyone who competes in the games exercises self-control (*engkrateuomai*) in all things' (1 Cor. 9:25). The one, therefore, who is most under the control of the Holy Spirit will be the one who is in most control of himself. J H McIlvaine makes the observation:

> Self-control is essential to the consciousness and manifestation of reserved force in speaking – 'the spirit of the prophets must be subject to the prophets'.... The orator also is a prophet in a true through

> limited sense, and it is equally necessary that his ardor and passion, however high they may rise, should never be allowed to get the better of reason and propriety. He must never allow himself to be transported wholly out of himself, but there must always be a clear method in his prophetic raptures. It was said of Demosthenes, that even in his most impassioned eloquence, he never was known to lose control of himself; and this enabled him to control and direct the storm which he raised, and on which he rode. In like manner, all truly great orators, in their noblest flights, whilst transporting their audiences, keep the mastery of the situation by remaining masters of themselves.[243]

These principles demand critical analysis and conscious effort for correction, cultivation and improvement. However, with few exceptions this effort must not be carried on in the pulpit. Self-forgetfulness should characterize the preacher as his mind is taken up with the passage before him, the God in whose presence he speaks and those to whom he is speaking. The highest form of self-control is self-forgetfulness. Perhaps, on occasion, if a man has been working on his enunciation, and notices in the act of preaching that he is slurring some of his words, he may catch himself and make quick reparations. Or if a man has the tendency to make angry facial expressions, he may become aware of it during a sermon, and make the necessary alterations. By and large though, any such efforts should take place away from pulpit because the goal is self-forgetfulness.

Broadus notes:

> Above all, be yourself. Speak out with freedom and earnestness what you think and feel. Better a thousand faults than through dread of faults to be tame. Some of the most useful preachers, men in a true and high sense eloquent, have had grave defects of manner. Habitually correct faults as far as possible, but whether the voice and the action be good or bad, if there is something in you to say, speak it out. And by all means let there be no affectation, or even artificiality.[244]

William Taylor strikes the balance between being oneself and making the effort to improve the act of preaching:

> It is undeniable that effective utterance will give force even to a feeble sermon; while careless, hesitating, and indistinct speech, will make the finest composition fall flat and powerless upon the listeners' ears. In itself the manner may be far less important than the matter; but it is valuable, as giving its full force to the matter, and ought not to be lightly esteemed. You do well, therefore, to cultivate elocution. But here, as in other things, you must be on your guard against artificiality. What you have to do is not to imitate another, but to cultivate yourselves. Do not covet 'the stare and stark theatric practiced at the glass', but aim rather to cure yourselves of any awkwardness that may adhere to you, and to acquire any qualities in which you may be deficient. Do not make yourselves into clay-figures, which are the painter's poor substitute for living men, but be yourselves, only yourselves, purged from your faults, and clothed with as much power as you can acquire by laborious exercise.[245]

If the man of God does not keep this issue clear in his mind, he will find two errors militating against the cultivation of effective preaching: paralyzing fatalism and crippling preoccupation. The fatalism will be manifested in an unhealthy view of providence. 'Well, that's just the way God made me. If I grit my teeth, I grit my teeth. If I speak with an annoying shrill when I get excited, then that's just the way it is. The people are going to have to accept me the way I am.' Keeping the issue clear in his mind will prevent such folly, but it will also prevent an unhealthy preoccupation with these issues. The awareness of the issues, the desire to improve and the avoidance of all affectation should be carefully balanced in the preacher's mind. If he is unduly preoccupied with matters pertaining to the act of preaching, he will be crippled in his delivery and consumed with self-consciousness.

The goal of every preacher who wants to be used by God must be to bring every element of preaching, from preparation to delivery, under the umbrella of God's glory and the edification of men. This means there will be conscious efforts at correction, cultivation and improvement. Paul's admonition to Timothy is helpful, 'Take pains with these things, be absorbed in them, so that your progress will be evident to all' (1 Tim. 4:15).

The preacher's physical condition, appearance and bearing, or pulpit deportment

In the section on the life of the man of God, there was a thorough examination of the pastor's physical well-being. This need not be repeated here. However, a few reminders are in order. The act of preaching, as has already been noted, engages the whole man, including his physical body. If there is a neglect of the preacher's physical condition, it will begin to erode the confidence and esteem of the people toward him. As a result his ministry will become increasingly neutralized. Furthermore, the lack of discipline will be an issue which assaults the conscience of the man of God, and will internally neutralize his ministry to some degree. Externally there will be a decrease of ability to maintain the physical rigor which is required in preaching. Spurgeon, of all people, notes, 'Pardon my saying that the condition of your body must be attended to, especially in the matter of eating, for any measure of excess may injure your digestion and make you stupid when you should be fervent.'[246] Overall, the neglect of the physical condition will have many ramifications on the ministry of the man.

> Let the physical condition be as vigorous as possible. In order to achieve this seek good health in general; take abundant sleep the night before speaking; at the meal before speaking eat moderately, of food easily digested, and if you are to speak immediately, eat very little; and do not, if it can possibly be avoided, exhaust your vitality during the day by exciting conversation. A healthy condition of the nervous system is surpassingly important; not a morbid excitability, such as is produced by studying very late the night before, but a healthy condition, so that feeling may quickly respond to thought, so that there may be sympathetic emotion, and at the same time complete control.[247]

Of course there have been and are exceptions to physical vigor in the pulpit. Paul, with his thorn in the flesh, preached with great weakness. In that very weakness he discovered the power and sufficient grace of God (2 Cor. 12:7-10). However, if a man is going to preach in weakness, let him be sure that it is sovereignly imposed weakness, and not the laziness of an undisciplined body.

McIlvaine rounds out the issue with these words, 'For whatsoever is worthy of the name of preaching requires the exercise of the whole vital force of a sound and healthy man. To preach the gospel takes all there is or can ever be in any man.'[248] Whatever a man may carry into the pulpit, he carries nothing less than himself. The self he brings may enhance or detract from his message.

A few words may be said about clothing, grooming, posture and facial expression. The Apostle Paul had a few governing principles which dictated his life; they are found in 1 and 2 Corinthians.

> For though I am free from all *men,* I have made myself a servant to all, that I might win the more; and to the Jews I became as a Jew, that I might win Jews; to those *who are* under the law, as under the law, that I might win those *who are* under the law; to those *who are* without law, as without law (not being without law toward God, but under law toward Christ), that I might win those *who are* without law; to the weak I became as weak, that I might win the weak. I have become all things to all *men,* that I might by all means save some. Now this I do for the gospel's sake, that I may be partaker of it with *you* (1 Cor. 9:19-23).

> We give no offense in anything, that our ministry may not be blamed. But in all *things* we commend ourselves as ministers of God (2 Cor. 6:3-4a).

These principles should apply to the way the man of God dresses. His clothing should be culturally compatible. The gospel does not war with that which is neutral in culture, and neither should the preacher. The clothing must be in keeping with the times. To wear a sports jacket with six-inch lapels would be cause for ridicule.[249] The clothing worn preaching in Latvia or New Jersey may differ radically from the clothing worn in Nevada or Pakistan. His dress should be with Christian modesty, avoiding the gaudy, the provocative or the bizarre. He should also have some degree of aesthetic sensitivity (or at least have a wife who does). A simple awareness of the compatibility of colors and patterns is a necessity. He must also have a sanctified flexibility and common sense.

The man of God must also pay attention to other 'mundane'

details such as grooming. His hairstyle should exhibit the same cultural compatibility, Christian modesty, aesthetic sensibility and sanctified flexibility that his clothing habits do. He should have care for his fingernails, shoes, and even spectacles. Although he cannot be absorbed in these things, he must be sensitive enough to keep them from being a distraction.[250]

The man of God should also be conscientious of his posture. He should approach the pulpit in a way that bespeaks dignity and certainty. He is the ambassador for the holy God. 'And if the honour of an ambassador be in proportion to the power and glory of the sovereign who employs him, what is the dignity of him who is the ambassador of the King of Kings and Lord of Lords; and at the same time, what ought to be the sanctity of his conduct, and the elevation of his character?'[251] One should also be aware of how he sits, keeping in mind that modesty is important in this body-crazed culture. Although this may sound unspiritual, the man of God must not wear trousers that are so tight and sit in such a way that he gives a lesson on anatomy to the congregation as he sits on the platform. The preacher should not be always self-conscious about his posture, but it should be so ingrained in him that he automatically carries himself in dignity.

Finally, the man of God must pay some attention to his facial expressions. There is much in Scripture which reveals that the face is the window of the soul, the thoughts and emotions of the inner man (Gen. 4:5-6; Matt. 6:16; Prov. 15:13; Isa. 3:9; Acts 6:15; 2 Cor. 3:7). A preacher's face should be characterized by a sobriety and seriousness. Pastor Martin again quotes Tozer, 'A man cannot be both a prophet and a clown.' The man who always has the giddy look will not command respect in the pulpit. Do the people know he is serious? Do they know that he knows what he is there to do? His face must also be characterized by joy. He is not the angel of death, he is a messenger of life, one who lives in the presence of God where there is joy and pleasure for evermore. He is a herald of good news. The look of confidence and certainty in God should also be seen in his face. A man who is timid because of uncertainty about his message will show it in his face. A man who has been called, knows his commission, knows his message and knows what the goals are will show that in his face too.

Finally, the man of God should reveal goodwill toward men. He is a shepherd, a counselor, and a friend. The look of tenderness and acceptance should mark his expression. Obviously, all of these expressions do not manifest themselves at once. The point, however, is that the man of God must be conscious of his facial expressions. Does he always look mad? Does he always look as though the world is about to end? Does he look as if he is lost? Does he look aggressive and unapproachable? Inappropriate facial expressions can be a hindrance to the ministry.

When all has been said, none of these principles can be absolutized and set in concrete. These principles cannot and should not negate personal taste and style. But the point is well made that men in the ministry should conduct themselves, in dress, grooming and even facial expressions, as dignified Christian gentlemen. In everything they should strive to avoid being a stumbling block (bad breath or a 50s' hairstyle included), so that Christ would not be eclipsed in their ministries.

The preacher's emotional constitution and activity

The fervency, earnestness and passion in preaching have to do with the emotions of the preacher. This subject requires attention because it is so vital to the act of preaching itself. 'Real success is proportionate to the preacher's earnestness.'[252] John Murray noted, 'To me, preaching without passion is not preaching at all.'[253] Therefore, an examination of the emotions, their origin and moral and sinful qualities, their place and function in communication, especially preaching, and the moral obligations in relation to their expression, is much needed. Although many of the older writers deal with the emotions in relation to preaching and will be drawn from, Pastor Martin takes a thorough and penetrating look at this neglected subject. Although it may seem like a digression, a working definition and description of the emotions and the origin and quality of the emotions will form the foundation for the more directly relevant issues: the strategic place and function of the emotions in preaching and the moral obligations the man of God has in conjunction with his emotions.

A working definition and description of the emotions

Man is a rational creature who thinks, perceives and receives information in his mind. He is also a volitional creature who wills and makes choices. In addition to this he is an emotional creature who feels and experiences emotions.

> The emotions are an aspect of the mind. They are experienced within the soul, but have physical manifestations. Anger, for example, affects the adrenal glands, sorrow the tear glands, worry the digestive glands, fear the circulatory system, etc.... Emotions, like sensations, elude precise definition. As the idea of sweetness, sourness, or bitterness can be conveyed only by reference to an object which possesses these qualities, so the meaning of a specific emotion can be communicated to another only by a reference to that emotion. Everyone knows what is meant by love, fear, anger, worry, etc. But it is most difficult to convey the meaning of any one of these emotions by an attempted definition. However, all emotions have in common the general idea of being stirred up, excited, perturbed.[254]

What pain is to the nerve endings, what sweetness is to the taste buds, what light is to the eye, the feelings are to the soul. Feelings are the emotions aroused to the point of consciousness. Thus, Pastor Martin defines the emotions as, 'the diversified, conscious sensibilities of the soul'.[255]

The origin and moral quality of the emotions

The emotional constitution of man is a created reality, which is part of the image of God. Although many of the scholastic theologians spoke of the 'impassibility' of God, hopefully it is recognized that God is not without emotions. Rather, God is the epitome of perfect emotion.[256] Pastor Martin cautions, 'In contemplating such realities the safest path to walk in order to avoid entangling ourselves in philosophical subtleties is to remember that the God whom we worship, love, and serve, is the God revealed in Jesus Christ (John 1:18, 14:7-9).'[257] On this point, B B Warfield has spoken eloquently and persuasively.[258]

Man made in the image of God is an emotional being. There is an obvious difference between man's pre-fall and post-fall emotional constitution. Before the fall, Adam and Eve each had a mind which perceived reality accurately, and emotions and a will which responded accordingly. Prior to the fall, Adam and Eve's emotions were completely holy, even as the Lord Jesus's were in the days of His flesh. Jonathan Edwards notes: 'God has given to mankind affections, for the same purpose which He has given all the faculties and principles of the human soul, viz., that they might be subservient to man's chief end, and the great business for which God created him, that is, the business of religion.'[259] For Adam and Eve, their affections were properly placed and proportioned.

However, the fall brought radical disruption to man's faculties, so that his mind and will are depraved, as well as his emotions. Man, in his state of sin, loves what he should hate and hates what he should love (Jer. 2:13; John 3:19).

> The natural man's affections are wretchedly misplaced; he is a spiritual monster. His heart is where his feet should be, fixed on the earth; his heels are lifted up against heaven, which his heart should be set on. His face is towards hell, his back towards heaven; and therefore God calls him to turn. He loves what he should hate and hates what he should love; joys in what he ought to mourn for, and mourns for what he should rejoice in; glories in his shame, and is ashamed of his glory; abhors what he should desire, and desires what he should abhor.[260]

In redemption, the restorative and recreative work of God's grace in Christ renovates the whole man, including his emotions (Matt. 5:3, 11-12; Rom. 14:17; Gal. 5:22; 1 Pet. 1:8). The emotions, then, most certainly are employed in the great work of religion. The above quotation from Edwards confirms that, as well as the following observation by Dabney:

> Good brethren write to religious journals grateful accounts of a work of grace in their charges, and tell the editors that 'they are happy to say, the work has been purely rational and quiet, and attended by not the slightest excitement'. They forget that the efficacious (not possibly, tempestuous) movement of the feelings is just as essential a part of a true religious experience, as the illumination of the intellect by divine truth; for indeed, there is no such thing as the implantation

> of practical principle, or the right decisions of the will, without feeling. In estimating a work of divine grace as genuine, we should rather ask ourselves whether the right feelings are excited, and excited by divine cause. If so, we need not fear the most intense excitement.... On practical subjects, truth is only influential as it stimulates some practical feeling. There is no logical appeal of the rhetorical nature which does not include and appeal to feeling.[261]

The strategic place and function of the emotions in oral communication in general and in preaching in particular

It is indisputable that the emotions cause great physiological effect in general. It is equally indisputable that the emotions exert a powerful influence on all the factors and faculties involved in oral communication. Various emotions will have varying effects on the voice, the vocabulary and physical action. The people at a college football game, the man being scorned by his girlfriend, the woman facing an intruder, a mother with a child in a burning house, or a husband grieving over the loss of a wife will all have their particular emotions impact voice, vocabulary and physical action.

These emotional effects also have an influence on those who hear them. Whether it is the sobs of a grieving parent or the uncontrollable laughter of an entertained audience, these emotional manifestations will impact those who hear and see them. There is a contagion in emotion itself. That contagion is even more acutely felt in a group setting. Dabney has noted this:

> The Creator has formed man with this law of feeling, that the mere witnessing of any human emotion colors the soul of the spectator with a similar emotion, in a less degree. In the object of the sympathy, the emotion was propagated according to the laws of the understanding, which presents to the heart some view of the facts rationally adapted to be the motive or occasion for feeling. But in the subject of the sympathetic feeling, there is no acting of the understanding, no view presented to it by the heart, unless we call the mere perception of emotion in the other person a view of the understanding. The sympathetic emotion is wholly unintelligent, is superinduced by the mere sight of the feeling in another, and usually vanishes when that is removed. In proof, we point to the facts that

> we are saddened when we see a person weep, although we do not know the cause of his grief, and if we see persons angry or fighting, we partake of their excitement though we know and care nothing of them or their quarrel. In a word, our sympathetic feeling is provoked, not by the rational cause of the feeling we behold, but by the mere beholding of the feeling.[262]

So what is the legitimate place and function of the emotions in communication in general and preaching in particular? Is it not this very understanding of human nature, and the influence of the emotions, which has led men like John Murray to note that, 'preaching without passion is not preaching at all'? Pastor Martin brings these strands together with a powerful summary:

> If all of these perspectives on the relationship between the emotions and oral communications are valid, is it not unthinkable that a man should stand before his fellow mortals with a mind impregnated with the truth, his own affections warmed by the truth, and under the peculiar present assistance of the Holy Spirit promised in connection with preaching – is it not unthinkable that emotional energy should not pulsate throughout his discourse?[263]

Gardiner Spring cannot be surpassed in his eloquence in stating this truth:

> He (the preacher) must feel his subject. It is as marvelous as it is mournful, that the weighty and thrilling truths of God's Word lose so much of their force from the little interest the preacher himself feels in his theme. George Whitefield was probably the most remarkable man in this respect, whom the world has seen. Rich as his discourses were, they do not compare with the discourses of some other preachers in richness of thought. But in intensity of feeling, he had no equal. He enchained his auditory by his intense interest in his subject. A ship-carpenter once remarked, that 'he could usually build a ship from stem to stern, during the sermon; but under Mr. Whitefield he could not lay a single plank'. It is of themselves ministers should frequently complain, rather than of their hearers; it is they who are cold and inanimate.... No preacher can sustain the attention of a people unless he feels his subject; nor can he long sustain it, unless he feels it deeply. If he would make others solemn, he himself must be solemn;

> he must have fellowship with the truths he utters. He must preach as though he were under the eye of God, and as though his own soul were bound up in the souls of those who hear him. He must preach as though he were in sight of the cross, and heard the groans of the Mighty Sufferer of Calvary; as though the judgment were set, and the books opened; as though the sentence were just about to be passed which decided the destinies of men; as though he had been looking into the pit of despair, as well as drawing aside the veil, and taking a view of the unutterable glory.[264]

'Is it not the height of an unsound theology of the constitution of man as created and redeemed that would assert that intense emotional energy in preaching is unwarranted, indiscreet, and unnecessary?'[265] Obviously, the manner of emotion will differ in every preacher. Some men will be very animated, and have a wide range of decibels. Others will grow quiet and still. The presence of emotion in the act of preaching, that zeal, fervor and passion, is not a canned item that looks the same in every man. Just as every man is different in his personality, background, experience and so forth, so there will be difference in the expression of emotion. Nevertheless, an emotionless, robotic, unfeeling man who preaches Christ, heaven and hell, sin and grace, repentance and faith, is a contradiction of nature and grace.

> The world also will suffer as well as the church if we are not fervent. We cannot expect a gospel devoid of earnestness to have any effect upon the unconverted around us.... The whole outside world receives serious danger from the cold-hearted preacher, for it draws the same conclusion as the individual sinner: it perseveres in its listlessness, it gives its strength to its own transient objects, and thinks itself wise for so doing. How can it be otherwise? If the prophet leaves his heart behind him when he professes to speak in the name of God, what can he expect but that the ungodly around him persuade themselves that there is nothing in his message, and that his commission is a farce.[266]

God Himself is perfect in His emotions. The Lord Jesus manifested perfect emotions in His incarnation. The redemptive process realigns the affections, as the inner man is brought into conformity with Christ. The affections indeed are central in the Christian's life. Although the emotions, or affections, play a central part in true religion, remaining sin still influences the emotions in the direction of excesses or 'short circuits'.

If the emotions play a role in Christian experience, then it must also be true that they play a role in the life and ministry of the preacher. Emotions tainted with sin can betray the preacher in the act of preaching. Earnestness, zeal, fervency and passion can become excessive, manipulative and sinful. Yet, lack of these emotional qualities in preaching kills preaching. Could it even be said that the absence of such emotion is sinful? Thomas Murphy thought so, 'To preach in a cold, unfeeling manner, to preach without earnestness, is sinful.'[267] So what are the moral duties and obligations with respect to the emotions?

The moral duties and obligations with respect to the emotions

It is the duty of every Christian, and especially the man of God, to cultivate, control and appropriately express his emotions. Since self-control is a biblical duty (Prov. 14:29, 16:32; Gal. 5:23), and the emotions are a part of the God-given self, then the control of the emotions is a biblical duty. Throughout the Scriptures God has commanded His people to be in control of their emotions, and also to display or curtail certain emotions. This is significant in a day when most people think that they have no control over their emotions. Even in Christian circles, many have been taught that the emotions are a law unto themselves. The Scripture, however, presents God as directing man how he should feel.

'Return to Me with *all your heart*, and with fasting, *weeping* and *mourning*; and *rend your heart* and not your garments.... Let the priests, the LORD's ministers, *weep* between the porch and the altar' (Joel 2:12, 13, 17. NASB).

'Also the word of Jehovah came unto me, saying, Son of man, behold, I take away from thee the desire of thine eyes with a stroke: yet *thou shalt neither mourn nor weep, neither shall thy tears run down. Sigh, but not aloud, make no mourning for the dead*; bind thy headtire upon thee, and put thy shoes upon thy feet, and cover not thy lips, and eat not the bread of men. So I spake unto the people in the morning; and at even my wife died; and *I did in the morning as I was commanded*' (Ezek. 24:15-18, ASV).

'Be *devoted* to one another in *brotherly love*.... Not lagging behind in *diligence*, *fervent* in spirit.... *Rejoicing* in hope.... *Rejoice* with those who rejoice, and *weep* with those who weep' (Rom. 12:10, 11, 15). (See also Neh. 8:9-12; Eccles. 3:1-4; Matt. 5:11-12; Luke 23:28-31; 1 Cor. 7:29-30 and Jas. 4:9 for some other examples.)

'In these passages God calls men to come to grips with the realities which, if consciously and powerfully present in the soul, cannot but produce the commanded emotional state and its appropriate expression.'[268] These commanded expressions may be in the manifestation or restraint of any given emotion. By God's grace and Spirit, His people can and must obey His commands concerning certain emotions. It is in the grace-empowered obedience to these commands that the people of God exercise the fruit of the Spirit of self-control. It is this grace-empowered bearing of the fruit of self-control which is the duty of the preacher. Passion in preaching will be destructive when there is a lack of self-control. However, when passion is governed by self-control, it is a powerful tool in conveying the truth. J W Alexander aptly noted, 'Passion is eloquence.'[269]

Some practical guidelines for the cultivation and appropriate expression of the emotions in preaching

It should be recognized that because God has wired every man differently there will be different needs for the cultivation of the emotions and their expression in preaching. The man who is expressive, highly strung, and emotionally 'dynamic' may need to cultivate more self-control than anything else. The man who may be as cold and seemingly indifferent as the guards at Buckingham Palace may need to work on actively expressing his emotions. The following guidelines are given in general.

1) *Engagement in regular biblical meditation*

'My heart was hot within me, *while I was musing the fire burned*;[270] then I spoke with my tongue' (Ps. 39:3, NASB). There is an emotional power in meditation. The very act of meditation engages not only the mind, but also the affections. Contemplative meditation on great biblical truths can cultivate the emotions so that truth becomes felt. It is the felt power of truth which gives rise to the appropriate expression of emotion in preaching.

2) *The exercise of the imagination and empathetic faculties*
While reading the narratives of Scripture or the riveting events of Christian biography, the man of God should exercise a sanctified imagination, placing himself within earshot of the groans of Gethsemane, the weeping of the overwhelmed Joseph, the sobs of a grief-stricken David after losing Absalom, and the cry of dereliction from the Mighty Sufferer of Calvary. The imagination can transport the man of God to the hall at Worms, where Christ-centered courage and Biblical reformation won the day. The imagination needs to hear the words above the flames at the stake at Oxford, 'Be of good comfort, Master Ridley, and play the man; we shall this day light such a candle by God's grace, in England, as I trust shall never be put out.' The waves covering the heads of the two Margarets at Solway Firth, or the heads of Covenanters on the Netherbow, should grip the imagination. The mind should move the heart as the five missionaries sang, 'We Rest on Thee' the morning of their martyrdom on the beach of the Curaray River. These are real events and the imagination should lock into the reality of them, playing them in the theater of the mind. The use of the imagination in this way cultivates the emotions and their proper expression.

3) *Reading aloud, seeking to allow the appropriate emotional impact to be felt and expressed*

This is a manner in which the preceding point can be exercised. However, there is more to it than just that. In reading aloud the reader can begin to allow the content to impact the emotions which should impact the voice. For instance, reading Latimer's words to Master Ridley can be a good exercise to cultivate the proper emotional impact and expression. For a man to read those words aloud without pause, emphasis, and inflection, but simply to drone through it, diminishes the depth of the words. However, to read the words aloud, allowing the depth of them to sink into the soul, will impact the way they are read.

4) *The seeking of emotional engagement, during the preparation process*

For some, this is rather natural. Others will need to work on it. In the process of sermon preparation itself, meditation on the truths at hand, the engagement of the imagination, thoughts on the necessity of this truth for the congregation, and proper emotional expression in prayer (Ps. 62:8) can begin to warm the man of God's heart so that he is emotionally primed before he enters the pulpit. The eagerness to preach should be fuelled by the felt power of the truth to be preached. The felt power of the truth to be preached can be cultivated through engaging emotionally in the preparation process. The man who doesn't feel in the study will probably not feel much in the pulpit.

Miscellaneous observations and cautions relative to this subject

Some men will need the bridle while others will need the spur. Therefore, as has been noted throughout this project, accurate self-assessment is vital (Rom. 12:3). The man of God must evaluate his basic emotional constitution and deal with himself accordingly. The man of God must consciously work at mending any broken circuits between proper emotions and their appropriate expression. For some, passion will obscure reason and the man of God will need to correct this. For others, any restraint will obscure all expression. Christ must be the pastor's example.[271] The repairing of broken circuits can be worked at home with his wife, children and other close friends. The assessment of other competent Christians should be sought. Practical and real improvement can be made.

An important caution needs to be noted. The man of God should beware venting emotions beyond the level appropriate to the mental and emotional state of his hearers. Dabney notes:

> The disclosure of your own emotion must not too far outrun the temper of the congregation, lest it should appear to them from their cooler position extravagance. The effect of such an impression would be that the chasm between them and yourself would be widened, instead of being closed by their elevation to your level.[272]

Another caution is for the man of God to beware his peculiar vulnerability after the emotional expenditure of preaching. He may find himself given to discouragement, despondency or even sensuality. Simply being aware of his tendencies can go a great length in guarding against these vulnerabilities.

A final caution is to avoid all affectation. All emotional display must be genuine. Any attempts at improvement must at the same time be a rejection of affectation. People despise the affected. True emotion in preaching must exist because of the realities at hand, not because of the histrionics demanded by today's vaunted theories of 'effective' communication.

> But the emotions which the preacher aims to propagate are the moral and spiritual. It is these, then, by which he must be possessed and animated. In other words, in order to be capable of any power of persuasion, you must be men of ardent and genuine religious affections. You must be men of faith and prayer; you must live near the cross and feel 'the powers of the world to come'. We thus learn again the great truth that it is divine grace which makes the true minister.[273]

The preacher's vocal powers and their employment in the act of preaching

Relative to the subject matter of preaching, the voice used to convey that matter is of secondary importance. Relative, also, to the character of the preacher, the voice is of secondary importance. Both truth and character are vastly more important than the vocal powers which herald the truth. 'Any view of the place and importance of the vocal powers in preaching which does not begin with these perspectives and is not continually conditioned by them is doomed to be unscriptural and dangerous.'[274] Spurgeon summarizes this in his usual way.

> Our first rule with regard to the voice would be – do not think too much about it, for recollect the sweetest voice is nothing without something to say.... A man with a surpassingly excellent voice who is destitute of a well-informed head, and an earnest heart, will be 'a voice crying in the wilderness'; Such a man may shine in the choir, but he is useless in the pulpit.... You are not singers but preachers: your voice is but a secondary matter.[275]

Content and character are supreme. Relative to the mechanics of preaching, however, the vocal powers are extremely important. 'The voice is the speaker's great instrument. Nothing else in a man's physical constitution is nearly so important.'[276]

> Every sensible Christian knows well that voice and delivery have a great deal to say to the effectiveness of a speaker, and above all of one who speaks in the pulpit. A sermon faultless both in doctrine and composition will often sound dull and tiresome, when tamely read by a clergyman with a heavy, monotonous manner. A sermon of little intrinsic merit, and containing perhaps not a half-dozen ideas, will often pass muster as brilliant and eloquent, when delivered by a lively speaker with a good voice. For want of good delivery some men make gold look like copper, while others, by the sheer force of a good delivery, make a few halfpence pass for gold.[277]

The various dimensions of the vocal powers ought to be used in the act of preaching. None of the God-given dimensions of the vocal powers should be omitted or poorly regulated in preaching. Rather, all of the God-given dimensions of the vocal powers ought to be wisely employed in the proclamation of the truth. The dimensions include compass or range, volume or force, distinctness, speed or tempo, emphasis and intensity. 'Brethren, in the name of everything that is sacred, ring the whole chime in your steeple, and do not dun your people with the ding-dong of one poor cracked bell.'[278]

There are a number of practical guidelines for the improvement of the vocal powers in the act of preaching.

(1) *Avoid all vocal affectations*

Unfortunately, most people today think that any inflection, any drama, any emphasis, any volume, is affected. This is simply not the case. The prophets were commanded to cry out and lift up their voice. A fireside chat tone when a trumpet blast is in order is the real affectation. Affectation is artificial, unnatural, and consciously forced. Spurgeon, quoting Abbé Mullois, strongly states,

> A man who has not a natural and true delivery, should not be allowed to occupy the pulpit; from thence, at least, everything else that is false should be summarily banished.... The instant you abandon the natural and the true, you forego the right to be believed, as well as the right of being listened to.[279]

(2) *Correct all vocal distractions where possible*

There may be some nasality in the voice. This is a great distraction. The writer well remembers an associate pastor, who whenever he preached, would click his tongue against the back of his front teeth. Perhaps others may have indistinct speech patterns, where their 'm's and 'n's sound the same. Whatever the case may be, the man of God may have distracting vocal habits, which must be worked on. Just as physical distractions must be taken care of, so must vocal distractions. Spurgeon's humor on this subject cannot be neglected.

> Moreover, brethren, avoid the use of the nose as an organ of speech, for the best authorities are agreed that it is intended to smell with. Time was, when the nasal twang was the correct thing, but in this degenerate age you had better obey the evident suggestion of nature, and let the mouth keep to its work without the interference of the olfactory instrument. Should an American student be present he must excuse my pressing remark upon his attention. Abhor the practice of some men, who will not bring out the 'r', such a habit is 'vewy wuinous and wediculous, vewy wetched and wepwehensible'.[280]

(3) *Cultivate sufficient volume so as to be heard, commandingly and comfortably*

Speech is addressed to the ear. Its first requisite is, therefore, audibility: we must so utter it as to be heard. This simple remark will suggest to your good sense the rule as to the general gauge of loudness. The voice should be always loud enough to be heard throughout the audience, and, except in animated passages, it should not be much louder. To secure that result, it is well to direct the eyes generally toward the farthest circle of hearers; for the voice will naturally adjust itself to the distance of those we address. This rule is useful also in guarding against the distraction of our attention and the loss of our thread of thought, by noting too closely any individual countenance or trivial event in the audience near us. But there is an element more essential to audibility than loudness: this is distinctness. By distinctness I mean these traits: clearness or purity of tone, due deliberation or separation of the syllables, and especially careful articulation.[281]

(4) *Cultivate a variety of tone, pace, intensity and correctness of pronunciation*

The tone must be varied if the hearers are not to drift off to sleep. The droning monotony of a static tone is death to a sermon's power. The pace must also be varied. Sometimes verbal torrents will be very appropriate. Other times a methodical, slow emphasis on each syllable will be most useful. The pace varies through the course of the sermon. Intensity also must vary. If a sermon takes off at 10.0 on the Richter scale, and maintains that for forty-five minutes, the people will be either so uninterested or so worn out that the sermon loses all effect. Additionally, correct pronunciation must be cultivated. 'Take great care of the consonants, enunciate every one of them clearly; they are the features and expression of the words. Practice indefatigably till you give every one of the consonants its due; the vowels have a voice of their own, and therefore can speak for themselves.'[282]

Finally, the man of God cannot spare himself the real labor of fully engaging all the faculties connected with an effective use of his vocal powers. He should be cognizant of how the stomach muscles are used; how to employ the diaphragm in projecting the voice; how to use and protect the larynx; the mechanics of the tongue, teeth and lips in enunciation. He must also open himself up to competent critics and practical disciplines in order to improve his vocal efficiency.

The preacher's physical action in preaching

As the theme of the man of God in relation to himself in the act of preaching is considered, the actual physical action comes into focus. Although much has been said which is relevant to this subject, it is necessary to examine a few salient principles. Just as men differ emotionally and vocally, so they differ in their physical actions. The range of legitimate physical action is broad and subjective. Yet one cannot ignore that physical action in communication is somewhat of a window into the speaker. The exterior often reveals the interior realities (Gen. 4:1-6; 2 Sam. 6:12-16; Dan. 5:1-7; Matt. 2:11 cf. 4:9; Luke 24:50; John 17:1; Acts 3:8, 26:1; 1 Cor. 14:25). Therefore, a few general principles concerning physical action in preaching are warranted.

(1) *Forget yourself, be yourself*

This principle was expanded in detail previously in 'The Preacher in Relationship to Himself in the Act of Preaching', with appropriate quotations by Broadus and Taylor. The physical action of the man of God must be ultimately determined by self-forgetfulness and naturalness. Out of this ultimate principle flow others which are vital.

(2) *Never premeditate any physical action or consciously force such action while preaching*

This applies to the use of the voice and the body. All voice inflection and bodily action cannot be premeditated or it will appear to be affected. Pastor Martin relays a story of the one and only time when he premeditated an act in preaching. He was a nineteen year old student preacher and he was going to preach on the resurrection. He had planned to bring some drama to the resurrection by dropping his voice with 'appropriate' physical action, as he spoke of the crucifixion and burial. Then, in order to capture the drama of the resurrection he would burst forth with a great shout. After he did the deed, he said he felt like a young man who had just been defiled in the worst sort of way. He felt as if he had cheapened the pulpit. And with the feeling of defilement on his heart, he vowed to never premeditate any action ever again.[283]

(3) *There should be a conscious goal to rid oneself of all distracting physical actions and mannerisms*

'It is not so much incumbent upon you to acquire right pulpit action as it is to get rid of that which is wrong.'[284] Nervous gestures and habits, such as twiddling the fingers, fidgeting, tightening shoulders, and others, should be identified and broken. Incongruent physical actions, such as a clenched fist when offering Christ freely or pointing downward while speaking of the glory of heaven should be avoided. Any physical action which distracts ought to be avoided. This includes any strained action. Pastor Martin tells of a bad habit he was broken of through the smile and slight chuckle of Mrs. Martin. He had the habit of buttoning and unbuttoning his coat while preaching. On one occasion, he put the buttons in the wrong holes, creating a lopsided appearance. His wife smiled and perhaps even chuckled, and so Pastor Martin slipped behind the pulpit to check his belt and zip, and then noticed his uneven coat. It cured him once and for all.

This illustration brings out the necessity of having someone close enough to the man of God who can point out the distractions. If the man of God is going to be serious about glorifying God in his delivery, then he must seek the counsel of those close to him for open and honest evaluations regarding any habits, gestures or actions which may detract from the preaching of the Word.

(4) *Some specific guidelines for the more naturally animated are necessary*

The more naturally animated can sometimes get carried away and need to remember that they are heralds and proclaimers, not actors or mime artists. The issue of self-control, which has already been expounded, is necessary here as well. This may be necessary, for instance, if some action prohibits the preacher from being distinctly heard. There may be a microphone which has a limited range. If the animated preacher is all over the platform, he may need to harness his body closer to the microphone for the sake of audibility which is always more important than the physical dynamics. The animated, physically active preacher may also get carried away into indecorous or ludicrous actions. That too, should be avoided. J W Alexander makes the point, 'Every excess of manner over matter hinders the effect of the delivery, on all wise judges. Where there is more voice, more emphasis, or more gesture, than there is feeling, there is waste, and worse; powder beyond the shot.'[285]

(5) *Some specific guidelines for the less naturally animated are also necessary*

The less animated need to be convinced of the necessity of cultivating some physical activity. The less animated should pray for some liberation in their redeemed humanity. They should be willing to yield themselves as a vehicle for conveying truth. Pastor Achille Blaize was reported to pray, 'Lord, I offer up to you my eyes, my eyelids, my mouth, my arms, my hands, my legs, my feet. May you take it all and use it for your service.'

The man of God should also pray for more truly felt earnestness in preaching. The real issue often times, is not the lack of physical ability, but rather the lack of emotional earnestness in preaching. It was said of Baxter, who preached with such great feeling, 'The only teacher that gave him lessons in action and attitude was feeling, real, genuine, holy, feeling, and this taught him how to look, how to move, how to speak.'[286] Alexander identifies the proper solution,

> Every man may be said to have his quantum of animation, beyond which he cannot go without fireworks and affectation. Hence, to exhort a young man to be more animated, is to mislead and perhaps spoil him, *unless you mean to inculcate the cultivation of inward emotion.*[287]

The less animated preacher may work at developing animation in congenial, non-ministerial situations. When he reads to his children, he can develop animation and vocal passion. He may actively seek the judicious evaluation of people in the congregation. Most certainly he should expose himself to different models. Although all people are imitative and preaching is somewhat an imitative art, there should be no intention of deliberately mimicking another.[288] However, there is a great value in seeing others, in order to help oneself. Whatever he does outside the pulpit to help develop animation, he must remember that when he comes into the pulpit, 'forget yourself, be yourself.'

18

THE MAN OF GOD AND HIS RELATIONSHIP TO HIS HEARERS IN THE ACT OF PREACHING

This section grows out of the soil of 'The life of the man of God in relationship to his people'. The act of preaching is a dynamic act not merely accomplished through one man. Rather, the act of preaching takes place in the mutual empathetic involvement between the preacher and his congregation. The empathy that is being spoken of here is the kind which could be described as being under somebody else's skin, so that one feels what that person feels; or getting behind their eyeballs so that one can see what that person sees. It is the interpersonal dynamic which could be described as alternating currents. This empathetic element in the act of preaching has not gone unnoticed by those writing on preaching in the past.

> When a man who is apt in teaching, whose soul is on fire with the truth which he trusts has saved him and hopes will save others, speaks to his fellow-man, face to face, eye to eye, and electric sympathies flash to and fro between him and his hearers, till they lift each up, higher and higher, into the intensest thought, and the most impassioned emotion – higher and yet higher, till they are borne as on chariots of fire above the world, – there is a power to move men, to influence character, life, destiny, such as no printed page can ever possess.[289]

> Speaking directly to the audience brings the speaker into the true vital relations to them, by which he is enabled to grasp them with his mind, and exert a direct mental influence upon them.... He grasps them thus with his mind, and holds them steadily in his mental grasp. This enables him to gain their attention and sympathy, and bring all his personal power, as a man to bear upon them, as men and women of like passions with himself. Thus he pours his thoughts and feelings into them through the open, but ever mysterious channels of the sympathetic affections.[290]

> Eloquence is not the mere communication of a set of dry notions; it is a sympathy, a spiritual infection, a communion of life and action between two souls, a projection of the orator's thought, conviction, emotion and will into the mind and heart of the audience. Nothing, therefore, is a true oration which is not a life, a spiritual action, transacted in the utterance.[291]

> But what is of greater importance, the instructions of the living teacher are beyond measure more impressive and affecting than any other method of instruction. Men are the creatures, not of thought only, but of feeling; they have susceptibilities which seek to be gratified, and which ought to be turned to good account. Nature demands the presence, the sympathy, the eye, the voice, the action, the expressive countenance of the living teacher.... The most powerful appeals ever made to the reason, the conscience, the interest, or the passions of men, are not made from the press, but from the warm heart and glowing lips of the living speaker.[292]

> Another element to which I attach importance is that the preacher while speaking should in a sense be deriving something from his congregation. There are those present in the congregation who are spiritually-minded people, and filled with the Spirit, and they make their contribution to the occasion. There is always an element of exchange in true preaching.[293]

> The look, attitude, manner of address of the extemporary Preacher, is more direct, personal, and arresting. His habit is more ready to improve passing occasions, or to introduce a striking hint to rouse his careless hearers. The reality before his eyes at the moment of action inspires a warmth, which, abstracted from the scene of work, he could never impart. The sight of his people in the presence of God – their very countenances – their attention or listlessness – their feeding interest or apparent dislike – suggests many points of animated address, which did not occur in the study; excites many visible impressions, which awakens corresponding sympathy and interest in his congregation.[294]

This exchange, as Lloyd-Jones put it, is vital in the act of preaching. It is part of unction, the sacred anointing, the felt presence of God, and so on. It is indispensable if the preached Word is to 'spread rapidly and be glorified' (2 Thess. 3:1), and if there is to be a 'demonstration of the Spirit and of power' (1 Cor. 2:4). Therefore, some practical directives for attaining and maintaining profitable mutual empathetic involvement between the pastor and his congregation are necessary.

(1) *The man of God must always seek to master the essential content, structure and thrust of any given sermon*

The congregation cannot feel as if the preacher is preoccupied with the sub-processes of the sermon. If he is constantly looking at notes, or worse, a manuscript; or if he is struggling for words to express himself properly, then that vital mutual empathy will be lost. The man of God must be thoroughly prepared, not just in his exposition, but in his soul, if he is to give the congregation his full attention. To be sure, there are times when the Spirit shores up shortcomings such as lack of preparation due to emergencies and so on. However, the Spirit shores things up by giving liberty to the preacher, not by causing the preacher to stumble around for words on paper or in his head. The preacher must have the content and structural flow mastered. He must have the purpose of the sermon thoroughly settled. It is in this discipline of mastering the message that great freedom comes to the man of God.

(2) *The man of God also needs to be mastered by the biblical truths and practical implications he is preaching if there is to be this exchange*

'Your subject must weigh so much upon your own mind that you dedicate all your faculties at their best to the deliverance of your soul concerning it and then when your hearers see that the topic has engrossed you, it will by degrees engross them.'[295] The preacher has to feel deeply about the truth he is preaching if the congregation is going to empathize, that is, feel deeply with him. Just as he has grappled with the truth and mastered it, so also the truth has grappled with him, and laid hold of him. When the truth has his heart, when it has his mind, then the man in the pulpit has something to give and the congregation has something to receive. The great impassioned exchange, the giving and receiving of felt truth, is indeed glorious.

(3) *The man of God must also seek to establish and maintain conscious sensitivity to the congregation*

The preacher must open his spirit to the congregation. He needs to be willing to be vulnerable to them. In Paul's terms, 'we were well-pleased to impart to you not only the gospel of God but also our own lives' (1 Thess. 2:8). In cultivating mutual empathy, the preacher needs an unusual sensitivity to the congregation. It is a 'sixth sense' which the preacher must have. This sensitivity is a part of unction; it is definitely the work of the Spirit within; but it is also vital if any exchange is going to take place. McIlvaine recognized this very point when he noted,

> The sensibility of the true orator to the mental state of the audience is very great. In fact the degree of this sensibility is an infallible test of natural genius for public speaking. For he who does not feel the need of the attention and sympathy of his audience, who hardly knows whether he has it or not, and who can speak about as well without it as with it – for there are such speakers – that man is incapable of eloquence, and ought to dismiss all thoughts of becoming an orator. The speaker who has any natural adaptation or genius for this art, seems to reflect, as it were, all the states and changes of mind and feeling which take place in those to whom he is speaking. He seems to know by instinct whether he is heard by the whole audience, whether he has their attention, whether they understand what he is saying, and whether they are favorably or unfavorably affected by it; and he feels as if it were almost impossible for him to proceed in his discourse, until he has succeeded in fixing their attention, and in gaining their sympathy.[296]

This conscious sensitivity occurs when the preacher engages the congregation with real eye contact. The eye contact needs to begin when the sermon begins, and be maintained throughout the message. The direct eye contact is the preacher's way of saying, 'I demand your attention. I will not settle for less. I am here to speak. You are here to listen.' The eye to eye contact can convey earnestness, tenderness, invitation, exhortation, rebuke and all other feelings which the preacher may legitimately experience in the act of preaching.

> What a variety of emotions the eye can appropriately represent! It sparkles with intelligence, flashes with indignation, melts with grief, trembles with pity, languishes with love, twinkles with humor, starts with amazement, or shrinks with horror, according to the impulse given to it by the soul within. A dog knows from his master's eye whether he is about to be caressed or kicked.[297]

(4) *The man of God must seek to establish and maintain undivided attention*

The kingdom of Satan is threatened most when the Word is preached in the power of the Spirit. Therefore, Satan intends to snatch the seed (Mark 4:4, 15). How does Satan snatch the Word and make it ineffective? Most experienced preachers would answer by 'inattention'. The wandering mind is the devil's biggest weapon of defense in protecting his kingdom. McIlvaine once again makes the observation of an experienced speaker,

> The attention of the audience is indispensable to this sympathy. In order to secure results, it is necessary that the attention of the audience should first be gained, and concentrated upon the thoughts of the speaker, as they are delivered. This is indispensable to the free play, and greatest effect of the sympathetic action. For even a single person who is inattentive, or whose mind is otherwise occupied, not only fails to contribute his share to the effect, but he presents an obstacle to the propagation and flow of the common feeling, and exerts a positive influence in crossing and confusing the mysterious currents of sympathy and thought.[298]

Undivided attention can be established by the man of God speaking in a simple, artless, frank, manly way. In the day of stereotypical clerical wimps, the man who stands and speaks directly to the heart without the professional clergy tone or liturgy can arrest the attention of the congregation. Once again, if the strong tone of 'I am here to be heard', comes across in the preacher's voice and demeanor, he will more likely have the attention of even the young. If he is a man with a message, a commission, and it is stated plainly and without affectation, he will probably have the ears of most. However, there are those times when even the best don't have the attention of everyone.

The man of God has to be sensitive enough to know when to use a judicious pause, or other rhetorical devices. Pounding the pulpit or making some noise may revive attention. Once in a while, the exceptional use of a direct appeal or gracious rebuke may even be in order. The pastor may notice some drifting, and he may stop and say, 'Dear people, I have labored over this text this whole week. I have prayed for the Spirit to use it for your good. I am pouring my heart out to you, the beads of sweat on my brow prove it. Will you please, for the sake of your own soul and out of respect for God's holy Word, give me your attention.' Spurgeon, of course, was a master at this, and testifies to his method on this matter:

> Sometimes the manners of our people are inimical to attention; they are not in the habit of attending; they attend the chapel but do not attend the preacher. They are accustomed to look round at every one who enters the place, and they come in at all times, sometimes with much stamping, squeaking of boots, and banging of doors. I was preaching once to a people who continually looked round, and I adopted the expedient of saying, 'Now, friends, as it is so very interesting to you to know who comes in, and it disturbs me so very much for you to look round, I will, if you like, describe each one as he comes in, so that you may sit and look at me, and keep up at least a show of decency.' I described one gentleman who came in, who happened to be a friend whom I could depict without offense as 'a very respectable gentleman who had just taken his hat off', and so on; and after that one attempt I found it was not necessary to describe any more, because they felt shocked at what I was doing, and I assured them that I was much more shocked that they should render it necessary for me to reduce their conduct to such an absurdity. It cured them for the time being, and I hope for ever, much to their pastor's joy.[299]

> Andrew Fuller had barely commenced a sermon when he saw the people going to sleep. He said, 'Friends, friends, friends, this won't do. I have thought sometimes when you were asleep that it was my fault, but now you are asleep before I begin, and it must be your fault. Pray wake up and give me an opportunity of doing you some good.'[300]

The man of God who stands to deliver God's Word must have the mutual empathetic involvement between himself and his hearers. He must be the master of his message, and he must be mastered by his message. He needs to stand as a man who knows what he is talking about, certain of what he is saying; but he also must be a man possessed, that is, possessed by the truth he speaks. He must stand in the pulpit and establish and maintain a conscious sensitivity to the congregation, being open with them, looking them in the eyes, penetrating their souls with his soul which is on fire with truth. He must stand in that pulpit and have their attention. He cannot go on unless he has their ears, and he will not be satisfied until he has their hearts, too. It is this dynamic which is vital for God-owned preaching.

19

THE MAN OF GOD AND HIS RELATIONSHIP TO HIS PAPER IN THE ACT OF PREACHING

What is under consideration here is not what takes place in the study itself, but rather the issue at hand is the preacher's relationship to the paper in the act of preaching. It is crucial that the nature of this seemingly unimportant issue be identified. Pastor Martin states the issue both negatively and positively.

> The issue is NOT how much written composition is done in the study or how much written material is brought into the pulpit. The issue is how much dependence upon and preoccupation with written material is manifested in the act of preaching. To state the matter another way, the issue is how much mental and physical attachment is there to one's paper. At the end of the day we are NOT so much concerned with issues of paper and print, but with the issues of eyes and brains.[301]

This issue deeply impacts the mutual empathetic involvement between the preacher and his hearers. In light of the vital importance of the previous section, this subject begins, by implication, to take on significance. Therefore, some general guidelines are in order, assuming most men will take some paper with them into the pulpit. Also, some practical counsels on any actual reading which may take place in the pulpit will be given.

(1) *The man of God should never read a full manuscript from the pulpit*

Some may immediately object, pointing to those giants among men, Jonathan Edwards and Thomas Chalmers. Iain Murray has given a convincing refutation to the allegation that Edwards read his sermons.[302] Be that as it may, Etter's comments are thoroughly appropriate to such an appeal.

> Chalmers and Edwards, perhaps were exceptions [i.e., to extemporaneous preaching]; but these 'sons of thunder' possessed such an ungovernable flood and luxuriance of feeling that they needed the curb of the manuscript in order to keep them within legitimate bounds; and yet Chalmers read his paper in tones of enthusiasm that 'made the rafters roar'. 'During the reading of his sermons, Dr. Chalmers was absolutely terrible. His heavy frame was convulsed, his face was flushed; the veins on his forehead and neck stood out like whipcords; the foam flew from his mouth like flakes. He hung over his audience, menacing them with his shaking fist, or stood erect, manacled and staring.' No one will object to that kind of sermon-reading, so far as animation is concerned. 'His manuscript *burned*, but some of our modern manuscripts *ought* to be burned.'[303]

Again, the man of God should not ordinarily read a full manuscript in the pulpit. To avoid the temptation of reading a manuscript, would it not be wise simply to avoid taking a full manuscript into the pulpit? Although this is dogmatic and not by any means accepted by all, it is nevertheless non-negotiable. Dabney is no less dogmatic when he states:

> Reading a manuscript to the people can never, with any justice, be termed preaching.... In the delivery of the sermon there can be no exception in favor of the mere reader. How can he whose eyes are fixed upon the paper before him, who performs the mechanical task of reciting the very words inscribed upon it, have the inflections, the emphasis, the look, the gesture, the flexibility, the fire, or oratorical actions? Mere reading, then, should be sternly banished from the pulpit, except in those rare cases in which the didactic purpose supersedes the rhetorical, and exact verbal accuracy is more essential than eloquence. [304]

There may be others who object, claiming that what they do is not 'mere reading', but they 'speak' from a manuscript. To that McIlvaine addresses the following:

> Reading and speaking from manuscript, are so nearly allied, and the sub-processes in the two cases differ so little, and the light they throw upon each other is so important, that they require to be treated together. For in both the sub-processes are those of taking in the

> sense of the manuscript, or printed page, through the eye; and these processes are the reverse of those which belong to the giving out of the sense by the voice, and to the impressing of the thought and sentiment upon other minds. The mental operations of giving out, and taking in the sense, are in the highest degree incompatible with each other. Certainly they cannot both go on together as leading states of the same mind; one or the other must fall into the rank of a sub-process.[305]

McIlvaine's point may be illustrated by a sponge. A sponge is either soaking in water or wringing out water. It cannot do both at the same time. The manuscript preacher is by the very nature of reading, soaking in, and thus cannot be giving out. The extemporaneous preacher has no such relationship to his notes; he is not taking in; he is giving out. Perhaps nobody has made this point better than the French Calvinist, Pierre Ch. Marcel:

> If the preacher is and remains dependent upon his manuscript or upon his memory, there is not *just one* prisoner – there are two: the preacher and the Spirit, and through the Spirit Christ. The written or memorized text of the sermon at this moment exercises its dominance; Christ through the Spirit is not free.[306]

(2) *The man of God ought to aim at reducing the sermon to a one page skeleton to be carried into the pulpit*[307]

This idea reflects that the preacher is only minimally dependent on the skeleton for his flow of thought. Although it is recognized that other notes, such as quotations and perhaps exegetical data might be present, the sermon itself should be at the barest minimum. The practical wisdom of this suggested guideline is exemplified by Spurgeon.

> If for two successive Sundays I make my notes a little longer and fuller than usual, I find on the third occasion that I require them longer still; and I also observe that if on occasion I lean a little more to my recollection of my thoughts, and am not so extemporaneous as I have been accustomed to be, there is a direct craving and even an increasing necessity for pre-composition. If a man begins to walk with a stick merely for a whim, he will soon come to require a stick;

> if you indulge your eyes with spectacles they will speedily demand them as a permanent appendage; and if you were to walk with crutches for a month, at the end of the time they would be almost necessary to your movements, although naturally your limbs might be as sound and healthy as any man's. Ill uses create an ill nature. You must continually practice extemporizing.[308]

(3) *The preacher should look at his paper only as much as is absolutely necessary*

If eye contact is to be maintained, as well as that dynamic exchange, then the eyes cannot be continually drifting to the paper. Therefore the preacher should look at his paper at those times which are least likely to break off living contact with the congregation. A good time would be during a transition of mood or intensity. If the preacher has been intensely applying the truth, and is going to drop his tone, he might then pause and glance at his notes. The pause would give the congregation the opportunity to drop with him. Or after a lengthy explanation of a passage or theme when the pastor is about to apply the text, he may pause and glance at his notes, before launching into the application. Another judicious time would be when the congregation is turning to a passage of Scripture.

Finally, since reading quotations requires paper, some practical counsels concerning the reading of quotations in the act of preaching are briefly given. Quotations should be sparse. Even though a congregation may be a reading congregation who loves the old paths, it is difficult to hear a man like the Scribes: 'Matthew Henry says ... Calvin noted ... As Baxter said ... And of course, Owen addressed this issue....' The sermon is not a doctoral dissertation, or an anthology, or even a lecture. It is the living communication of the Word of God. Too many quotes make listening difficult.

The quotations should be copied and in order before bringing them into the pulpit. Lugging ten pounds of books might strike terror into the hearts of God's people. Shuffling through seven pages to find that brilliant quotation will frustrate the people of God and cause them to lose their concentration. Furthermore, the quotation should be mastered before it is used in the sermon. How the preacher reads it in his head may not be the way it comes out verbally. The preacher should be familiar enough with it that he can read it and maintain the same flow of speech that he had before. Too many pastors start to read, sound stilted, and then the congregation switches off. Also, there is nothing wrong with paraphrasing a quotation. It often will give a better flow to the sermon than actual reading. Whether read or paraphrased, archaic words should be replaced. A recondite word will break the flow of thought, and may appear pedantic.

Whatever paper may be on the sacred desk is there only as a silent servant. It should never be in the place of the master. The act of preaching should be the living communication between the living preacher and the living congregation, empowered by the living Spirit. Therefore, the paper the man of God brings into the pulpit should in no way interfere with this Divine transaction. This will require that the man of God work on his extemporaneous abilities, sharpening mental and verbal skills. He should strive to be as free from the paper as he can possibly be. When he is free from his paper, he is more likely to experience the freedom of the Spirit in the act of preaching.

20

THE MAN OF GOD IN RELATIONSHIP TO HIS PHYSICAL SURROUNDINGS IN THE ACT OF PREACHING

The man of God should do everything in his power to make sure that the act of preaching is used by God for the good of the souls of men and for the glory of Jesus Christ. This means that he preaches as in the sight of God and is aware of the fact that he is on his way to judgment. He is conscious that he stands as an ambassador, a herald and a chosen instrument in the hand of God, that his task is a divinely appointed one. The man of God also preaches with self-control and self-forgetfulness, striving for optimum effect in the act of preaching. He wants to make certain that everything about himself does not detract from the Word preached. His clothing, his hair, his posture, even his facial expressions, are concerns. His emotions are stirred by the truth, but they are also appropriately expressed. Again, his concern is the exaltation and promotion of the truth. His voice and his physical actions must be compatible with the truth he is expressing. The preacher's relationship to his congregation is also vital. That glorious exchange, that mutual empathetic involvement is sought after and guarded. Even such detail as the preacher's relationship to his paper should be a concern. Nothing can detract from the preaching of the Word!

With such great concerns ever before the serious Christian preacher, it is incongruous then to ignore the physical surroundings where the act of preaching takes place. The act of preaching, no matter how Spirit-empowered, is done before bodily creatures. No preacher has ever stood and preached before disembodied spirits or insensitive bodily creatures. Almost everyone who will hear the Word preached will have eyes which can see. The mind will not engage if the eyes are distracted. Almost everyone who sits under the ministry of the Word will have ears. If the ears are distracted, the mind will not stay focused. Everyone will have lungs, which will be taking in oxygen. If the oxygen supply is wanting, the brain will not function as it should. Everyone will have a back and buttocks. It is next to impossible to break hearts when the buttocks or lower back are hurting because of the torturous influence of uncomfortable chairs or pews.

The Enemy of the souls of men will do everything he can to hinder the reception of the Word preached (Mt. 13:19). But the man of God cannot be ignorant of his schemes (2 Cor. 2:11). So the issue of physical surroundings is ultimately a matter of spiritual warfare (Eph. 6:11f.). Our heavenly Father, furthermore, is aware of inherent human weaknesses and He keeps them in mind (Ps. 103:13-14). He does not demean His creatures' weak physical constitutions. Therefore the man of God ought to reflect his heavenly Father's beneficent character. This requires that the physical context where the act of preaching takes place be thought out and well-planned.[309]

The pulpit and its setting are a central feature to the unhindered act of preaching. The structure of the pulpit itself is important. The pulpit must be aesthetically and architecturally compatible with the rest of the building. The functionality of the pulpit is also a critical consideration. A church may have a wonderful Gothic motif, with a pulpit which beautifully fits that motif, and yet it may bury the small-framed preacher because of its great size. Spurgeon humorously noted, 'A deep wooden pulpit of the old sort might well remind a minister of his mortality, for it is nothing but a coffin set on end: but on what rational ground do we bury our pastors alive?'[310]

On the other hand, a pulpit may be too low for a tall preacher, or too high for a short preacher. The pulpit must be designed to be functional for the regular preacher.[311] It also needs to be materially substantial. It must be strong and firm. It is not a prop for the invalid who cannot hold himself up on his own two legs, but it must not be flimsy and rickety. A flimsy pulpit does not reflect the manly, strong, authoritative, bold preaching of the Word of God. The bottom line is that the pulpit needs to be made for the optimum impression on the congregation, which means it must be compatible with the building and the preacher and it needs to bespeak a strong ministry of the Word.

The placement of the pulpit is also important. The Reformation's symbolism of pulpit placement is nearly forgotten today. 'The Reformation gave centrality to the sermon. The pulpit was higher than the altar, for Luther held that salvation is through the Word, and without the Word the elements are devoid of sacramental quality, but the Word is sterile unless it is spoken.'[312] The pulpit is central because preaching is central. Preaching is central because God's Word is central. Whatever the layout of the building, the pulpit needs to be placed centrally, so that when one walks into the building, he can see that the people gather in this place around the preached Word.

The placement is not only central, it must be visible. The visibility of the pulpit, and thus the preacher, is no small matter. When creatures with eyeballs are visually distracted, they by nature are hindered from concentrating. In a room of sixty people, a twelve inch platform may be perfectly suitable. In a room of two hundred, the platform will need to be higher for good visibility. Proper lighting is also necessary, not only for the preacher's Bible and notes, but for the congregation to see the whites of the preacher's eyes and for him to see theirs. Easy and safe accessibility as well as unrestricted mobility for the preacher are also non-negotiable.

Seats and their arrangement are also another crucial consideration. Many places of worship actually undermine the preaching of the Word by their hard seats or pews which were evidently designed for a torture chamber. Comfortable seating is vital. The heart and mind will only absorb what the seat can endure. The chairs or pews should be strategically situated for maximum visibility. This may mean that the chairs need to be staggered for a clear view. They will also need to be arranged to keep visual distractions such as movement to and from the rest room, or late arrivals, to a minimum. Many who have to rent a building and have only limited space will need to secure the help of some serious minded engineers who understand the dynamics of worship. These can lay out the building to maximize space and minimize distractions.

Acoustics and voice assistance are also a serious concern. The number of audible distractions is nearly limitless. The goal is to have an acoustic situation which allows for the full range of the preacher's voice to be heard with comfortable audibility. No one in the congregation should have to strain to hear his lows, or experience pain when he hits the highs. In an existing building, the church may need to add sounding boards or sound absorbent material such as drapes, carpet, and acoustic tiles. If the luxury of building a facility exists, professional advice should be sought. The voice assistance equipment should always be viewed as just that, voice assistance, as opposed to a public address system. The congregation should not be aware of any amplification of the voice. The sound of the voice should be as natural as possible. Finally, all equipment should allow for the preacher's full range of movements in the act of preaching.

For optimum effectiveness in the act of preaching, good ventilation and temperature control are an absolute necessity. Every person who walks through the doors into the place of worship is an oxygen consumer, a humidifier and a radiant heater. If the brain is starved of oxygen, the listener will grow drowsy. If the heat and humidity are high, concentration is laborious. 'A gust of fresh air through the building might be to the people the next best thing to the gospel itself, at least it would put them in a fit frame of mind to receive the truth.'[313] Some quiet overhead fans may be needed. Quiet exhaust fans and air intake louvres may also be installed for good air movement. A deacon who watches the temperature and adjusts the thermostat performs a great act of mercy. Even in the middle of the sermon, a merciful word which may open the heart may be, 'Deacon, would you please open those windows.' Whatever devices are used for the physical comfort, they cannot be audible or visual distractions.

Conclusion

The ultimate end which all elements of preaching serve is the glory of God and the good of men, in their salvation and edification. The act of preaching, therefore, is a vital subject which requires the attention of all who would claim to speak in the name of Christ.

That sermon which is conceived and gestated in the study and closet will be either born or still-born in the act of preaching. As a result, the man of God must be thoroughly acquainted with and growing in his understanding of the act of preaching, as it relates to God, to himself, to his hearers, and even to his paper and physical surroundings.

Epilogue and Resources

The ultimate goal of this project is to stir afresh a desire for powerful, Spirit-anointed, God-owned preaching among men of God. It is the great need for today. Albert N Martin has been an instrument used by God not only to demonstrate powerful preaching, but also to develop and articulate a theology of preaching. It is my prayer that the Lord Jesus Christ would be pleased to use these efforts to help strengthen His Kingdom heralds in the greatest task of all – preaching His eternal gospel.

The number of resources which are available from Trinity Pulpit are almost staggering. For more information on Pastor Martin's preaching tapes or the Pastoral Theology lectures, call 1-800-722-3584 or 1-973-334-6272 or write Trinity Pulpit, P.O. Box 395 Montville, NJ 07045 USA.

REFERENCES

1. Iain Murray, 'The Life of John Murray' in *The Collected Writings of John Murray*, Volume 3 (Edinburgh: Banner of Truth Trust, 1982), 134.
2. A letter from John MacArthur to the writer, dated June 23, 1997.
3. A letter from J I Packer to the writer, dated July 31, 1997.
4. A letter from Iain Murray to the writer, dated March 19, 1997.
5. E-mail from Joel Beeke to the writer, dated September 27, 1997.
6. A letter from Edward Donnelly to the writer, dated May 20, 1997.
7. Donnelly correspondence.
8. Charles Spurgeon, *Lectures to My Students* (Pasadena, TX: Pilgrims Publications, reprint, 1990. First published, 1881). I, 120. All of the quotations from this volume will be identified by a Roman numeral, indicating which of the four books they come from, followed by the page number.
9. Brian Lee interview with Joyce (Martin) Maltbee, Albert and Marilyn Martin. June 8, 1995.
10. Brian Lee interview.
11. This was the Salvation Army's equivalent of the 'altar'.
12. Brian Lee interview.
13. Brian Lee interview.
14. Brian Borgman interview with Albert Martin, October 23, 1998.
15. Brian Borgman interview, Oct. 23, 1998.
16. Brian Borgman interview, Oct. 23, 1998.
17. Trinity Pulpit, TOC0116. All further references to tapes will be from the Trinity Pulpit with only the tapes numbers being listed.
18. A letter from Achille Blaize to the writer, June 25, 1997.
19. This figure must be considered in the light of the discounted prices at Trinity Book Service.
20. Trinity Ministry Academy Prospectus, 5th Edition, 4-5.
21. Letter from Randy Pizzino to the writer, May 20, 1997.
22. Letter from Lois (Martin) Shannon to the writer, October 30, 1997.
23. Albert Martin, 'Essential Elements of a Biblical Call' MI-MA-84 to 94.
24. Spurgeon, I. 22.
25. Albert N Martin, *What's Wrong with Preaching Today?* (Edinburgh: Banner of Truth, 1967, reprinted, 1992), p. 5.

26. Andrew Bonar, *The Memoi* [illegible] *bert Murray M'Cheyne* (Edinburgh: Banner [illegible] irst published in 1844.), 150.
27. Edmund Clowney, *Called to th* [illegible] : Presbyterian and Reformed, 1964), 79.
28. Robert Lewis Dabney, *Discuss* [illegible] *bney, Volume 2* (Edinburgh: Banner of Trut [illegible] n 1891), 27.
29. Clowney, 68.
30. Dabney, 29.
31. Quoted in Arnold Dallimore, *C* [illegible] *ife and Times of the Great Evangelist of the* [illegible] Volume One (Edinburgh: Banner of Truth, [illegible]
32. This was the Corinthians' view, which Paul had to correct.
33. 'Ignorant beings they must be if they look for wealth in connection with the Baptist ministry.' Spurgeon, I. 24.
34. R C H Lenski, *The Interpretation of St. Paul's Epistles to the Colossians, to the Thessalonians, to Timothy, to Titus and to Philemon* (Minneapolis: Augsburg Publishing House, 1937), 576.
35. One thinks here of St. John Chrysostom's hair-raising story of being dragged to the ordination council, after trying to hide from the church officers.
36. The two verbs, *oregetai* (be eager for, long for) and *epitumeô* (to strongly desire) are both in the present tense, indicating that the desire is not weak and intermittent, but strong and prevailing.
37. Spurgeon, I. 23-4.
38. Spurgeon, I. 29.
39. It is this focus of the desire that, in times past, drove Pastor Martin to maintain an incredibly busy preaching schedule. Although he was more than content to preach solely to the congregation of Trinity Baptist Church, nevertheless, God has so gifted him and granted him a stewardship that he would have believed himself negligent if he did not minister to the body of Christ at large.
40. Charles Bridges, *The Christian Ministry* (Edinburgh: Banner of Truth, 1959; first published 1830), 95.
41. Bridges, 27.
42. James Stewart, *Heralds of God* (Grand Rapids: Baker Book House, 1972 reprint. First published, 1946), 217.
43. Quoted in Stewart, 56.
44. John Owen, *The Works of John Owen, The Church and the Bible, Volume XVI* (Edinburgh: Banner of Truth, 1968. First published 1850-53), 76.

45. John Newton, *The Letters of John Newton* (Edinburgh: Banner of Truth, 1960), 55.
46. Owen, XVI, 86.
47. *presbeuō*, 'to function as a representative of a ruling authority'. Johannes P Louw and Eugene A Nida, *Greek-English Lexicon of the New Testament: Based on Semantic Domains* (New York: United Bible Society, 1988, 1989), I, 482, 37.888.
48. *kērux*, 'a person who preaches – preacher'. Louw and Nida, I, 417, 33.259.
49. John R W Stott, *The Preachers Portrait* (Grand Rapids: Eerdmans, 1961), 42.
50. Some appeal to Moses and Exodus 4:10. For a discussion of this, see Acts 7:22 and Walter Kaiser's comment in the *Expositor's Bible Commentary*, Volume 2 (Grand Rapids: Zondervan, 1981), 328.
51. Spurgeon, I. 35. See also Dabney, II. 37.
52. Martyn Lloyd-Jones, *Preaching and Preachers* (Grand Rapids: Zondervan, 1971), 305.
53. Pierre Ch. Marcel, *The Relevance of Preaching* trans. Rob Roy McGregor (Grand Rapids: Baker, 1963), 100-1.
54. ibid.
55. *episkopos*, 'one who serves as a leader in the church – ... In translating this word it is important to try to combine the concepts of both service and leadership, in other words, the responsibility of caring for the needs of a congregation as well as directing the activities of the membership.' Louw and Nida, I, 542, 53.71.
56. Dabney, *Discussions*, Vol. 2, 35.
57. Albert N Martin, Trinity Ministerial Academy, 'Pastoral Theology Outline' April 1997, 11.
58. Furthermore, Proverbs gives aphoristic insight into this principle (see Prov. 11:14, 15:22, 18:1, 24:6).
59. Clowney, 85.
60. Newton, 55.
61. Albert N Martin, 'Essential Elements of Effective Pastoral Ministry: In the Man' MI-MA-2 to 14.
62. There is obviously more to pastoral ministry than preaching, but it is beyond the scope of this work to include issues relating to pastoral oversight.
63. Spurgeon, I. 1-2.
64. Thomas Murphy, *Pastoral Theology* (Audubon, NJ: Old Paths Publications, reprint, 1996. First published, 1877), 37-9.
65. Octavius Winslow, *The Precious Things of God* (Pittsburgh, PA:

Soli Deo Gloria reprint, 1993. First published, 1860), 272.
66. John Piper, *Desiring God* (Sisters, OR: Multnomah Books, 1996), 224. Parenthesis is added for clarity.
67. Murphy, 76.
68. Thomas Brooks, *The Works of Thomas Brooks*, Volume II (Edinburgh: Banner of Truth reprint, 1980), 166.
69. Bridges, 60.
70. Jonathan Edwards, *The Works of Jonathan Edwards*, Volume 2 (Edinburgh: Banner of Truth, reprint, 1974. First published, 1834), 73.
71. For detailed teaching on this subject, see A N Martin's three sermons on 'The Attaining and Maintaining of a Good Conscience' tape # TX-F-4-6).
72. For a further development of this subject, see sermon tapes TP-L 15-24, from the series, 'The Perseverance of the Saints'.
73. Erroll Hulse, 'The Preacher and Piety', in *The Preacher and Preaching*, ed. Samuel Logan (Philipsburg, PA: Presbyterian and Reformed, 1986), 62-3.
74. Murphy, 93-4.
75. J W Alexander, *Thoughts on Preaching* (Edinburgh: Banner of Truth reprint, 1975. First published in 1864), 173.
76. Charles Spurgeon, 'Paul's Books'. *Free Grace Broadcaster*, 125 (May-June 1988): 14.
77. Although thousands of examples could be used, one thinks of Calvin's treatment of the truth of God's providence, which he warmly applies to believers and the world around them, and in fact, criticizes those who don't feelingly appreciate this truth. 'Indeed, although they subscribe to Paul's statement that we have our being and move and live in God (Acts 17:28), yet they are far from that *earnest feeling* of grace, which he commends, because they do not at all *taste* God's special care, by which alone His fatherly favor is known.' John Calvin, *Institutes of the Christian Religion*, translated by Ford Lewis Battles, Book I, Chapter XVI, 1. (Italics added).
78. Albert N Martin from the jacket cover of R L Dabney, *R L Dabney on Preaching: Lectures on Sacred Rhetoric* (Edinburgh: Banner of Truth reprint, 1979. First published, 1870).
79. Alexander, 128. See also Alexander's further comments on general preparation and study habits on pages 167-8, 170-93.
80. We would not want to limit our exposure only to Puritans of the seventeenth century. We would be remiss if we neglected such giants as Winslow, Ryle, Spurgeon and a host of others.

81. Dr. Jay Adams said that one of the reasons the Doctor of Ministry program in homiletics at Westminster Seminary did not have more students is because most pastors think they preach as well as they can and there is little room for improvement!
82. This is not to say that the Pastor must become an expert in postmodern thought or the rise of neo-paganism. However, such books as Gene Veith's *Postmodern Times* (Wheaton: Crossway Books, 1994) and Peter Jones' *Spirit Wars* (Escondido: Winepress Publishing, 1997) can be very helpful.
83. Author's note: I am including all of us today, in comparison to that titanic intellect of Jonathan Edwards. To be contemporary, we are operating on much smaller hard drives than did Edwards!
84. Pastors would do well to read Mortimer Adler's *How to Read a Book* (Simon and Schuster, 1972) every couple of years. Listen to Adler on this issue on reading and thinking, 'The fourth and highest level of reading we will call Synoptical Reading. It is the most complex and systematic type of reading of all. It makes very heavy demands on the reader, even if the materials he is reading are themselves relatively easy and unsophisticated.

    Another name for this level of reading might be comparative reading. When reading synoptically, the reader reads many books, not just one, and places them in relation to one another and to a subject about which they all revolve. But mere comparison is not enough. Synoptical reading involves more. With the help of the books read, the synoptical reader is able to construct an analysis of the subject that may not be in any of the books. It is obvious, therefore, that synoptical reading is the most active and effortful kind of reading' (20).
85. Quoted in Bridges, 50.
86. *Westminster Confession of Faith* (Glasgow: Free Presbyterian Publications, first published, 1646), 217-21. (Italics are added for relevant emphasis).
87. This theme of the body in preaching will be greatly expanded under 'The Act of Preaching'.
88. R C Sproul, 'The Whole Man', in Logan, 107.
89. Andrew Thomson, *Prince of the Puritans, John Owen* (Fearn, Great Britain: Christian Focus Publications, 1996. Also in *The Works of John Owen*, Vol. I), 14.
90. Quoted in J Oswald Sanders, *Spiritual Leadership* (Chicago, IL: Moody Press, 1967), 176.
91. Pastor Martin's series, 'Warning Against Ministerial Backsliding

and Burnout' (TP1008) has helped many men in the ministry.

92. Jonathan Edwards, *Charity and its Fruit* (Edinburgh: Banner of Truth, reprint, 1969. First published, 1852), 167.
93. Edwards, *Charity and Its Fruit*, 158-9.
94. Benjamin B. Warfield, 'The Emotional Life of Our Lord', in *The Person and Work of Christ* (Philadelphia, PA: Presbyterian and Reformed, 1950), 106.
95. Richard Baxter, *The Reformed Pastor* (Edinburgh: Banner of Truth reprint, 1974. First published, 1656), 117-8.
96. Lloyd-Jones, 92.
97. Baxter, 131-2.
98. As to the showing of affection to women, one must certainly use discretion and be above reproach. But there is still a very real and unambiguous demonstration of affection towards those of the opposite sex which exists within the family of God: treat 'older women as mothers, younger women as sisters, in all purity' (1 Tim. 5:2).
99. This principle is so beautifully exemplified by Pastor Martin. On one occasion when I and my family were visiting Trinity Baptist Church, I was standing in the foyer watching the people file out past Pastor Martin. My attention was riveted when I saw him get down on both knees and give a little girl a big bear hug. To my surprise, Pastor Martin was hugging my eight year old daughter who is painfully shy! She came walking over to me with a huge smile and said, 'I like Pastor Martin's hugs, I think I'll ask for another one.'
100. Bridges, 297.
101. Gardiner Spring, *The Power of the Pulpit* (Edinburgh: Banner of Truth, reprint, 1986. First published, 1848), 72.
102. Maurice Roberts, 'Acceptable Service'. *Banner of Truth* (July 1989): 3.
103. Baxter, 71.
104. There may be necessary times when he must deal with his salary, but let it be done in a straightforward, manly way; not in mousy comments dropped here and there, nor in a whining, self-serving manner.
105. Baxter, 74-5.
106. Owen, VI, 40.
107. Owen, VI, 42.
108. Owen, VI, 56.
109. Owen, VI, 58.
110. The author heartily recommends John Piper's *Future Grace* (Sister,

OR: Multnomah, 1995) especially chapter 27 on lust (Multnomah, 1995).

111. This list is an edited compilation of a seminary chapel session given by Randy Alcorn at Western Conservative Baptist Seminary in Portland, OR.
112. Spurgeon, I. 184.
113. Spurgeon, I.185-6.
114. Spurgeon, I.185
115. John Murray, *The Epistle to the Romans*, NICNT (Grand Rapids: Eerdmans, 1959, 1965), 117-8.
116. Charles Bridges, *Proverbs* (Edinburgh: Banner of Truth reprint, 1968. First published, 1846), 507-8.
117. Alexander, 160.
118. Geoffrey B Wilson, *The Pastoral Epistles* (Edinburgh: Banner of Truth, 1982), 51.
119. Paul stereotypes Cretans with a cliché from his day. The point is that sometimes the stereotypes, if true, set some guidelines in ministry.
120. This is not to deny real and valid emergencies where plans need to be rearranged, rather it is the inexcusable act of putting others before one's family.
121. Tedd Tripp's *Shepherding a Child's Heart* (Wapwallopen, PA: Shepherd Press, 1995) and Paul Tripp's *Age of Opportunity, A Biblical Guide to Parenting Teens* (Philipsburg, NJ: Presbyterian and Reformed, 1997) are highly recommended as particularly helpful.
122. Walter Chantry, *The Shadow of the Cross, Studies in Self-Denial* (Edinburgh: Banner of Truth, 1981), 66.
123. The author has heard Dr. John Piper, pastor of Bethlehem Baptist Church, Minneapolis, MN, say many times that he has never owned a TV because he knows his own weaknesses and the TV dries up his soul. Obviously we cannot legislate owning and watching television, but this author is convinced that many pastors would experience tremendous liberty and depth in their walk with God if they would get rid of the TV, or at least did not turn it on so much.
124. Horatius Bonar, *Words to Winners of Souls* (Philipsburg, PA: Presbyterian and Reformed, reprinted, 1995. First published, 1860), 38-40.
125. Albert N Martin, 'Essential Elements of Effective Pastoral Ministry: In the Message' MI-MA-15 to 26.
126. John Stott, *Between Two Worlds* (Grand Rapids: Eerdmans, 1982), 92.
127. Quoted in John Piper, *The Supremacy of God in Preaching* (Grand Rapids: Baker Book House, 1990), 22.

128. Sydney Greidanus, *The Modern Preacher and the Ancient Text* (Grand Rapids: Eerdmans, 1988), 9.
129. Joel R Beeke, 'Reformed Experiential Preaching' classroom notes, Westminster Theological Seminary in California, January 1997.
130. Stephen Charnock, *The Doctrine of Regeneration* (Grand Rapids: Baker Book House, reprint, 1980. First published, 1840), 276.
131. ibid. 287.
132. John Calvin, *Calvin's New Testament Commentaries, Volume 5*, translated by T H L Parker (Grand Rapids: Eerdmans, 1959), 145.
133. W Robert Godfrey, 'What Do We Mean By Sola Scriptura?' in *Sola Scriptura: The Protestant Position on the Bible,* ed. Don Kistler (Morgan, PA: Soli Deo Gloria, 1995), 6-7.
134. Spring, 36.
135. Greidanus, 8-9.
136. Greidanus, 13. Italics are his.
137. B B Warfield, 'The Purpose of the Seminary', in *Selected Shorter Writings of Benjamin B Warfield–I*, ed. John E Meeter (Nutley, NJ: Presbyterian and Reformed, 1970), 377.
138. ibid, 378.
139. Piper, *The Supremacy of God in Preaching*, 86.
140. RL Dabney, *R.l. Dabney on Preaching: Lectures in Sacred Rhetoric* (Edinburgh: Banner of Truth, rpt. 1979. First published, 1870), 27-8.
141. Donald Macleod states that systematic theology has four characteristics. '*First* it is thematic. Its interest is not in a particular text or a particular book or in an author or personality, but in the doctrinal themes of Scripture. *Second*, it is comprehensive. It draws upon all that Scripture and historical theology have to say on particular topics. *Third*, it is normative. It regards its own conclusions as representing not what a particular biblical author thought or what theologians believe or what may be inspiring for the church to accept, but the truth. *Fourth*, it is systematic. It seeks to arrange topics in the best possible order, to analyze and synthesize individual doctrines as lucidly as possible, and to relate them as coherently and cogently as possible to the life of both the church and world.' 'Preaching and Systematic Theology' in Logan, 248.
142. Spurgeon, I, 74.
143. Lloyd-Jones, 66.
144. Dabney, *Lectures in Sacred Rhetoric,* 30.
145. Jay Adams, *Preaching With Purpose* (Grand Rapids: Zondervan, 1982), 147.

146. Murphy, 169.
147. Under axiom four, which deals with application, some of the excesses of the redemptive-historical approach will be treated briefly, and how these excesses sometimes undermine pointed application. However, under this particular heading, the warnings are valid if balanced and qualified.
148. Quoted in Bridges, 264.
149. Erroll Hulse, 'The Living Church' in *Local Church Practice*, (Hayward Heath Sussex: Carey Publications, 1978), 35.
150. R B Kuiper, *The Glorious Body of Christ* (Edinburgh: Banner of Truth, 1967), 121.
151. Spurgeon, I. 89.
152. Martyn Lloyd-Jones, 189.
153. William Gurnall, *The Christian in Complete Armor* (Edinburgh: Banner of Truth, reprint 1964. First published, 1662 and 1665), 231.
154. Baxter, 113.
155. Owen, VII, 263.
156. John A Broadus, *A Treatise on the Preparation and Delivery of Sermons*, 29th edition, edited by Edwin Charles Dargan (New York: A C Armstrong and Son, 1899), 258-9.
157. Broadus, 260.
158. Edwards, *Works,* I, clxxiv.
159. Broadus, 260.
160. Tape EX-H-17, Eph. 2:7, 'The Riches of His Grace'.
161. J C Ryle, *The Upper Room* (Edinburgh: Banner of Truth reprint, 1977. First published, 1888), 41.
162. Ryle, 42
163. Broadus, 263.
164. ibid.
165. Spurgeon, I, 141.
166. John Flavel, 'The Fountain of Life' in *The Works of John Flavel Volume I* (Edinburgh: Banner of Truth reprint, 1968. First published, 1820), 33.
167. Andrew Bonar, 45.
168. Comment is made with full knowledge and agreement with Geoffrey Thomas's statement, 'Preaching that lacks application is the bane of the modern Reformed pulpit.' ('Powerful Preaching' in Logan, 380.)
169. John Angell James, *An Earnest Ministry, The Want of the Times* (Edinburgh: Banner of Truth, 1993. First published, 1847), 86-7.
170. Albert N Martin, Trinity Ministerial Academy, Pastoral Theology Outline, April 1997, p. 38.

171. William G T Shedd, *Homiletics and Pastoral Theology* (Edinburgh: Banner of Truth reprint, 1965. First published, 1867), 220.
172. Bridges, 272.
173. Bridges, 270-1.
174. John Newton, 'Letter on the propriety of a ministerial address to the unconverted', in *The Christian Pastor's Manual*, ed. John Brown (Ligonier, PA: Soli Deo Gloria reprint, 1991), 372.
175. Bridges, 269.
176. Bridges notes, 'Some have thought that the doctrine of Christ crucified is of far greater moment than the details of obligation – as if the one did not necessarily belong to the other', 264.
177. Bridges, 271.
178. ibid, fn. 1, 271.
179. Quoted in Peter Lewis, *The Genius of Puritanism* (Morgan, PA: Soli Deo Gloria reprint, 1996. First published, 1977), 49.
180. *Westminster Confession of Faith* (Glasgow: Free Presbyterian Publication, 1958, first published, 1646), 380. See also the entirety of 'Of the Preaching of the Word' in the *Directory for Publick Worship* and *LC*, Q/A 159.
181. John Calvin, *Sermons on Job*, trans. Arthur Golding (Edinburgh: Banner of Truth reprint, 1993. First published, 1574), 103.
182. Calvin, *Sermons on Job*, 104.
183. 'Massillon's preaching is said to have been so pointed, that no one stopped to criticize or admire. Each carried away the arrow fastened in his heart, considering himself to be the person addressed, and having neither time, thought, nor inclination to apply it to others' (Bridges, 270).
184. Bridges, 271
185. For a helpful analysis of the debate see Hendrik Krabbendam, 'Hermeneutics and Preaching' in Logan, 228-36, and Jay Adams, *Truth Applied* (Grand Rapids: Zondervan, 1990), 20-1.
186. Michael Horton, 'What Are We Looking for in the Bible? A Plea for Redemptive-Historical Preaching', *Modern Reformation* Volume 5, Number 3 (May/June 1996), 7.
187. This is the short coming of the so-called redemptive-historical approach. The advocates assert, 'When done properly, the redemptive-historical exposition of *the biblical text is supposedly at the same time its application*' (Krabbendam, 'Hermeneutics and Preaching' in Logan, 233. Italics added).
188. Bridges, 268.
189. Bridges, 260-1.

190. Murphy, 79-80.
191. Pastor Martin is obviously recommended. In addition to Pastor Martin, good examples can be found in the preaching (contained in books and tapes) of Pastors Edward Donnelly, Sinclair Ferguson and Jim Boice (especially Dr. Boice's exposition of the Psalms). Of special note is Dr. Martyn Lloyd-Jones, whose diagnostic and applicatory insights into the mind-set of society and cultural trends, are well worth being familiar with.
192. Pastor Albert N Martin, 'Are You For Real? A Study in Self-Deception'. TT-D-1 to TT-D-22
193. See also William Perkins, *The Art of Prophesying* (Edinburgh: Banner of Truth, 1996. First published, in Latin 1592, in English, 1606), 54-63.
194. An invaluable tool for this kind of research is Robert Paul Martin, *A Guide to the Puritans* (Edinburgh: Banner of Truth, 1997).
195. An excellent example of this very practice was exhibited by Pastor Edward Donnelly when he preached two sermons on the temptation of Christ. The first sermon was theological and didactic, examining the redemptive-historical significance of the passage. The second sermon was almost completely applicatory, in exhortation and consolation (TD-E-1 and 2).
196. Spurgeon, I, 148.
197. J C Ryle, *The New Birth* (Grand Rapids: Baker Book House reprint, 1977), 106-53.
198. For a whole sermon dedicated to this method of application see 'Do You Love Christ?'(TO-Q-30). It is significant to note that this sermon follows nineteen sermons on the person and work of Christ (TO-Q-11 to 29).
199. Marcel, 91, 95.
200. In seminary I had a professor who had an incredible gift for telling stories. However, we never remembered the truths he was illustrating, only the illustrations themselves. Here is a good test of illegitimate usage: does the illustration eclipse the truth?
201. Lloyd-Jones, 232.
202. This phrase comes from Robert Murray McCheyne's poem, 'Jehovah Tsidekenu' (Andrew Bonar, 632).
203. Ryle, *The Upper Room*, 48.
204. Broadus, 228-9.
205. Lloyd-Jones, 233.
206. Ryle, *The Upper Room*, 48.
207. Jay Adams, 'Sense Appeal and Story Telling' in Logan, 350.

208. Spurgeon, II, 2-3.
209. 'The God of Absolute Perfection', TO-Q-3
210. In transcribing this illustration, I have edited very little, wanting to capture the verbal style.
211. Broadus, 228.
212. Spurgeon, II. 5.
213. Lloyd-Jones, 233-4.
214. Jay Adams, 'Sense Appeal and Storytelling' in Logan, 357.
215. 'Back to the Basics' #4-6 (TX-F-4, 5, 6).
216. Adams says that a preacher can learn something about story telling from Norman Vincent Peale, but certainly not preaching content! (Logan, 352). There are many gifted story tellers, such as Garrison Keeler, who can be learned from.
217. Bridges, 312.
218. 'It is a frequent mistake to take too much for granted' Bridges, 312-3.
219. J C Ryle, *Christian Leaders of the 18th Century* (Edinburgh: Banner of Truth, 1978. Originally published, 1885), 24-5.
220. *Parrēsia* in *A Greek-English Lexicon of the New Testament and Other Early Christian Literature* (Chicago: University of Chicago Press, 1957), 635. This word is a favorite of the Apostle John, who uses it in connection with speech (*laleō*) seven times in the Gospel of John (John 7:13, 26, 10:24, 11:14, 16:25, 29, 18:20). For a thorough discussion see Schlier in Gerhard Kittel and Friedrich Gerhard, *Theological Dictionary of the New Testament*, trans. Geoffrey Bromiley (Grand Rapids: Eerdmans, 1967), V. 879-82.
221. Jay Adams, *Truth Applied*, 110.
222. Quoted in Bridges, fn. 2, 311.
223. Ryle, *The Upper Room*, 51-2.
224. Charles Spurgeon, *An All-Round Ministry* (Edinburgh: Banner of Truth, 1960. First published, 1900), 353-4.
225. Ryle, *The Upper Room*, 38. This quotation is given, knowing that in some circles, it is sadly thought that being crude and uneducated is a better conduit for the Holy Spirit.
226. Quoted in Bridges, 316.
227. Spurgeon, *Lectures to My Students*, I, 145.
228. Lloyd-Jones, 241-2.
229. It should not be deduced from this principle that the better the preacher, the longer he should preach. The principle should be taken in balance with the rest of the section.
230. Spurgeon, I. 145.

231. E-mail correspondence between the author and Dr. Beeke, December 19, 1998.
232. Spurgeon, I. 144-5.
233. Broadus, 536.
234. Marcel, 95.
235. Lloyd-Jones, 80.
236. Albert N Martin, 'Essential Elements of Effective Pastoral Ministry: In the Act of Preaching' MI-MA-38 to 49.
237. The Greek grammatical construction is clear, *lalēsai houtōs hōste pisteusai*. The speaking (*lalēsai*) was done in a certain manner (*houtōs*, adverb of manner) that a result was accomplished (infinitive of result, *hōste pisteusai*), many believed.
238. Broadus, 480-1.
239. Spurgeon, II. 9.
240. The term Paul uses in 2 Corinthians 2:17 is *eilikrinia*, indicating unmixed substances, unalloyed, pure.
241. Quoted in Broadus, 483. Two archaic words were changed, line 17, 'avaunt' to 'away!', and in line 18, 'glass' to 'mirror'.
242. Geoffrey Wilson, *1 Corinthians* (Edinburgh: Banner of Truth, 1978), 207.
243. J H McIlvaine, *Elocution: The Sources and Elements of Its Power* (New York: Scribner, Armstrong & Co., 1873), 165.
244. Broadus, 482.
245. William Taylor, *The Ministry of the Word* (Grand Rapids: Baker Bookhouse, reprint, 1975), 72.
246. Spurgeon, II, 152.
247. Broadus, 482.
248. McIlvaine, 164.
249. It is realized that six inch lapels might come back into style though.
250. Recently the writer was talking to a man who visited a church in his area, and found an unseemly patch of hair on the preacher's head a constant distraction. Although he admitted that being distracted by this odd patch of hair wasn't a mark of spirituality, he wanted to hear the sermon but found that his eyes kept straying to the preacher's head.
251. John A. James, *An Earnest Ministry: The Want of the Times*, 24.
252. Spurgeon, II, 11.
253. John Murray, *The Collected Works of John Murray*, Volume 3 (Edinburgh: Banner of Truth, 1982), 72.
254. Alfred M Rehwinkel, 'Emotion' in *Baker Dictionary of Theology*, ed. E F Harrison (Grand Rapids, MI: Baker Bookhouse, 1960), 181.

255. Albert N Martin, 'Pastoral Theology Outline/Pastor's Conference 1996', 5.
256. On the subject of God's emotions and impassibility, see Robert Reymond, *A New Systematic Theology of the Christian Faith* (Nashville, TN: Thomas Nelson publishers, 1998), 178-9; John Piper, 'Are There Two Wills in God? Divine Election and God's Desire for All to Be Saved' in *The Grace of God and the Bondage of the Will*, Volume I, eds. Thomas Schreiner and Bruce Ware (Grand Rapids: Baker Bookhouse, 1995), especially pages 126-7; John Piper, *The Pleasures of God* (Portland, OR: Multnomah Press, 1991).
257. Albert N Martin, ibid.
258. See B B Warfield, 'The Emotional Life of Our Lord' in *The Person and Work of Christ* (Philadelphia, PA: Presbyterian and Reformed, 1950), 93-145 and Pastor A N Martin, 'Christ – The Pattern for our Emotional Life' four tapes (TP1037).
259. Jonathan Edwards, *Religious Affections* (Edinburgh: Banner of Truth reprint, 1961. First published, 1746), 51.
260. Thomas Boston, *Human Nature in its Fourfold State* (Edinburgh: Banner of Truth, reprint, 1964. First published, nd), 127.
261. R L Dabney, 'Spurious Religious Excitements' in *Discussions*, Volume Three, 1.
262. R L Dabney, 'An Exposition of 1 Corinthians 3:10-15' in *Discussions*, Volume One, 559-60.
263. Albert N Martin, 'Pastoral Theology Outline/Pastors' Conference 1996', 6.
264. Spring, 131-132.
265. Albert N Martin, ibid.
266. Spurgeon, II, 147-8.
267. Murphy, 191.
268. Albert N Martin, 'Pastoral Theology Outline/Pastors' Conference 1996', 7.
269. Alexander, 20.
270. 'While I meditated, the fire burned' (NIV).
271. Once again, Warfield's essay, 'The Emotional Life of Our Lord' is highly recommended.
272. Dabney, *Lectures on Sacred Rhetoric*, 250.
273. Dabney, ibid.
274. Albert N Martin, Trinity Ministerial Academy, Pastoral Theology Outline, April 1997, 63.
275. Spurgeon, I. 117.
276. Broadus, 483.

277. J C Ryle, *Christian Leaders of the 18th Century*, 201.
278. Spurgeon, I. 118.
279. Spurgeon, I. 119.
280. Spurgeon, I. 122.
281. Dabney, 304-5.
282. Spurgeon, I. 131.
283. Albert N Martin, 'The Preacher's Physical Action.' Pt. 1 (MI-MA-44). Many over the years have accused Pastor Martin of histrionics. This writer is convinced, through listening and watching him preach, as well as discussing this very issue with him, that what one sees and hears is simply the unfettered display of felt truth.
284. Spurgeon, II. 98.
285. Alexander, 30.
286. Murphy, 194.
287. Alexander, 30. Italics are added.
288. 'Such was Al Martin's closeness to John Murray that at one Leicester Ministers' Conference he allowed himself the liberty of mimicking the Professor's best-known gesture – that gaze turned downwards to the finger nails of a half-clinched hand – *his object being to illustrate in an address on preaching how easily we can fall into the mannerisms of those we esteem*. John Murray was chairing that session and sitting with his usual grave countenance, which slowly gave way to a smile!' Iain Murray, 'Life of John Murray,' in *The Collected Writings of John Murray*, volume 3, fn. 134. Italics are added.
289. Broadus, 2.
290. McIlvaine, 95-6.
291. Dabney, 333.
292. Spring, 57-8.
293. Lloyd-Jones, 84.
294. Bridges, 286.
295. Spurgeon, I, 146.
296. McIlvaine, 105.
297. William Garden Blaikie, *For the Work of the Ministry: A Manual of Homiletical and Pastoral Theology* (London: J Nisbet and Co., 1890), 162.
298. McIlvaine, 110-1.
299. Spurgeon, I, 139-40.
300. Spurgeon, I, 149.
301. Albert N Martin, 'Pastoral Theology Outline/Pastors' Conference 1996', 11-12.

302. Iain Murray, *Jonathan Edwards: A New Biography* (Edinburgh: Banner of Truth, 1987), see pages 189-91.
303. John Etter, *The Preacher and His Sermon* (Dayton, OH: United Brethren Publishing House, 1888), 444.
304. Dabney, 328-9.
305. McIlvaine, 138-9.
306. Marcel, 95.
307. This is a target which Pastor Martin himself has failed to hit in the bull's eye.
308. Spurgeon, I, 164.
309. For further thoughts on this subject from a building perspective see Albert N Martin, 'A Theology of Christian Architecture' TE-21.
310. Spurgeon, II, 102-3.
311. A brief word of wisdom for visiting preachers is to check the pulpit beforehand in order to make sure that the height is compatible. Some alterations might need to be made in order for the preacher to see his notes and Bible, and this needs to be done *before* he starts preaching.
312. John Stott, *Between Two Worlds*, 23-4.
313. Spurgeon, I, 139.

BIBLIOGRAPHY

Adams, Jay. *Preaching with Purpose*. Grand Rapids: Zondervan, 1982.

Adams, Jay. *Truth Applied.* Grand Rapids: Zondervan, 1990.

Adler, Mortimer. *How to Read a Book*. New York: Simon and Schuster, 1972.

Alexander, J W. *Thoughts on Preaching*. Edinburgh: Banner of Truth, reprinted, 1975. First published, 1864.

Bauer, Arndt, Gingrich. *A Greek-English Lexicon of the New Testament and Other Early Christian Literature*. Chicago: University of Chicago Press, 1957.

Baxter, Richard. *The Reformed Pastor*. Edinburgh: Banner of Truth, reprinted, 1974. First published, 1656.

Beeke, Joel. 'Reformed Experiential Preaching.' Classroom notes, Westminster Theological Seminary in California, January, 1997.

Blaikie, William Garden. *For the Work of the Ministry: A Manual of Homiletical and Pastoral Theology*. London: J Nisbet and Co., 1890.

Bonar, Andrew. *The Memoirs and Remains of Robert Murray McCheyne*. Edinburgh: Banner of Truth, reprinted, 1966. First published, 1844.

Bonar, Horatius. *Words to Winners of Souls*. Philipsburg, PA: Presbyterian and Reformed, reprinted, 1995. First published, 1860.

Boston, Thomas. *Human Nature in Its Fourfold State*. Edinburgh: Banner of Truth, reprint, 1964.

Bridges, Charles. *The Christian Ministry*. Edinburgh: Banner of Truth, reprinted, 1959. First published, 1830.

Bridges, Charles. *Proverbs*. Edinburgh: Banner of Truth, reprinted, 1968. First published, 1846.

Broadus, John A. *Treatise on the Preparation and Delivery of Sermons*. 29th edition, edited, Charles Dargan. New York: A C Armstrong and Sons, 1899.

Brooks, Thomas. *The Works of Thomas Brooks*, Volume II. Edinburgh: Banner of Truth, reprint, 1980.

Calvin, John. *The Institutes of the Christian Religion*, 2 Volumes, translated by Ford Lewis Battles. Philadelphia: The Westminster Press, 1960.

Calvin, John. *Calvin's New Testament Commentaries*, Volume 5. Translated by T H L Parker. Grand Rapids: Eerdmans, 1959.

Calvin, John. *Sermons on Job*, translated by Arthur Golding. Edinburgh: Banner of Truth, reprint, 1993. First published, 1574.

Chantry, Walter. *The Shadow of the Cross: Studies in Self-Denial*. Edinburgh: Banner of Truth, 1981.

Charnock, Stephen. *The Doctrine of Regeneration.* Grand Rapids: Baker Book House, reprint, 1980. First published, 1840.

Clowney, Edmund. *Called to the Ministry*. Philipsburg, PA: Presbyterian and Reformed, 1964.

Dabney, Robert Lewis. *Discussions of Robert Lewis Dabney*, 3 Volumes. Edinburgh: Banner of Truth, reprint, 1967. First published, 1891.

Dabney, Robert Lewis. *R L Dabney on Preaching: Lectures on Sacred Rhetoric*. Edinburgh: Banner of Truth, reprint, 1979. First published, 1870.

Dallimore, Arnold. *George Whitefield: The Life and Times of the Great Evangelist of the 18th Century*, 2 Volumes. Edinburgh: Banner of Truth, 1970.

Edwards, Jonathan. *The Works of Jonathan Edwards*, 2 Volumes. Edinburgh: Banner of Truth, reprint 1974. First published, 1834.

Edwards, Jonathan. *Charity and Its Fruit.* Edinburgh: Banner of Truth, reprint, 1969. First published, 1852.

Edwards, Jonathan. *Religious Affections*. Edinburgh: Banner of Truth, reprint, 1961. First published, 1746.

Etter, John. *The Preacher and His Sermon*. Dayton, OH: United Brethren Publishing House, 1888.

Flavel, John. *The Works of John Flavel*, Volume I. Edinburgh: Banner of Truth, reprint, 1968. First published, 1820.

Godfrey, W. Robert. 'What Do We Mean By Sola Scriptura?' *Sola Scriptura: The Protestant Position on the Bible*, ed. Don Kistler. Morgan, PA: Soli Deo Gloria, 1995.

Greidanus, Sydney. *The Modern Preacher and the Ancient Text.* Grand Rapids: Eerdmans, 1988.

Gurnall, William. *The Christian in Complete Armor.* Edinburgh: Banner of Truth, reprint, 1964. First published, 1662, 1665.

Harrison, E F Ed. *Baker Dictionary of Theology*. Grand Rapids: Baker Book House, 1960.

Horton, Michael. 'What Are We Looking For? A Plea for Redemptive-Historical Preaching'. *Modern Reformation* Volume 5, Number 3 (May/June 1996).

Hulse, Erroll. 'The Living Church', in *Local Church Practice.* Hayward Heath Sussex: Carey Publications, 1978.

James, John Angell. *An Earnest Ministry.* Edinburgh: Banner of Truth, reprint, 1993. First published, 1847.

Kaiser, Walter. 'Exodus' in *The Expositor's Bible Commentary*, volume 2. Grand Rapids: Zondervan, 1981.

Kittel, Gerhard. *Theological Dictionary of the New Testament*. 10 Volumes. Trans. Geoffrey Bromiley. Grand Rapids: Eerdmans, 1967.

Kuiper, R B. *The Glorious Body of Christ*. Edinburgh: Banner of Truth, 1967.

Lenski, R C H. *The Interpretation of St. Paul's Epistles to the Colossians, to the Thessalonians, to Timothy, to Titus, to Philemon.* Minneapolis, MN: Augsburg Publishing House, 1937.

Lewis, Peter. *The Genius of Puritanism.* Morgan, PA: Soli Deo Gloria, reprint, 1996. First published, 1977.

Logan, Samuel, editor. *The Preacher and Preaching.* Philipsburg, PA: Presbyterian and Reformed, 1986.

Louw, Johannes P and Eugene A Nida. *Greek-English Lexicon of the New Testament: Based on Semantic Domains*, 2 Volumes. New York: United Bible Society, 1988, 1989.

Lloyd-Jones, D Martyn. *Preaching and Preachers.* Grand Rapids: Zondervan, 1971.

Marcel, Pierre Ch. *The Relevance of Preaching.* Translated by Robert Roy McGregor. Grand Rapids: Baker Book House, 1963.

Martin, Albert N. *What's Wrong With Preaching Today*? Edinburgh: Banner of Truth, 1967.

Martin, Albert N. 'Pastoral Theology Outline', Trinity Ministerial Academy, April 1997.

Martin, Albert N. 'Pastoral Theology Outline/Pastors' Conference', 1996.

Martin, Robert P *A Guide to the Puritans.* Edinburgh: Banner of Truth, 1997.

McIlvaine, J H *Elocution: The Sources and Elements of Its Power.* New York: Scribner, Armstrong & Co., 1873.

Murphy, Thomas. *Pastoral Theology.* Audubon, NJ: Old Paths Publications, reprint 1996. First published, 1877.

Murray, Iain. *Jonathan Edwards: A New Biography.* Edinburgh: Banner of Truth, 1987.

Murray, John. *The Collected Writings of John Murray*, 4 Volumes. Edinburgh: Banner of Truth Trust, 1982.

Murray, John. *The Epistle to the Romans*, NICNT. Grand Rapids: Eerdmans, 1959, 1965.

Newton, John. *The Letters of John Newton.* Edinburgh: Banner of Truth, 1960.

Newton, John. 'Letter on the Propriety of a Ministerial Address to the Unconverted', in *The Christian Pastor's Manual*, ed. John Brown. Ligonier, PA: Soli Deo Gloria, reprint, 1991. First published, 1826.

Owen, John. *The Works of John Owen, Volume VI.* Edinburgh: Banner of Truth, reprint, 1968. First published, 1850-1853.

Owen, John. *The Works of John Owen, Volume VII.* Edinburgh: Banner of Truth, reprint, 1968. First published, 1850-1853.

Owen, John. *The Works of John Owen, Volume XVI.* Edinburgh: Banner of Truth, reprint, 1968. First published, 1850-1853.

Perkins, William. *The Art of Prophesying.* Edinburgh: Banner of Truth,

reprint, 1996. First published, Latin ed. 1592, English ed. 1606.
Piper, John. *Desiring God.* Sisters, OR: Multnomah Books, 1996.
Piper, John. *Future Grace.* Sisters, OR: Multnomah Books, 1995.
Piper, John. *The Supremacy of God in Preaching.* Grand Rapids: Baker Book House, 1990.
Piper, John. *The Pleasures of God.* Portland, OR: Mulnomah Books, 1991.
Piper, John. 'Are There Two Wills in God? Divine Election and God's desire for All To Be Saved'. in *The Grace of God and The Bondage of the Will,* Vol. I, eds. Thomas Schreiner and Bruce Ware. Grand Rapids: Baker Book House, 1995.
Reymond, Robert. *A New Systematic Theology of the Christian Faith.* Nashville, TN: Thomas Nelson, 1998.
Roberts, Maurice. 'Acceptable Service'. *Banner of Truth.* (July, 1989).
Ryle, J C. *Christian Leaders of the 18th Century.* Edinburgh: Banner of Truth, reprint, 1978. First published, 1885.
Ryle, J C. *The New Birth.* Grand Rapids: Baker Book House, reprint, 1977.
Ryle, J C. *The Upper Room.* Edinburgh: Banner of Truth, reprint, 1977. First published, 1888.
Sanders, J Oswald. *Spiritual Leadership.* Chicago: Moody Press, 1967.
Shedd, William G T. *Homiletics and Pastoral Theology.* Edinburgh: Banner of Truth, reprint, 1965. First published, 1867.
Spring, Gardiner. *The Power of the Pulpit.* Edinburgh: Banner of Truth, reprint, 1986. First published, 1848.
Spurgeon, Charles. *Lectures to My Students.* Pasadena, TX: Pilgrims Publications, reprint 1990. First published, 1881.
Spurgeon, Charles. *An All-Round Ministry.* Edinburgh: Banner of Truth, reprint, 1960. First published, 1900.
Spurgeon, Charles. 'Paul and His Books'. *Free Grace Broadcaster,* 125 (May-June, 1988).
Stewart, James. *Heralds of God.* Grand Rapids: Baker Book House, reprint, 1972. First published, 1946.
Stott, John R W. *The Preacher's Portrait.* Grand Rapids: Eerdmans, 1961.
Stott, John R W. *Between Two Worlds.* Grand Rapids: Eerdmans, 1982.
Taylor, William. *The Ministry of the Word.* Grand Rapids: Baker Book House, reprint, 1975.
Thomson, Andrew. *Prince of the Puritans, John Owen.* Great Britain: Christian Focus Publications, 1996.
Warfield, Benjamin B. *The Person and Work of Christ.* Philadelphia: Presbyterian and Reformed, 1950.
Warfield, Benjamin B. *Selected Shorter Writings of Benjamin B Warfield – I,* ed. John Meeter. Nutley, NJ: Presbyterian and Reformed, 1970.
Westminster Confession of Faith. Glasgow: Free Presbyterian Publications. First published, 1646.

Wilson, Geoffrey B. *1 Corinthians*. Edinburgh: Banner of Truth, 1978.

Wilson, Geoffrey B. *The Pastoral Epistles*. Edinburgh: Banner of Truth, 1982.

Winslow, Octavius. *The Precious Things of God*. Pittsburgh, PA: Soli Deo Gloria, reprinted, 1993. First published, 1860.

Subject Index

Persons' Index

Scripture Index